Gerard Hallock

History of the South Congregational Church, New Haven : from its origin in 1852 till January 1, 1865

Gerard Hallock

History of the South Congregational Church, New Haven : from its origin in 1852 till January 1, 1865

ISBN/EAN: 9783337263096

Printed in Europe, USA, Canada, Australia, Japan

Cover: Foto ©ninafisch / pixelio.de

More available books at **www.hansebooks.com**

HISTORY

OF THE

South Congregational Church,

NEW HAVEN,

FROM

ITS ORIGIN IN 1852 TILL JANUARY 1, 1865.

BY GERARD HALLOCK.

CLERK OF SAID CHURCH.

NEW HAVEN.
PRINTED BY TUTTLE, MOREHOUSE AND TAYLOR.
1865.

TABLE OF CONTENTS.

CHAPTER I.
	Pages
Preliminary History of South Church,	5–18

CHAPTER II.
Ministry of Rev. Dr. Stiles,	19–50

CHAPTER III.
Ministry of Rev. Mr. Noyes,	51–70

CHAPTER IV.
Ministry of Rev. Mr. Carroll,	71–102

CHAPTER V.
The Ex-parte Council,	103–104
"Result of Council,"	104–111
Reply of South Church to do.,	111–133
Rejoinder to Reply,	133–140
Remarks on the Rejoinder,	140–161
Strictures on the "Remarks" by a Member of the Council,	161–162
Reply to the Strictures—Rev. Dr. Dutton on Female Voting,	163–166
Effects of the Action of Council,	166–176

CHAPTER VI.
New Year's Address (1864) to Rev. Mr. Carroll,	177–183
Mr. Carroll's Reply—Rev. Mr. Barrett,	184–185

Parting Interview with Rev. Mr. Barrett, 185–187
State and Progress of the Church, 187–204
South Church Finances, 204–206
Resolutions concerning the Bell, 206–207

CHAPTER VII.

Rev. Mr. Carroll's Memorial Sermon, 209–257

CATALOGUE.

Comprising   Pages

Confession of Faith, 1–3
Covenant, 4
Standing Rules, 5–7
Officers of Church and Society, 9–10
Chronological List of all who are or have been Members of
   South Church, 11–23
Alphabetical List of Present Members, 25–31
Alphabetical List of Ex-members, 33–41
Chronological List of do., 43–46
Summary of Admissions and Dismissions, 47–48

HISTORY OF THE SOUTH CHURCH.

CHAPTER I.

PRELIMINARY HISTORY.

Prior to the erection of the South Church edifices, in 1851 and 1852, there was no house of worship of any Protestant denomination, in the south-western section of the city. The nearest Protestant church, at the date mentioned, was that in College street, distant, by the course of the roads, about three-quarters of a mile from the site of the South Church. For two or three years, a few individuals had been mooting the question, whether it was not possible to provide a place of worship for this destitute section, too many of whose inhabitants excused themselves from attending public worship on account of distance, poverty, and other circumstances, which served to quiet their consciences and keep them aloof from the means of grace. True, there was a small Sabbath School held in the Mount Pleasant School-house a part of the time, and occasionally some clergyman from town, or theological student, would come over and hold a meeting for prayer, or preach a sermon. The few pious people who resided in the vicinity, encouraged these efforts, and did what they could to promote them. But they were poor, as well as few in number, and could really do nothing, or next to nothing, towards the erection of a house of worship. Some individuals who belonged to churches in town, were too much attached to them to be willing to engage in any new enterprise looking to a disruption of existing relations.

Thus, in one way or another, the projectors of the South Church enterprise met with discouragement at every step. The first idea was, to have a Mission Chapel, erected by subscription, and free to all. But on this basis there would be no revenue, and a constant outlay would be required to support the minister and defray other necessary expenses.

Next, a small church edifice was contemplated, in which the slips should be rented, and thus the expense of supporting the establishment be in part defrayed. But this plan was found to be no more acceptable than the other. A personal application to all those persons in the vicinity who were deemed most likely to be able and willing to aid the enterprise, produced but one subscription, ($50,) and an offer on the part of a farmer to assist in digging the cellar.* These

---

* It should, perhaps, be mentioned that a lady offered to give a site for the church, not far from the present location, on condition that the edifice to be erected on it, should be used *forever* as a *Congregational* church. This offer, generous as it was in some respects, the parties interested felt obliged to decline, as they could not run the risk of losing their whole investment, in case the church enterprise, which was altogether an experiment, should not succeed.

subscriptions were afterwards respectfully declined, and the plan was adopted which was finally carried into effect. It was simply this,—for the projectors of the undertaking to take the work into their own hands, do it at their own expense, and hold the property in their own right, until such time as the church and society should be able to redeem it. But then the question arose, how large a building should be erected,—whether of wood, or brick, or stone,—whether only large enough to accommodate such of the existing population as might be expected to attend, or having reference also to prospective wants. If we built a small church, we should be likely to have a small minister, small congregations, and a small income. But if we should be prospered beyond our hopes, then would come the necessity of a larger house, and we should have to lengthen it, or in some way add to its dimensions. This would violate its architectural proportions, and otherwise deform it,—at the same time increasing the expense.

Suffice it to say, the result of our deliberations was, to build a church of the first class, whether as to dimensions, materials, architectural beauty, or other basis of comparison; one that should do honor, not only to the neighborhood, but to the city; one that should be suited to the wants of the community half a century hence. This conclusion was aided and encouraged by the eminent architect, SIDNEY M. STONE, to whom we applied for a plan, and who subsequently took the contract for building the church.

and became a proprietor to the extent of $1,000. The contract was dated January 25, 1851, and called for the completion of the building by the first of March in the following year. With the exception of a lot of land worth $2,000, all the payments were to be made, and were made, in cash, as the work proceeded. A very eligible site had been purchased one week previous, for $1,015, of Mrs. Hannah Tuttle and her daughters Lucy and Elizabeth, at the corner of Columbus and Liberty streets, described in their deed as containing "ninety square rods, more or less." It is bounded Northerly 115 feet 6 inches by Columbus street, Easterly 206 feet by Liberty street, Southerly 115 feet 8 inches, Westerly 203 feet 9 inches.

The walls of the church above ground are of Portland (Connecticut River) stone, 64 feet front and rear, by 90 feet from outside to outside, and 34 feet high from top of water-table to line of eaves. Recess for pulpit in rear end of the church, 7 feet by 22, and 26 feet six inches high from top of water-table to line of eaves. Tower 21 feet by 21, and 87 feet high from top of water-table to top of stonework. From the surface of the ground to the top of battlement, 98 feet 6 inches. As the tower projects 10 feet from the main building, the entire length of the structure is 107 feet. The audience room is 75 feet by 59 feet 8 inches in the clear, exclusive of the recess for pulpit, and organ-loft in front. The foundation walls of the tower are six feet thick at bottom, and four feet at top. Walls of tower, above the foundation walls, 2 feet 3 inches thick 35 feet **upward, then** 2 feet thick 27 feet upward to bell-deck, **then 1 foot and 6 inches thick** 25 feet upward to **top of stone-work.** The foundation walls of the building proper are 3 feet **6 inches** thick at bottom, **and 2 feet 10 inches at top ;** the side and front walls 2 feet thick from top of **foundation walls** to the height of **two feet** above the tops **of the windows ;** then **1 foot 9 inches** thick **to eaves.** The rear wall, including recess, **1 foot 6 inches thick.** All the interstices in the walls as they were being **built,** were filled **with soft** mortar **or cement.** The mason-work was let out **by** the contractor **to Messrs. Perkins & Hine ;** the wood-work to **Nicholas Countryman.** The whole was done to the entire **satisfaction of the parties interested, and unless destroyed by** fire or some other extraordinary **visitation, the building will** stand for ages.

Scarcely had the main **edifice been opened for public worship, on the** last Sabbath **in June, 1852,** when there was found to be an urgent necessity **for** smaller rooms, suitable for **conference and prayer meetings,** and for the **Sabbath School, which had been transferred to** this church **from the Mount Pleasant school-house. Accordingly THE CHAPEL, fronting on Liberty street,** directly in the rear of the Church, was projected **and built by day's work, 57 feet by 35,** from outside **to outside, in the same style and of the same kind of material as** the main edifice. Both buildings are rigidly plain, **but** the effect is, to give them an air of dignity and permanence, rather than cheapness ; to please the eye with beautiful proportions and a simplicity that never tires, rather than tickle it with ornament for a time, to be disgusted in the end. A single enclosure embraces both buildings,—the fence on both streets being a substantial cast-iron railing, resting upon, or rather entered into, a massive dressed-stone coping, of the same material as the walls of the buildings. The entire lower floor of the Chapel, except the vestibule, is fitted up as an Audience Room, being provided with a pulpit and slips, and will comfortably seat from 250 to 300 persons. The upper story is occupied chiefly as the "Ladies' Room" ; being neatly carpeted, and provided with seventy or eighty chairs, settees, work-tables, tea-tables, sideboards, crockery, and other apparatus, for the convenience of the Sewing Society and other meetings. In this "large upper-room furnished," the church prayer meetings are held. Over the vestibule is the Pastor's study, carpeted and furnished in an appropriate manner. The Sabbath School Library, comprising about 500 well-selected volumes, is kept in a little room set off from the vestibule. A Melodeon is used in common by the Sabbath School and other meetings in the Chapel and Ladies' Room.

The following schedule shows the cost of the South Church property, both real and personal, distinguishing as far as practicable, between the Church and the Chapel :—

SOUTH CHURCH.—Main Edifice.

Cost of Lot,	$ 1,015 00
Contract with Sidney M. Stone, for main edifice,	19,000 00
Variations and extras,	235 16
Richard Carse, windows for church, complete,	654 00
Bell, (2,504 lbs.) and rigging, from Holbrook's Foundry, East Medway, Mass.,	686 00
Gas pipes, meter, &c.,	38 70
Grading, turfing, trees and vines, about the church,	195 37
Paving in front of church,	35 76
Carpets for church, and putting down,—Marble & Foster,	632 38
Church furniture,—Blair's bill,	1,270 17
Psalm books and Music books for church,	32 63
Mats, &c., for church,—Walker's bill,	22 81
Curtains for pulpit windows,—Doolittle's bill,	88 50
Organ, from Erben's Factory, New York,	2,500 00
Carting do., and trimmings for pulpit,	32 09
Countryman's bill for out-buildings, benches, and sundries about church,	332 06
Communion Service, and Baptismal Vase,	75 00
Cloths for do.,	18 50
Wm. M. Hubbard, for work, &c. at church, before occupancy,	21 23
Iron Railing Company's bill for fences, &c.,	918 38
Painting iron fences,—Andrews' bill,	25 00
Countryman's bill for vestibule.	48 81
Total cost of church edifice and furniture complete, including ground,	$27,877 53

SOUTH CHURCH CHAPEL.

Sidney M. Stone's bill for Chapel,	$6,076 31
Ventilators for do.,	11 00
Carting stone for do.,—Hull & Wallace's bill,	132 00
Stones left after building church,—bought of Perkins & Hine.	21 00
Carse, for Chapel windows,	249 00
Carpets for lecture room of Chapel, Marble & Foster.	149 79

Mats, &c. for Chapel,—Walker,			·	·	·	5 71
Blair's bill for sundries in furnishing Chapel and Pastor's Study,						230 00
do. do. furniture for Ladies' Room,					·	190 00
Side-board for	do.	do.	Bowditch,		·	7 00
Carpets for	do.	do.	Marble & Foster,		·	109 73
Oil cloth for	do.	do.	Fairman,		·	4 13
Stove, &c.	do.	do.	Cannon,	·	·	18 27
Crockery and tea urn for do.	do.		Minor,	·	·	23 51
Gas extension to Chapel,			·	·	·	46 50
Bible and 127 Hymn Books, (red covers,) for Chapel,					·	14 45
Six missionary maps for do.		·	·	·	·	28 00

Total cost of chapel and furniture complete, · · $7,346 40
"   " church, &c., as above,* · · · 27,877 55
"   " Church and Chapel, including ground,† $35,223 95

Of which was paid by Thomas R. Trowbridge
  and Brothers, · · · · $3,500 00
By Sidney M. Stone, · · · 1,000 00
By Amos Smith, · · · · 1,000 00
                                        ———— 5,500 00

By Gerard Hallock, · · · · · $29,723 95

who, accordingly, on the 23d of April, 1853, conveyed to Thomas R. Trowbridge, for the latter and his brothers, Henry and Ezekiel, one undivided tenth of all the property aforesaid, and to Sidney M. Stone

---

* This distinction in the cost of Church and Chapel is not strictly accurate, as some of the bills are charged to the Church which belong, in part, to the Chapel, and *vice versa*. For instance, the iron railing is all charged to the Church, while the stone coping on which it rests, is all charged to the Chapel. So, likewise, the horse-sheds and other out-buildings are all charged to the Church, while all the side-walk pavement on Liberty street is charged to the Chapel. On the whole, the variations from exactness about balance each other.

† Many small items, amounting to several hundred dollars in the aggregate, were paid by the principal proprietor, without being included in this account.

and **Amos Smith**, each an undivided thirty-fifth. In 1855 he re-purchased the shares of Messrs. Stone and Smith, and on the 20th October, 1864, those of the Messrs. Trowbridge; thus becoming sole proprietor. As soon as a *church* was organized, November 8, 1852, the buildings were placed at its disposal, for use and occupancy, at the nominal rent of a barley-corn a year, and have continued in its possession, or in that of the church and society, to the present time, at the same nominal rent,—the principal proprietor keeping the property insured at his own expense for about $30,000, and doing most of the repairs. As he is the only one of the original proprietors who is now connected with the church and society, and as he is identified with them in all their sympathies and interests, they have every reason to be satisfied with the present state of things, until they shall be disposed to take the property into their own hands, and sustain the establishment after the usual manner of such organizations. Whenever that time shall come, it is fair to presume that they will find him ready to meet their wishes on satisfactory terms.

It may not be generally known that the South Church was erected with a view to the occupancy of its pulpit by Rev. E. N. SAWTELL, now seamen's chaplain at the port of Havre, France. He had previously occupied the last named position for seven years,—had officiated for about an equal period as pastor of a Presbyterian Church in Louisville, Ky., and for several years had been one of the Secretaries of a Society in New York, now known as the American and Foreign Christian Union. In every sphere in which he had been called to act, he had acquitted himself with distinguished ability; and being now at the zenith of his intellectual powers, with a warm, Christian heart, and rare speaking talents,—withal longing to engage again in his Master's service as a preacher and pastor,—it was a great disappointment to those of us who knew his worth, to find ourselves cut off from all prospect of consummating the proposed arrangement; and equally so to himself, as will be seen by the following extracts from his letters:

"CLEVELAND, *December* 30, 1851.

"For several weeks it has been in my heart to write you fully and frankly on the precarious state of my health, or rather, the almost entire loss of my speaking powers. * * You are aware, I think, that an attack of bilious fever which I had in New York last February, was succeeded by an inflammation of the throat, which troubled me more or less through the summer. It however gave me but little anxiety, as I thought time and care would eradicate the complaint. In this I have been mistaken. On the return of cold, frosty weather, it seized my throat with increased virulence; and since leaving New York, I have not been able to preach at all. Even in conducting family worship, or reading an article aloud in a newspaper, my voice has so utterly failed me, that I could finish it only in a whisper. I have availed myself of the best medical advice, but to very little purpose; physicians give me but little encouragement.

* * * * * * * * *

"Now, my dear sir, what shall be done? The Lord's hand is evidently in this matter, and while it is our duty to bow submissively to His will, it is equally our duty to inquire what He will have us to do. * * * O, what a world of uncertainties and disappointments! How easy for the Lord to thwart all our plans! It does indeed require much grace to say at all times and under all circumstances, 'The will of the Lord be done.' Lord, increase our faith. * * * Mrs. Sawtell has often felt that the Lord might tear me away from what she sometimes feared was my idol. Though not conscious of idolatry, I am aware that my soul has been wrapped up in that one object. But the Lord can do without me. That He intends to have a church there, I have not the least shadow of doubt, though my voice may never be heard in that pulpit. May God bless you and yours, and the enterprise you have so much at heart."

"CLEVELAND, *Feb.* 18, 1852.

"*Messrs. Hallock, Trowbridge, Smith, Stone, and others.*

"DEAR SIRS:—The recent intelligence which I have received of the near completion of your church edifice, has filled my heart with mingled emotions of joy and grief; of joy, that the Lord has enabled you to do so much; grief, at the prospect of my doing so little, or, perhaps as I ought rather to say, *of my doing nothing*, in advancing that noble enterprise in which you are engaged. I have before intimated to some of my friends, my fears on this subject, owing to the precarious state of my voice. But hoping at the return of each day, that some favorable change or symptoms might manifest themselves, and unwilling to be convinced that I was to have no part nor lot in that matter, I have deferred writing to you jointly, until I dare defer no longer. I think it due to you all, as well as to myself, to make known to you the whole truth in this matter, and keep nothing back, that is in the least calculated to shed light upon your path and mine. During the whole winter I have been a great sufferer, with an inflammation of the throat, accompanied with an entire exhaustion or prostration of my speaking powers. I have recently made two attempts to speak in public, in both of which I failed, and had to cut short my remarks, and from the effects of which I have not yet recovered. One was simply a short address, at the anniversary of the Society for National Popular Education; and although I yielded reluctantly to the solicitations of Governor Slade to make this address, I finally did it rather as an experiment, to see what effect it would produce upon my throat, that it might shed light upon my future path, and enable you the better to judge whether it would be prudent and wise for me to enter upon that inviting and important field of labor which you have, at so much expense, opened before me. To my own mind, the testimony furnished by this experiment, has been most painfully conclusive. I did not spend over an hour in jotting down the few thoughts I offered on that occasion, and yet, when I entered the church, my whole frame was agitated, my nerves unstrung, my throat inflamed and almost closed up, and when I returned home, I had a high fever, and for three days was confined to the house. There seems to be a connection, a strange sympathy, between my throat and all mental efforts. The least excitement only enhances the disease; and as it is impossible for me to speak in public, and much less to preach the Gospel, without mental effort, and strongly excited feelings, I can see but little hope for me,—and I write this with a feeling heart and weeping eyes.

"I have earnestly prayed, that if it be for the glory of God, this cup of disappointment might pass from me. 'Yet, not my will, but Thine, O Lord, be done,' must, and I trust ever will be, the language of my heart. I have often pictured to myself the happiness I should experience in once more returning to the duties of a pastoral life, after the shifting scenes through which I have passed, and of having my family located in such a place as New Haven, and of closing my ministerial labors in what would seem to be as near an earthly paradise as any thing I could imagine this side of Heaven; and it may be that my Heavenly Father has seen some lurking sin in these anticipations, that needs to be eradicated, ere I can 'be made meet for the inheritance of the children of light.' Or, it may be, that He sees some other one that could better fill that place, and that He has other work for me to do. At any rate, we cannot, we *must* not, shut our eyes to the clear indications of His providence, however they may thwart our purposes or cross our inclinations. I need not say, that all that human skill can do or devise, has been done in my case

My physicians give but little encouragement of my ever being able to preach much more.

* * * * * *

"And now, my dear friends, may that God, 'whose path is in the deep,—whose ways are past finding out,' guide you, and bless you abundantly in your noble work, and send you a man after 'His own heart.' And should it please Him to restore me to health, and permit us to labor together, we will rejoice. If not, we will bow meekly at His feet, and say, 'Let the will of the Lord be done.'

"Your sincere friend and brother in Christ,

E. N. SAWTELL."

"CLEVELAND, Feb. 21, 1852.

* * "So long have I been in the habit of contemplating that church as my own child, beloved and longed for, that now, to give it up, seems at times like the plucking out of a right eye. But, my dear friend, let our daily prayer be, that our mutual disappointment may be mutually sanctified to us,—and teach us more and more our dependence on God, and the uncertainty of all human calculations. The Lord doeth all things well. 'How unsearchable are His judgments, and His ways past finding out.' * * * And now, my dear brother, I commend you to God, and to the word of His grace; praying that His grace may be sufficient for you, and for all who are laboring with you; and that God may, in His own good time, send you a man after His own heart, to preach faithfully the Gospel of His dear Son, and break unto you the bread of life."

"CLEVELAND, April 5, 1852.

"Your kind letter, announcing an invitation to Rev. Dr. STILES to take my place in the new Church, has been duly received, with heart-felt gratitude to God for directing your minds to that man of God,—a man of all others in the large circle of my acquaintance I should prefer. My sincere hope and earnest prayer is, that God will send him to you, and open for him a wide door of usefulness. I cannot doubt but a blessing,—a rich harvest is before him, if he enter that field. He is a good man and true; fervent, eloquent, full of holy fire and apostolic zeal,—simple as a child,—an eye single, a heart warm, and a whole body full of light. O, should I live to see him settled among you, I should feel that the Lord's hand, which is so heavily laid on me, had by it wrought the greater mercies for you, and for that dear infant church."

CHAPTER II.

MINISTRY OF DR. STILES.

At the time our application was made to Rev. Dr. Stiles, he was engaged in the service of the American Bible Society, as Secretary for the South; spending most of his time in the Southern States, in furtherance of the objects of that institution. Our application took him by surprise, and was successful only because, when we had ascertained his purpose never again to accept a permanent pastorship, we modified our overture accordingly. In a letter dated Savannah, April 1, 1852, he wrote as follows:—

"While I am comforted that good brethren should invite me to any field in my Master's vineyard, and especially so important a one, I must respond,—if the intent of your communication is to call me to officiate as the permanent minister of the church, I must, as at present advised, answer respectfully, but decidedly in the negative. From constitutional structure rather than holy principle, I habitually over-work. Youthful vigor and inordinate effort may agree for a time, but years and over-work have no congeniality. This has long been my experience. * * * I think I may say that no agency in the Kingdom could content me for a moment, if it denied me the opportunity of so *preaching the Gospel* as to promise, under God, the conversion of sinners. For this reason, why should I wish to exchange my present occupation for a regular pastorship? I think I have seen many, many conversions this winter; thirty or forty in one place, and occasional instances all along down to my very last preachings; and my conviction is, not to the detriment, but rather to the advantage, of my official work. You understand from this extended sketch, what my response is to any application to accept the permanent pastorate of a church. * * * Had the call been to a *temporary* service, (and such the early language of your letter seemed to indicate, when you said, 'to dedicate this church or assist in dedicating it, and then go on preaching in it until such time as you may see fit to organize a church,')"—had such been the nature of the call. Dr. Stiles leaves it to be inferred that his difficulty on this head would have been obviated. He adds, "Now my brother, let me say in conclusion, I honor you and your three coadjutors in my heart. You are doing a good work. Surely the Lord will in due time point out His man for your church. I need not say that I will take a special interest in your enterprise,—shall delight in its prosperity—shall love at any time to speak the Master's messages to your people,—and do now pray, The Lord be with you."

MACON, GEO., April 14, 1852.
* * * "'The Lord lead us, in the matter of the church,— command my services if He so directs,—forbid my connexion with you if *this* is His will."

"P. S. I have this moment received your last. God bless my dear brother Sawtell. My friends everywhere think too much of me."

Not to extend these extracts, suffice it to say, that on reading them, our application was so modified as only to invite Dr. Stiles to come and dedicate the church, and then to remain with us so long as his sense of duty, under all the circumstances, as seen by himself, should seem to require. The reader will bear in mind that there was at this time no church organization,—much less an ecclesiastical society. Whatever arrangements were to be made for the supply of the pulpit, must be made by the proprietors, for there was no one else to do it. Well, Dr. Stiles at length came. Mr. Sawtell also came. The dedication had been fixed for the last Sabbath in June, 1852, and these good men, as if moved by an invisible attraction, were here the day previous, and stopped at the house of one of the proprietors, where they were thrice welcome. The new church and its prospective dedication and promise of usefulness, were the absorbing theme of their conversation and prayers. On the (Saturday) evening previous to the dedication, Mr. Amos Smith called to see them, and nearly the whole evening was spent in fervent addresses to the Throne of Grace,—each of the three brethren officiating in turn,—or in serious conversation suggested by the occasion which had brought them together. It was an evening long to be remembered; for if ever a church was thoroughly and honestly dedicated to God in advance, it was then and there, in that impromptu meeting of four persons. They prayed that God would own and bless that sanctuary from its very beginning; that his Holy Spirit might ever dwell in it and overshadow it; that the faithful Gospel might ever be faithfully preached there, and blessed to the conviction, conversion, and salvation of a multitude of souls. There was no formality about the exercises,—no effort,—nothing pre-concerted; it was the spontaneous outflow and overflow of Christian hearts, united in one object, and moved by a heavenly influence. To these prayers, and the answer to them, Dr. Stiles alludes in one of the extracts quoted below.

The first sermon ever preached in the South Church was by Rev. Dr. STILES, on Sabbath morning, June 27, 1852, from the text, "Why will ye die?" It was a deeply impressive discourse, and was preached to a very large audience. Not only the fame of the preacher, but the novelty of the occasion, drew together a crowd of hearers. In the afternoon the pulpit was occupied by some other clergyman. In the evening, Dr. Stiles preached the DEDICATION sermon, from the text, "I am not ashamed of the Gospel of Christ." He now laid out his full strength, stimulated alike by the greatness of his theme, and by the sea of up-turned faces which he saw before him. Every slip and aisle, every gallery and entry, every standing-place, and even the pulpit stairs of that spacious edifice, were filled to overflowing, and hundreds went away, from the impossibility of gaining admittance. Rev. Mr. Sawtell was present to enjoy the scene, but was unable to take any prominent part in the exercises. Several persons, who afterward obtained joy and peace in believing, date their first religious impressions from the solemnities of that day. One man in particular, then between 45 and 50 years of age, who had lived a very wicked life and gloried in his wickedness, was melted down under convictions of the truth, and never found rest until he found it in Christ. He has ever since witnessed a good confession,—always ready to lift up his voice in prayer or praise,—to do or to suffer for his Divine Master,—and is now an officer, as well as a most efficient member, of the South Church. Lest it should be thought that this statement is too highly colored, we here present his own account of the "great change" which took place in his views and feelings, as published in a little Tract, not very long after the date of his conversion. In that Tract he says,—

"From early boyhood, say for the last thirty six years of my life, I was a disbeliever in the Bible, the day of judgment, and even in the existence of God himself. I saw a controlling power all around me, but never connected it with a divine person. My creed looked to this world as the end of all things, and taught me, if happiness was to be found at all, it must be reached in this life. The fact is, at the age of thirteen years I discarded all the influence of my pious parents and friends, and claimed the right to control my own acts.

"As I advanced in life I denounced the clergy, closed my ears to all Christian advice, and my eyes to all the providences of God. I seldom entered a church. My Sabbaths were desecrated by devotion to boating, fishing, hunting, nay, to all sorts of amusements, which I took great pleasure in boldly prosecuting before the eyes of the public. I ridiculed and even abused those who were disposed to observe the Sabbath. I have a vivid recollection of the prevailing state of my mind when I heard the Sabbath bells, and looked upon the multitudes repairing to the house of God. I said in my heart, 'You fools, I never saw God, and you never did; why not act as sensible beings, and enjoy yourselves as I do?' In a word, I determined 'to sail the ship myself,' and for thirty-six years I did so. Was I happy? No; all was dark and gloomy in the prospect. Death and the grave were constantly before me, and though in perfect health, yet when thinking of the future I was always disturbed.

"My views and feelings are now greatly changed. And why? I gave a moment's honest attention to the salvation of my soul, and by the grace of God I am now happy. Dear fellow-sinner, whether you admit your accountability or not, if you will open your eyes and ears, and lift up your heart to God for mercy and salvation through Jesus Christ, you can secure that same change, and be happy too.

"I was induced to attend the dedication of a church in the place where I lived. The preacher was earnest and warm in his appeal to the consciences of the audience. I was a close listener to his words. Truth was permitted for the first time to light up my dark mind. The Spirit of God became an inmate of my heart. From a listener I became an inquirer. In due time the great truths of the gospel opened upon my agonized soul. I saw my sins and my ruin. The anguish of my spirit was awful in the extreme. I was actually on the very borders of despair. None but God knows the strugglings and sufferings of that hour, or, blessed be His name, the peace and comfort which I now enjoy. I can tell you of my present happy faith, and of the contrast between the hope of the unrepenting sinner and that blessed hope which by the grace of God now cheers my soul. I can tell you that the future now looks bright; that there is now no sting in death, no victory in the grave, no bliss in ignorance. Open your eyes and ears and heart, and God will give you the Holy Spirit, and with it a blessing so great that your soul cannot contain it."

This is a good beginning, it may be said; but did he hold out?—did his religion last? His old companions in sin, when they heard that he had been converted, predicted that in six months he would be as bad as ever. If he should not, they would be compelled (they said) to believe there was something in religion. Well, it is now *twelve years* since his conversion, and where does he stand? The following extracts will show. They are taken from letters which, on each anniversary of his spiritual birth, he has been in the habit of addressing to a friend who took a part in the erection of the South Church buildings.

NEW HAVEN, Nov. 23, 1861.

"Nine years ago, by the grace of God, I entered upon a new life, with strong promises that as the previous years of my existence had been a failure, the years to come should be to the glory of God, and the training of my soul to enjoy His presence hereafter. Every returning anniversary reminds me how poorly I have kept that promise, and how little I have done for Christ since it was made. I delight to see the return of this day and hour, because my heart goes out in gratitude, full to overflowing, towards God, that He then gave me such strong assurances of His love and favor, thus placing within me a Hope which has thus far been an anchor to my soul at all times. Yet while I am made happy under these assurances, I find one draw-back; and I ask, what have I done for Christ in return for his boundless love to me. I however still look up, and apply the only remedy which can carry me safely through. I have never for a moment doubted the beginning of a work of regeneration in my heart; and while the occurrences of nine years ago are so vividly before me, I never can. I am reminded of the faithfulness of our mutual friend, Dr. Stiles, who pleaded with and for me, and how he threw his whole heart into the work of kindling and fanning the faint glimmering light of hope in my soul. O how faithfully and perseveringly did he do his work! I love to remember him. I am also reminded of your many kind acts to me and mine; for, through the blessing of God and your liberal enterprise, we are looking *beyond*, for the rest that remaineth for those only that love our common Saviour. If at present the interests of this great enterprise appear neglected and tend to discouragement, may it not be a consolation that many souls *have been* saved through its instrumentality. I was in hopes that you would ere this have seen a great work done within its walls. But perhaps a greater is to come, after you have gone to your rest.—I am reminded at this hour, that a long life of wrong-doing is seldom repented of; or if repented of, the heart is in a poor condition to shuffle off evil associations and habits. The wounds are but partially healed, and I must carry through to the grave much that tends to hinder me in the Christian race. Almost all my companions in life, especially in middle life, have gone to the grave, full of sin, I fear. I am reminded especially to-night, as I reflect on former associations, that I am a monument of God's mercy; and I ask,—

> Why was I made to hear thy voice,
> And enter while there's room?

"With fresh resolutions and hopes, I trust to enter the new year stronger in Christ, richer in grace; and if before its close my soul shall be fully sanctified and fitted for a change, then God shall have the glory of my salvation in the new home where I hope to meet you."

"NEW HAVEN, November 23, 1862.

"Another year is gone, making *ten* in which I have tried to live worthily of the smiles and blessings of God, and with a hope of heaven. This anniversary is an eventful one,—for it comes freighted with bright hopes for our church, and evidently bearing testimony that God is with us, and is comforting us its members, removing from us the clouds which hung over us but a year since. It comes too, cementing our mutual friendship, begun ten years ago; and with my heart so full of gratitude to God and the kind souls instrumental in my welfare, I must let some of it escape by means of this letter. What wonderful kindness and mercy have been bestowed upon me, a poor, unworthy, wicked, blinded man! A few years ago my soul was unsuitable for the fellowship of God or godly men. It now sees mercy and love unmeasured, and light has taken up the darkness, revealing almost two heavens,—one begun on earth, and the other to come. * * * We have rejoiced together that our church (and I know as but few know how dear the whole enterprise is to you) is now in the hands of a good shepherd, and its prospects glorious for the future. The roots of bitterness over which we have mourned, are dead; and with God's help, I pray they may never be seen again. * * * Now, blessed with spiritual comforts,—blessed in my 'basket and store,'—with numerous friends to give me encouragement, I step into the new year with a thankful heart, and a firm reliance on Christ, that he will perfect in His own time and way, the good work begun November 23, 1852."

"NEW HAVEN, Nov. 23, 1863.

"The return of this hour is to me a comforting one. It reminds me of the dreadful pit from which I was digged just eleven years ago. It seems but a dream,—a new life, and one that gives me good cheer as I look forward. I feel that with all my short-comings and failings I can look back to the testimony that was mine eleven years ago, and onward I go with new hopes and renewed exertions. O what shall I render unto God for all His mercies to me in the space of eleven years! What changes—what blessings—what love!"

"NEW HAVEN, Nov. 23, 1864.

"This anniversary hour brings to my mind circumstances that occurred just twelve years ago; and they are before me now as vividly as at that moment. But it is twelve years (and they seem but a few days) since the light of God's forgiveness and love shone so brightly in my heart. The years have been short, but eventful; full of changes, intermixed with prosperity and adversity; and yet through them all to this present hour, not one doubt in the religion of Jesus and the work of His good Spirit in man's heart, (and by God's grace I can say in my own,) has ever crossed my mind. The testimony then given me by those influences, was just what my dark, wicked heart needed, to stay it in its new life. O the goodness of God in leading me to repentance, that I might see my obligations, my flagrant sins, and a way of escape from a just retribution.—This anniversary never comes, in its welcome round, without thoughts of that man of God, our mutual friend, Dr. Stiles. Though almost a stranger to me, yet knowing the value of a soul better than I did, he seemed to me almost as an angel of mercy standing between me and an offended God, and there earnestly and faithfully pleading that the light might illumine the darkness of my wicked soul, and salvation be given me. How often since I have obtained a knowledge of this great plan of salvation through Christ, (for until then I could not spiritually discern it,) have I thought of his anxiety and earnest pleadings with his Master in my behalf, as resembling the attitude in which Christ now stands toward me, as my Mediator. It would be a happy day could I meet this good friend again; but should it be ordered otherwise, I feel the consolation that we shall know each other there, in Christ's kingdom. Blessed thought, and thrice blessed hope!"

We have followed out this case to such a length, not only as one of special interest in itself, but as an illustration of the transforming power of religion in the soul; and also as showing the character of the ministrations with which the South Church was favored at this early period of its history. By a comparison of dates, it will be seen that the person alluded to, was struggling with convictions nearly *five months* before he yielded. During all this period his anxious Pastor was bearing him on the arms of faith to the Throne of Grace, often conversing and praying with him personally, and, as we have reason to believe, passing many sleepless hours of night, and sometimes nearly the whole night, in mingled emotions of hope and fear as to what would be the result. Verily he watched for souls as one who knew he must give an account. Other cases of conviction and conversion occupied his thoughts also; but he seemed to feel that "*this* kind" of possession was not to be overcome except by extraordinary effort. And when at length a flood of light broke in upon the hitherto darkened mind of the convicted man, it was hard to say which most rejoiced, the new-born babe in Christ, or he who had so long travailed in birth for his salvation. A knowledge of the fact that the Spirit of God was moving upon the minds of the people, gave tone and direction to the preaching, as the preaching and other attendant means had been blessed to the descent of the Holy Spirit. It was not, however, the rushing, mighty wind, but the still, small voice. Profound attention and deep solemnity pervaded the large assemblies, especially under the powerful preaching of Dr. Stiles. Some of the texts from which he spoke, are as follows; and the very mention of them will recall to the minds of many who heard him, the general scope of his remarks :—

July 4, 1852. If then I be a Father, where is mine honor? *Matt.* i. 6.

Evening. "To-morrow." *Exod.* viii. 10. Subject, Procrastination.

July 11. Christ in you the hope of glory. *Col.* i. 27.

Evening. That there should be time no longer. *Rev.* x. 6.

July 18. See, I have accepted thee concerning this thing also. *Gen.* xix. 21. Subject, Intercessory Prayer.

Afternoon. The redemption of the soul is precious, and it ceaseth forever. *Ps.* xlix. 8.

Aug. 8. All my springs are in thee. *Ps.* lxxxvii. 7.

Afternoon. What could I have done more to my vineyard that I have not done in it? *Isa.* v. 4.

Aug. 15. And Pharaoh said unto Jacob, How old art thou? &c. *Gen.* xlvii. 8, 9. Subject, Life's Pilgrimage.

Afternoon. Thou shalt guide me with Thy counsel, and afterwards receive me to glory. *Ps.* lxxiii. 24.

Aug. 22. And the multitude of them that believed were of one heart, and of one soul, &c. *Acts* iv. 32, 33.

Afternoon. Behold the Lamb of God, that taketh away the sin of the world. *John* i. 29.

Aug. 29. Hear, O heavens. and give ear, O earth, for the Lord hath spoken: I have nourished and brought up children, and they have rebelled against me. The ox knoweth his owner, &c. *Isa.* i. 2, 3.

Sept. 5. And again, when He bringeth in the first begotten into the world, He saith, And let all the angels of God worship Him. *Heb.* i. 6.

Afternoon. And declared to be the Son of God with power, according to the Spirit of Holiness, by the resurrection from the dead. *Rom.* i. 4.

Sept. 19. For there is one God, and one Mediator between God and man, the man Christ Jesus, who gave Himself a ransom for all, to be testified in due time. 1st *Timo.* ii. 5, 6.

Afternoon. Same text.

Sept. 26. Then said Jesus unto His disciples. If any man will come after me, let him deny himself and take up his cross and follow me. *Matthew* xvi. 24.

Afternoon. And they that be wise, shall shine as the brightness of the firmament, and they that turn many to righteousness, as the stars forever and ever. *Dan.* xii. 3.

Oct. 3--*afternoon.* Sow to yourselves in righteousness, reap in mercy; break up your fallow ground, for it is time, &c. *Hosea* x. 12.

Oct. 10. And it came to pass the same night, that the Lord said unto him. Arise, get thee down unto the host, for I have delivered it into thy hand, &c. *Judges* vii. 9, 10, 11. Subject, God's tenderness to His people.

Oct. 24. And they all with one consent began to make excuse. The first said unto him, &c. *Luke* xiv. 18.

Oct. 31. Take my yoke upon you and learn of me, for I am meek and lowly in heart, and ye shall find rest unto your souls. *Matt.* xi. 29.

Nov. 8. That they all might be one; as Thou, Father, art in me, and I in Thee, that they also may be one in us. *John* xvii. 21.

These are all the discourses preached by Dr. Stiles in the South Church pulpit prior to the organization of the Church on the evening of Nov. 8th, 1852. On those Sabbaths when he did not preach, he was absent from the city, fulfilling engagements which he had made before coming to New Haven. By reason of impaired health, it was understood beforehand that he would not be expected to *preach* more than once on a **Sabbath**; besides which he would give an extempore address in the evening. But as yet the

Chapel was not completed, and the evening services, when there was not preaching in the church, were held at private houses, in some of which the voice of prayer and praise had never been heard before. There were also more or less meetings during the week; all of which were well attended, and many of them crowded. The Spirit of God was manifestly present. Those were happy seasons, as many who read these pages can testify, from their own recollection and experience.

We remarked above, that Dr. Stiles did not engage to preach more than once on a Sabbath. But, in point of fact, he generally did preach twice at this period of his ministry, as will be seen from the record of texts just quoted. His sermons, too, were generally long, occupying about an hour in their delivery, and sometimes more. Although not written out, they were well studied; and a page or two of manuscript, in addition to his mental resources, was all that he was accustomed to rely on, for the re-production of the most complicated processes of reasoning, often divided into heads and sub-heads, to an extent that would bewilder any but the most attentive hearers. To this argumentative character of his preaching and to his close analysis of subjects, is attributable the fact, which we believe is undeniable, that his discourses were more highly appreciated, and more effective for good, in the case of persons of vigorous minds and mature judgment, than among the young, or uneducated adults. We here speak of his discourses generally in the South Church. That he was *able* to adapt his preaching to the humblest capacities, is shown by his amazing popularity and success among the negroes in the low country of Georgia, where he labored for a considerable period between the date of his own conversion and his going to Andover Theological Seminary. When the negroes learned that he was about to leave them, they begged him not to go, manifesting toward him much the same feeling as the Ephesian elders did towards Paul, when they "fell on his neck and kissed him; sorrowing most of all for the words which he spake, that they should see his face no more." As, however, the Ephesian elders accompanied Paul to the ship which was to take him from them forever, so the negroes collected by hundreds at the landing from which their spiritual teacher was about to depart, to hear his last words and receive his benediction. He accordingly addressed them from the boat, telling them that he was a new axe which had never been ground. His edge was thick, and he had to pound away a long time before he could batter down even a small pine. He was going away to get sharpened; after which he hoped he should be able to cut down more trees in one day than he now could in a week. Carrying out this illustration, so familiar to the negroes, in such a manner as few other men could, they were convinced that it was best for him to go, and shouted "Go, massa, and de Lor be wid you," or to that effect. This is the merest outline of a most thrilling description of the scene, as related by Dr. Stiles, ten or twelve years ago, in the presence of the writer. And here we may be permitted to copy, briefly, from "Sketches of Western Men," as published in the N. Y. Evangelist of Feb. 7, 1856. Speaking of Dr. Stiles, the writer says :—

"In the Winter of 1842, it was my good fortune to hear this gentleman in Oxford, Ohio, several successive evenings and on the Sabbath. * * * He was at this time in the prime of a vigorous manhood, and his bearing was solemn without affectation and marked by a noble manliness. He seemed to feel 'how awful is this place!' and his whole demeanor betokened his sense of the responsibility of one who preaches the Gospel. His prayers, in their wrestling, pleading fervency, exceeded anything I had ever heard. There was no vaunt or cant in them, but they were of that style we see in Abraham's intercession for Lot. His tones of voice were reverent but earnest, and he literally 'filled his mouth with arguments,' as he approached the mercy seat. I have never seen any flagging of interest as he engaged in prayer. I have heard him in revivals, at communion season, in prayer meetings, once on the *Mayflower* on Lake Erie, with a little swearing French Catholic priest just opposite, and yet in all places his prayers have been so reverent, fervent, scriptural, and pertinent, that I put them down in my own mind as models.

"But in Oxford I heard him preach as well as pray, and some of those discourses are as vivid in memory as if uttered yesterday. This is specially the case with two sermons; the one on the words, 'For there is one God and one Mediator between God and man, the man Christ Jesus,' &c., (1 Tim. ii. 5, 6,) and the other on the expression of Pharaoh to Moses, 'To-morrow.' In these sermons were evidences of intense mental effort, and prodigious grasp of his subject. The analysis of the sin of procrastination, in the latter discourse, was exceedingly fine, and the illustrations admirable. Such an impression did this discourse make on my memory, that, on hearing it some years afterwards, a second time, at the East, I could anticipate his arguments and illustrations, without the least abatement of interest.

"Occasionally he illustrated particular points, either by anecdotes or comparisons, which were always in good taste, and told on his audience with prodigious power. Thus, I remember, he illustrated the necessity of a sinner's casting himself loose from every refuge, on the mercy of Christ, by the son of a stern sea captain. One day, when the ship was at anchor, the boy had climbed to the very top of a mast, and had lifted himself up so that he stood on the mast's top, on a place scarcely large enough for his feet, with nothing above him to cling to. To attempt to stoop, in order to catch something below, would be to lose his balance and fall to the deck. A cry of alarm ran through the ship as his perilous situation was perceived by the sailors. The father, coming from his cabin, saw that his son had no chance of life but to spring from that dizzy height into the water; and seizing his rifle with one hand, and the speaking trumpet in the other, standing where the boy could see him, he cried to him in piercing tones of command, 'Jump into the water, or I will shoot you!' For a moment the boy seemed wavering. Every eye was fixed on him with agonized intensity. The delay in obeying that stern voice was but momentary, and the boy sprang into the air. As he reached the water, several sailors sprang in and brought him in safety to the deck.

"This is a very meagre outline of a most thrilling illustration. The language, and tone, and manner, were highly dramatic, but perfectly natural, and the imagination was so stimulated, that it reproduced the scene, until it seemed an actuality, and not a narrative. So powerfully wrought up was the whole scene as to put the hearer into an excitement really painful; and yet the anecdote was not suffered to distract the mind from the point in hand, for instantly the preacher began to describe the danger of the impenitent sinner, with overpowering earnestness, and point to Christ as the only possible salvation. The effect here produced was a triumph of eloquence, at least so far as to kindle the emotions of an audience in a very high degree. * * *

"These illustrations formed but a small part of his discourses, and were always such as to administer to the great end aimed at. They were not introduced, as by some inferior men, to relieve the stupidity of a sermon, and to cover up grievous deficiencies in argument and substance, by some captivating narrative. The illustration was itself calculated to impress some valuable thought, to point an argument, or ren'er some truth overpowering. It has been my good fortune to hear Mr. Stiles many times since, but the impressions made by those discourses in Oxford have never been modified; and I can easily imagine the power of such a preacher in his early manhood, when addressing vast audiences, such as in revival seasons waited on his ministry in Georgia and Kentucky. He had all the elements of power for a southern audience. He was a most manly man in the pulpit, and in all the social relations of father, brother, friend and pastor; his piety was unquestioned, his prayers not merely appropriate but subduing, his emotions of the warmest and most generous character, his zeal apostolic, his mind logical and analytical, his imagination bold, and his view of his business as a preacher such as Paul had, 'woe is me if I preach not the gospel!'" Withal, he had a perfect freedom from all the trammels of manuscript, and at times, when in the full exercise of his gifts, seemed almost choked with the burning words which struggled for utterance."

We have copied the above as a truthful description of Dr. Stiles' preaching and praying, from a source less likely to be suspected of partiality than the present writer; who nevertheless may say, as he deeply feels, that whoever has had the opportunity of listening to such a preacher, not only on one occasion, but for some years, has incurred a weight of responsibility which it is not easy to estimate. But if some were unprofited and unblessed by his ministrations, through prejudice or other causes, many received the good seed into their hearts,—believed, and were saved. Others, who were already church-members, were attracted to and around him, and on the evening of November 8, 1852, *twenty-nine* of them, most or all of whom resided in the south-western portion of the city, were organized into a Christian church, in connection with his ministry. [For names, see Catalogue at the close of this volume.] They had previously appended their signatures to the following declaration :—

"We, the undersigned, having considered the increasing population of this section of the city, and its inconvenient distance from places of public worship, and having felt the consequent importance of Christian privileges in the midst of us, and being providentially provided with a sanctuary for the service of God; looking up to God for holy motive in our solemn work, and for His gracious blessing upon it, with a view to the constitution of a Christian church,—do hereby subscribe the above as our Confession of Faith and Church Covenant."

These documents are published in connection with the Catalogue, at the close of this volume. They were chiefly prepared by Rev. Dr. STILES, and are as good an epitome of Christian doctrine and fellowship as can well be found. On the evening aforesaid, the twenty-nine persons who had thus united themselves in covenant, although previously belonging to three religious denominations, and to churches in three different States, were publicly organized into a church, called "The South Congregational Church," by an Ecclesiastical Council whom they had invited to meet for that purpose, in which were represented by Pastor and Delegate, the Centre, North, Chapel Street, College Street, Howe Street, and Third Church, of New Haven; the First Church in Fair Haven, and the Church in Westville. The Council had previously approved of the Confession of Faith and Covenant, and had expressed themselves satisfied with the evidence presented of the regular standing of the applicants in Christian churches, and of their "dismission for the purpose of constituting themselves a Church of Christ." The exercises of the evening were as follows:—

Introductory, by Rev. WM. T. EUSTIS.

Sermon, by Rev. Dr. BACON.

Reading Confession of Faith and Covenant, by Rev. Dr. CLEAVELAND.

Address to the Church, by Rev. EDWARD STRONG.

Prayer, by Rev. Dr. DUTTON.

On the 18th of the same month, (November, 1852,) a Committee of the Church, who had been appointed on the 13th "to consult with Mr. STILES in reference to his official relations to the Church," reported, "that he regards himself, and wishes to be regarded by the Church, as sustaining the relation of an indefinite Stated Supply." Whereupon the following preamble and resolution were adopted:—

"WHEREAS the Rev. Dr. STILES had been engaged as stated preacher to the congregation assembling in Columbus Street Church, before this Church was constituted,—and whereas it is according to Congregational usage for the Church to express its concurrence in any arrangement that places a pastor over them; therefore—

"*Resolved*, That this Church do cordially accept the Rev. Dr. STILES as their Stated Minister, and do hereby invite him to attend all their meetings for business, as Moderator."

On the 19th of the same month, (November, 1852,) Benedict Burwell and Eastman S. Minor were chosen Deacons; and on the 3d of June, 1853, Thomas Horsfall was added to the number.

The first Communion of the Church was held on Sabbath forenoon, December 6th, 1852, on which occasion five persons were admitted by profession, and three by letter. At that Communion, as at all subsequent ones to the present time, the usual hours of worship in the forenoon were entirely devoted to Sacramental services. On the first Sabbath of each alternate month, from that date to the present, the Lord's Supper has been administered,—with this variation, that after the Communion in December, 1859, no other was held until the following March, (three months,)—the object being to change the order of the months in which the Communion was held. It is now held in January, March, and so on, each alternate month, to the end of the year. Many of these celebrations have been deeply solemn and impressive, and besides church-members, have attracted large numbers of other persons, to see and hear. In most, if not all the other Congregational Churches in the city, the Lord's Supper is administered every month.

The Chapel, which was completed and opened for use about the beginning of 1853, became at once the place for holding all religious meetings, except the regular preaching services of the Sabbath. Between those services was held the Sabbath School. On Sabbath evenings there was a large gathering in the Chapel proper, attracted by the powerful extempore addresses and prayers of Rev. Dr. STILES; on Tuesday evening there was a lecture or prayer meeting; on Wednesday afternoon and evening, in their room over the Chapel, a meeting of the Ladies' Benevolent Society, which was instituted November 11, 1852, (three days after the organization of the Church,) and which at this period assembled every week; and on Friday evening a prayer-meeting. The Ladies' Society devoted the afternoon to sewing for benevolent purposes; at tea-time they sat down to a plain but inviting supper, having all the apparatus for making tea and otherwise furnishing the tables, within their own precincts; after tea, an hour or two more was spent in sewing; then the Pastor took charge of the meeting, and the remainder of it was devoted to strictly religious exercises,—including an address, singing and prayer. These meetings were turned to excellent account by the Pastor, who conversed familiarly with the persons in attendance, and when he found cases of special seriousness, which he often did, he would invite them into his study, in the adjoining room, and talk and pray with them, after the usual manner of an Inquiry Meeting.

Quite a number of persons, now members of the church, trace their first permanent religious impressions to the influence of these meetings. The table was supplied by the ladies in rotation, or by such of them as were able to bear the expense, except that a gentleman of the congregation offered to provide sugar and tea, which he has continued to do ever since, of the choicest quality. One of the standing rules of the Society is, that "only one kind of cake be furnished, under penalty of one dollar." At the *anniversaries* of the Society this rule does not apply. On the contrary, every member, on such occasions, brings in what she pleases; and the consequence is, that there are not only several kinds of choice cake, but almost every thing else that a lady's ingenuity can think of, to make up a rich and inviting repast. The original number of members was only eighteen; but it has since very largely increased, and includes gentlemen as well as ladies,—the former paying an annuity of one dollar, and the latter of fifty cents. At some of the anniversary meetings, more than a hundred persons have sat down to the tea-tables, which, of course, in such cases, have to be spread more than once. The influence of these gatherings upon the *social* interests of the church and congregation is very valuable, as it brings and keeps the members acquainted with each other, and tends to do away those distinctions which so naturally creep in, even among the members of the same religious organization. This Society still continues to prosper, after twelve years of successful experiment.

So also does the Sabbath School. Originally transferred to the South Church from the Mount Pleasant School House, as before stated, it was in every respect a humble institution, if institution it could be called, but has since grown to liberal dimensions,—more than 200 teachers and pupils having sometimes been in actual attendance. Under the able superintendence of Deacon Warner, supported by a corps of faithful teachers, its numbers continue to increase. From it many plants of righteousness have been transferred to the church, thence, it may be hoped, to be transplanted into the Paradise above. Two or three years ago, one whole class of young ladies, five or six in number, who had for a considerable period enjoyed the instructions and counsels of Deacon Horsfall, were hopefully converted, and united with the church. It has long been customary, and still is, to have a Sabbath School festival on Christmas day, in the Ladies' Room, over the Chapel, where short addresses are made, hymns sung, and a prayer offered, at the close of which a bag of sweetmeats, fruits, &c. is distributed to each pupil. These are always interesting occasions, especially to the children, and are very largely attended. At the last festival of the kind, December 26th, 1864, (the 25th being Sunday,) there was a larger gathering than ever before on a similar occasion. The whole number of persons present, including children, must have been nearly or quite 400. About 165 bags of sweetmeats, fruits, &c., were given out,—and 160 or 170 persons, chiefly adults, sat down to tea. No person who accepted a bag, was allowed to take supper at the rooms. In the course of the evening, an hour or more was occupied in singing ; several accomplished musicians being present and participating. Rev. Mr. Carroll and his lady and *mother* were there, and added to the interest of the occasion. At a late hour the company separated, after an entertainment, moral, social and physical, which, taken all in all, has seldom been equaled in any church. There was a great abundance and variety of choice food, fruits, &c., including a barrel of fresh oranges, just arrived from Porto Rico ; and notwithstanding the bountiful repast enjoyed by so many, there was a handsome surplus of money and other good things, after supplying the wants of all. There are also quarterly meetings of the Sabbath School in the Chapel, which take the place of the regular Chapel services on those evenings, and are largely attended.

A Young People's Prayer Meeting was commenced at a very early date, in the Chapel, at the close of the afternoon service, and has been continued, with occasional interruptions, to the present time. Just now it is merged in the "Fulton street Prayer Meeting," so called, which is held in the Chapel on Sunday evenings.

But to go back to the thread of our narrative. While these collateral agencies, most **if not** all of them, **were in operation and** efficiently conducted, as long ago as the beginning of 1853,—that is to say, almost from the very organization of the South Church,—the Sword of the Spirit, which is the word of God, was powerfully wielded by Dr. Stiles, Dr. Nathaniel W. Taylor, and others; and as might be expected, God "left not himself without witness, in that he did good, and gave us rain from heaven." A few scraps from Dr. Stiles' letters written at that period, will show his estimate of the state of religious feeling in the congregation:

"NEW HAVEN, Dec. 13, 1852.

"A good meeting last night. Six persons among us now entertain hope. One or two interesting developments of this kind."

[From another letter without date, but which must have been written about the same time with the above.]

"Our seriousness has decidedly increased since Sabbath. The young person of whom I spoke as having taken a wrong direction, but whose early conversion I anticipated, rejoices in Christ. * * * It is a little remarkable that almost every awakened one says that he was impressed from the *very beginning* of our services. Remember two things:— our (perhaps) sincere prayers that God would descend and own that House as his accepted sanctuary, by the movements of his Spirit, at that earliest moment, and forever after. Call to mind your own frequent remark, when there was yet no outward manifestation of Divine influence, that the sermons preached would show their fruit by-and-bye. Mr. and Mrs. ———— said to me after meeting last night, that since their own conversion they had not seen such a demonstration of religious feeling as they then witnessed."

"NEW HAVEN, Dec. 22, 1862.

"One or two conversions this week; particularly a Miss ————, awakened last Sabbath. Prayer Meeting very crowded."

The same encouraging state of things continued for months, and with some variations, for years. It hardly amounted to a "revival," in the usual acceptation of the term; yet in the long run it produced the fruits of a revival. But one Communion passed, in the course of several years, say from 1852 to 1857, when there were not more or less admissions to the Church; [for particulars, see Catalogue at the close of this volume;] and we remember well what a cause of lamentation it was to the good man who had the interests of the Church so much at heart, that even one such season should pass without any visible in-gathering.

As a Southerner by birth and early education,—as a Christian, with a heart large enough to comprehend the wants of the whole country and the world,—Dr. Stiles was among the foremost in a movement commenced in the city of New York about a year after he came to New Haven, "for the diffusion of Gospel truth in the Southern and Southwestern States." A Society for that purpose, called the "Southern Aid Society," was organized at a Convention of clergymen and others from different parts of the country, held in said city, 28th and 29th of September, 1853. On the 27th and 28th of October following, the Society elected its officers, among whom was Rev. Dr. STILES as General Agent. The necessity for such an organization was very clearly set forth in an Address to the Christian Public, written by Dr. Stiles, and adopted by the Society, from which we can make room for only a few paragraphs, as follows :

"It may be asked,—'Why not accomplish your object through the American Home Missionary Society? Why form a new Society?' The answer is, that the course which the Home Missionary Society is understood to have marked out for itself, does not permit it to perform our work. First, because it is restricted by its rules, from aiding any minister or missionary, however faithful, laborious or self-denying, who, under any circumstances, is a slaveholder. And secondly, because the impression is general at the South, that the Home Missionary Society is closely allied to Abolitionism, so called. This impression, however erroneous, renders the aid afforded by that Society to churches in the Southern and South-Western States, of doubtful value in reference to success; insomuch that, in some cases where such aid had been rendered, it had been voluntarily relinquished by the recipients, needy though they were, as a damage rather than a benefit. While, therefore, we are convinced that the American Home Missionary Society, without a change of policy, is essentially unable, even if it were disposed, to perform our work, we desire still to cherish towards it the sentiments of kindness and good will, which, with some of us, date back to its organization, and even before; for some of us aided in its formation. Most of the members of the Southern Aid Society are, and long have been, supporters of the American Home Missionary Society; and some of them are among its largest contributors. They expect to aid it still. They rejoice in its efficient labors at the North and West, and hope, in some measure, to supply its lack of service at the South and South-West. The *whole country* is our field. In so far as it is occupied by the American Home Missionary Society, we gladly co-operate. Where that Society pauses or falters, there the Southern Aid Society begins its separate action, and thence proceeds. Thus, between the two, if Providence smiles upon our efforts, the *whole* of our beloved country will be cared for and aided, according to the measure of the benefactions of the churches."

"In the American Home Missionary Society's Annual Reports, the ministers or missionaries aided, are classed under the heads of New England, Middle, Southern, and Western States. The number so aided, for a few years past, in each of these geographical divisions, according to said Reports, is as follows:

	1848-9	1849-50	1850-1	1851-2	1852-3
New England States,	302	301	311	305	313
Middle do	239	228	224	213	215
Southern do	15	15	15	14	12
Western do	463	488	515	533	547
Total,	1,019	1,032	1,065	1,065	1,087

"The largest number aided in the Southern States, in any one of the last five years, is 15. It is proper, however, to remark, that in this (not unusual) classification, Kentucky and Tenessee, as well as Missouri and Arkansas, are ranked as Western States. Delaware and the District of Columbia are included among the Middle States. In *all* the slave-holding States, including the District of Columbia, the Society aided an aggregate of 56 ministers or missionaries, 30 of whom resided in Missouri, and nearly all the rest in other States bordering upon free territory. In all the *non*-slave-hoiding States, the Society aided 1,031 ministers or missionaries; being more than eighteen times as many as in the slave-holding States. In Maryland, South Carolina, Florida, Mississippi, Louisiana and Texas, comprising, according to the last census, a population of 2,675,-829 souls, and an area of 424,032 square miles, the Society, last year, aided not a single minister or missionary. In Georgia, Alabama and Arkansas, with an aggregate population of 1,887,309 souls, and an area of 160,920 square miles, it aided only three ministers or missionaries, one in each State.

"Without going further into particulars, is it extravagant or unkind to say, that the A. H. M. S. is not accomplishing in the Southern and South-Western States, all that might be reasonably expected from its national designation—much less all that is demanded by the immensity of the field,

(844,144 square miles, equal to 108 such States as Massachusetts,) the greatness of its population, (9,663,997 souls,) or the magnitude of the interests involved, both for this world and the next? And if such be the fact, need we any apology before a Christian people, for attempting, as God shall enable us, to occupy that most important and too long neglected missionary field, and to turn in that direction some portion of the zeal, effort, contributions and prayers, of the denominations with which we are connected. Precisely this is the object of the Southern Aid Society."

"We commend it to all who love the Church and the nation,—God and man. We dedicate it to the Lord Jesus Christ,—God and man, the Head of the Church and the Saviour of the world. And here we register our prayer, that its spirit may ever be Christian only, to all classes, and especially to Christian brethren; that its management may soon win the confidence of all Christian Societies toiling in the same cause; and that its work may thus be entered up, on the grand final record of the earth:—THE SOUTHERN AID SOCIETY,—IN THE SERVICE OF GOD,—THE SUPPLY OF THE NEEDY,—SALVATION TO THE LOST."

Notwithstanding the strong attachment of Dr. Stiles to his church and congregation, and his deep interest in their welfare, he felt it his duty to accept the General Agency of the new Society, at least in part, and it was finally arranged that he should devote one half his time to said Society, and the other half to his church in New Haven. This made it necessary that regular assistance should be provided for the supply of the pulpit in his absence, instead of depending, as had hitherto been done, upon casual engagements. Accordingly, three different clergymen, who occupied the position of Pastors in as many churches, were successively invited to this field as

Associate Stated Supply; but they all successively declined, although they had severally given us every reason to expect their acceptance of our invitation. In giving such encouragement, they were doubtless sincere, and spake as they meant. But the fact that they were wanted here, made them more highly valued by their people at home, who accordingly rallied around them, increased their salaries, paid up arrearages, and otherwise manifested so much kindness and affection, that their Pastors could not leave then. In announcing to his people the third of these successive disappointments, Dr. Stiles complimented them on their *money-power* [they were generally poor]; remarking that they not only paid a liberal salary to their own minister, but had raised the salaries of three other ministers, and how many more he could not say. In this state of things, Dr. Stiles deeming it of great importance that he should enter upon his new work without further delay, Rev. GURDON W. NOYES, a graduate of Union Theological Seminary, who for two or three years had ministered to a church in Portsmouth, Va., and more recently to a church in Cornwall, Vt., was engaged as temporary Supply, commencing his labors on the 2d of April, 1854. This engagement terminated on the 4th of June following. On that day, after the forenoon service, the church and congregation tarried, by request of Dr. Stiles, and on motion it was

"*Voted*, That we cordially approve of the employment of Rev. G. W. Noyes as Associate with Dr. Stiles in the ministry of this church and congregation."

On the 25th of June, in the same year, Mr. Noyes commenced his labors in the new relation. Under this arrangement affairs moved on quietly, without any thing very noticeable to record, (the two ministers coöperating when Dr. Stiles was present, and when he was absent, Mr. Noyes performing all the duties of the ministry,) until Sabbath evening, Nov. 15th, 1857, when Dr. Stiles, finding his whole time and energies required in behalf of the new Society, tendered his resignation in full as Stated Supply of the South Church. Whereupon the following preamble and resolutions were presented and adopted:

"*Whereas*, The Southern Aid Society having extended an earnest request to the Rev. Dr. Stiles, the Stated Pastor of this church and congregation, that he will devote his whole time to the interests of that Society, and learning from Dr. Stiles that it will be in accordance with his views of duty to accede to this request: Therefore,

"*Resolved*, 1st. That this Church acknowledge the principle to be of sacred obligation, for every servant of God to take that post of duty which will give him the widest sphere of influence.

"2d. That in the request made by the Southern Aid Society for the entire services of Dr. Stiles, we recognize his call to an extensive sphere of Christian labor, which, in the providence of God, he is peculiarly fitted to occupy.

"3d. That while we highly appreciate the services of Dr. Stiles as our Stated Pastor, and he enjoys our unabated confidence and esteem, we do approve of his acceding to the request of the Southern Aid Society, believing it to be a call from our Divine Master, for him to work in another part of His vineyard."

Thus was terminated a connection which to many of his people was fraught with inestimable blessings, and which afforded to thousands not belonging to his immediate congregation, and many of them from distant places, opportunity to hear the words of life and salvation from one of the most remarkable men of the age. And although now a wall of separation is built up between his former people and himself, so that neither he can come to them nor they go to him, yet they have the assurance in their own hearts that such of them as are true believers, will soon meet him in a world where wars and fightings and alienations are known no more.

Dr. Stiles left his people at a most interesting period, when the wave of religious revival which commenced in the Fulton street Prayer Meeting and afterwards spread over a great part of the land, had begun to flow, and had already, in its incipient influences, reached New Haven. The experienced shipmaster does not more clearly foresee the coming storm, than Dr. Stiles discerned in advance the signs of those times. Several weeks anterior to the date of his resignation, he remarked to the present writer that he believed we were on the eve of one of the greatest revivals ever known. He alluded to the manifestations of a pervading religious feeling in New York, Newark and other places, and expressed his belief that it was the precursor of events which would make heaven and earth rejoice.

CHAPTER III.

MINISTRY OF REV. MR. NOYES.

On the **29th of** November, 1857, the **South Church** passed the following resolution:

"*Resolved,* That Rev. G. W. Noyes, late Associate Pastor with Rev. Dr. Stiles, be requested to act as Stated Pastor until we can determine upon more definite arrangements."

December 1st, Mr. Noyes accepted the invitation. Dec. 27th, the following minute was presented by the Committee and adopted by the Church.

"Having been informed that the Ecclesiastical Society recently organized* in connection with this church, have voted to offer Rev. G. W. Noyes a salary of $1350 per annum for his ministerial services, this church do hereby request the Society to unite with them in a common invitation to Rev. G. W. Noyes to become their Pastor."

January 1, 1858, Mr. Noyes declined.

January 16th, the Church, in concurrence with the Society, voted to engage his services as Stated Supply until Spring; which they had previously learned would be agreeable to him. April 10th, 1858, at a meeting of the Church duly warned, and held in the Pastor's study, the call to Mr. Noyes to become their Pastor, was renewed, with a salary of $1500. The

---

* The Ecclesiastical Society was organized Dec. **5, 1857.** **See Appendix.**

Society concurred. April 18th, Mr. Noyes accepted the invitation. Accordingly, an Ecclesiastical Council, called by the parties jointly, was held on the 24th of May, in the South Church,—the following churches being represented, viz : Third, North, College Street, Chapel Street, Howe Street, Centre, Yale College Church, and South Church. Among other papers submitted to the Council, was one from the Fourth Presbytery of New York, certifying to Mr. Noyes' good standing in the church and in the ministry. The Council having decided that the examination and credentials of Mr. Noyes were satisfactory, proceeded to his installation on the evening of the same day, in the South Church, as follows :

Introductory Services, by Rev. Mr. ATWATER.
Sermon, by Rev. Dr. STILES.
Installing prayer, by Rev. Dr. CLEAVELAND.
Charge to the Pastor, by Rev. Dr. DUTTON.
Right hand of Fellowship, by Rev. Mr. HAMILTON.
Address to the People, by Rev. Mr. EUSTIS.
Benediction, by the Pastor.

Thus, for the first time since the organization of the church, it was provided with a regularly installed *Pastor*, technically so called. The winter and spring had been a season of special religious interest in his church and congregation, as well as in other churches of this city and elsewhere throughout the country. It was the season of "the great revival." On the 6th of June, 1858, the fruits of it, so far as the South Church was concerned, were gathered in,—26 persons being received by profession, and eight by letter. Unfortunately, for nearly a month (including three successive Sabbaths) when the revival was at its height, our minister was absent at the West. The Deacons and other members did what they could to direct inquiring souls to Christ; but it was felt to be a calamity, that in our time of greatest need, we were left destitute of ministerial aid, except as the pulpit was supplied by neighboring ministers on the Sabbath.

Occasionally, after Mr. Noyes became sole Pastor, Dr. Stiles, whose family still resided in this city, was invited to occupy his former pulpit. It was purely a "labor of love," without any visible motive but a desire to do good, and gratify his old friends in the Church and congregation, to whom his voice was always welcome. His official duties as General Agent of the Southern Aid Society kept him more and more away from the city, and about the close of 1859, one of the members of the South Church, learning that he was about to be absent several months, very innocently suggested to Mr. Noyes the propriety of inviting him to give us a sermon before his departure. The tenor of Mr. Noyes' reply will be gathered from the following letter, dated

NEW HAVEN, Dec. 24, 1859.

Rev. G. W. NOYES,

My dear Sir:—Your favor of the 14th inst. reveals a state of things in our Church and society which is much to be regretted. I have taken a little time to consider it.

The case is this: On the 12th inst. I ventured to suggest to you, that as Dr. Stiles was about to leave this part of the country, and to be absent several months, many of his former people would be gratified to hear him preach "at least once," before his departure. You reply in substance, that you "have no personal objections to such an arrangement," but that "many of the people have:" That some have impliedly or indirectly found fault with you for inviting him to preach so often already; and have said that if it continued, they should have to go elsewhere: That the last time he preached, a number of the choir left, and the remainder tarried reluctantly, as a matter of respect and duty: That others, on coming to the Church and learning that he was in the pulpit, went away elsewhere. In this condition of things you are pleased to ask my opinion as to the course most expedient for you to pursue. I will answer with all frankness, expecting you, after all, and wishing you, to exercise your undoubted right "to invite whomsoever you *choose*, to occupy your pulpit." But before I proceed, allow me to dispose of two or three preliminaries. And

1. As to the frequency of your inviting Dr. Stiles to preach. According to the best of my recollection and belief, he has preached in our Church but—[Here is a blank in the rough draft from which we copy, but on referring to a reliable record, we find that within the previous fifteen months Dr. Stiles had preached in the South Church five sermons; one of them during Mr. Noyes' absence on his annual vacation, when the pulpit was supplied by the Society's Committee.]

2. Notwithstanding the drawbacks of which you speak, is it not true that even now the audiences are larger *when the public are aware* that he is to preach, than at other times?

3. Have not some persons, including some members of the Church, left us, and gone to other Churches, under an impression that he has been discourteously treated.

And what is the demand of the class of persons of whom you speak? What is the condition on which they will consent to remain with us and be quiet? It is simply this; that the great and good man who laid the foundation of our spiritual edifice in faith and prayer,—such prayer, and such holy wrestlings as I never before heard from the lips of man; who dedicated our sanctuary to Almighty God, Father, Son and Holy Ghost, and in so doing, on the very first day of his ministrations, sent an arrow of conviction to the heart of an infidel and atheist, which was never extracted until he found joy and peace in believing; whose eloquent, faithful, pungent words of love and warning aroused the slumbering community around to the interests of the soul and eternity,—filled the house with profoundly attentive audiences, larger on an average, in the afternoon, (when he was expected to preach,) than those of any other sanctuary of our denomination in the city; who gathered our Church, drew up our Covenant and Confesssion of Faith, instituted or gave tone to our Ladies' Meeting, making it a centre of attraction to the whole neighborhood, and to many ladies in other parts of the city; who was the instrument, in the judgment of charity, of bringing scores of persons to Christ, including many individuals residing out of the city; who was the means, my dear Sir, of *your* coming to New Haven and holding the position you now occupy, and who, as the whole congregation can bear witness, treated you with uniform courtesy in all our public assemblies; and who to this day, although officially separated from us by calls to other fields of labor, does still often and earnestly remember us in his prayers, and is ready to serve us, in any way consistent with his other duties and our wishes; I say the class of persons of whom you speak, if I rightly understand their views, require that this holy man, who has done so much for us, shall be deliberately and permanently excluded from the pulpit which he so long and faithfully occupied. The question is not, as I understand it, whether he shall be invited to occupy the pulpit at this time, but at any time. The object seems to be, to fix a stigma upon him—to proscribe him; for what reason I do not know. I am not aware that he has done anything to forfeit the confidence of the Church and Society—much less their Christian courtesy. True, he was born South of Mason's and Dixon's line, has written a book, and has been an officer of the Southern Aid Society, whose object is simply and only to dispense the

Gospel of Christ to ten millions of people, including three and a half millions of slaves, from whom the American Home Missionary Society has withdrawn its aid. But I do not perceive that either of these facts, or all of them together, constitute a just ground of offence to a Christian congregation.

Viewing the matter in this light, I scarcely need add, that I can never be a party to such proscription, either actively or passively. If my own personal gratification were alone involved, I would cheerfully forego that gratification for the sake of peace. But if peace can be had, only on the condition of sacrificing a great and good man, of whom the world is not worthy, to the moloch of ultra Abolitionism, and of surrendering those noble edifices, that pulpit, and the institutions connected therewith, to the promotion of the same proscriptive and malignant spirit, then in my judgment the purchase is too dear, and I prefer to meet the issue as it stands. I well know that as a member of the Church and congregation, I have no more control over the action of either, than has the obscurest of our members. I am willing it should be so. And you will bear me witness that I have never sought to encroach upon the rights of the pulpit. At the same time I have some rights peculiar to myself. I have expended more than $50,000 upon the South Church enterprise, in the erection and furnishing of the buildings, and in supporting, in part, the expenses of the establishment for the last seven years. I have never, for a single moment, regretted the expenditure. On the contrary, I am ready to expend $50,000 more, if necessary, to carry out the objects of the enterprise as originally contemplated. What those objects are, you were early apprised; and your acceptance of the station which you now occupy, is proof that, substantially, they met your approbation. What they are, is evidenced by the history of the enterprise thus far, in connection with the fact that down to this day I have never complained of the manner in which they have been carried out. But if a new order of things is to be introduced; if the mad spirit of ultra Abolitionism, which has already divided so many churches, greatly damaged the interests of the slave, and brought our country to the brink of ruin, is to be infused into our church and to become dominant in its management,—which I do not believe, though I thus speak,—I have only to say, I shall want the buildings for their original purpose, and my money to sustain the enterprise on that basis.

It is but a few months since Rev. Dr. Bacon, seeing Dr. Stiles in his congregation, came down from the pulpit, and in the most cordial manner invited him to preach,—which he did. Are the South Church and congregation so much more intolerant than Dr. Bacon and his congregation, as the facts stated in your letter would seem to imply? I doubt it. I should like to see the experiment tried. I believe that a fair expression of the views of our people would show that they are generally conservative, and that the class of persons to whom you allude, are in a lean minority.

From what I have said, you are prepared for my *opinion*, which is, that such intolerance, discourtesy and ingratitude, towards a faithful soldier of the Cross, as would be exemplified in his exclusion from our pulpit, for no assigned cause, but, so far as appears, to gratify an unreasonable and cruel prejudice, *should not be yielded to*,—no, not for an hour. Three or four years ago, a few disaffected persons, of the same class, left us in disgust, and we have had peace ever since. If those who now threaten to leave, unless their wishes are complied with, should do so in fact, the probability is that the church and society will be stronger, happier, safer and better in the end, than by retaining them within its bosom. I know not who they are; I am glad I do not. But whoever they are, however many or however few, I cannot advise an act of palpable injustice and wrong, for the sake of retaining them. Let us protect and honor God's faithful ministers, and he will protect and bless us. As to temporalities I have no fear. And I am sure no spiritual blessing can be expected as the result of proscription such as is sought to be imposed upon us.

Should you, all things considered, conclude to invite Dr. Stiles into your pulpit once before he goes South, permit me to suggest that a notice of the fact be given in the newspapers. Then any who are unwilling to hear him, can stay away, and thus avoid the indecorum of leaving the house. As to the choir, or a portion of them, they must do as they think proper. For one, I would rather dispense with singing than yield to such dictation. What is it, in effect, but surrendering the pulpit to their control; or at least, giving them a veto upon the action of the pastor? I protest against such an invasion of his rights.

In conclusion, permit me to say, that at this time especially, any manifest slur upon a good man merely because he is a Southerner by birth, would be most unfortunate in its public bearing; and occurring in a church which has been generally supposed to be conservative, and is known as such all over the South, would have a very bad effect upon the public mind in that part of the country, which is in an excited and dangerous state. Do let us try to pour a little oil upon the troubled waters, and not let our glorious constellation go down in blood.

I remain with much respect,
Your friend and parishioner,
GERARD HALLOCK.

P. S. I have said nothing to Dr. Stiles about this whole matter. He does not know from me, that any correspondence has taken place between us.

On the receipt of this letter, and after consultation with some of his members, Mr. Noyes concluded to invite Dr. Stiles to preach, as proposed, and *did* invite him. Public notice was given in the newspapers, and on the 8th of January, 1860, Dr. Stiles preached to a very large and apparently gratified audience. The choir was as full as usual, and no persons left the house, that we are aware of, until the services were concluded. This is the last sermon but one that Dr. Stiles ever preached in the South Church.

The whole period of Mr. Noyes' ministry in connection with the South Church, was a little more than seven years; or say from April 2, 1854, till June 3, 1861. During the last half of this period, or say from Nov. 15, 1857, till the close of his labors, as above, he had the sole charge of the Church and congregation. Either to accompany or follow such a man as Dr. Stiles, was obviously a difficult undertaking. The wonder is, that Mr. Noyes was able to sustain himself so long and so well as he did, rather than that he finally failed to give satisfaction to a people, who, in the language of one of the other clergymen of the city, had been "spoiled by Dr. Stiles;" meaning, that the South Church people had been so accustomed to hear the powerful preaching of Dr. Stiles, that no minister of ordinary talents and resources could expect to satisfy them. On the 15th of May, 1861, Mr. Noyes tendered his resignation, as follows:—

To the South Congregational Church, New Haven, Conn.
DEAR BRETHREN:—
Learning that a small, yet influential minority among you, have recently become disaffected towards me, so as seriously to interfere with my comfort and usefulness, I felt it to be my duty to resign my charge; and do herewith resign it, to take effect on the 3d of next June; and request you to unite with me in calling an Ecclesiastical Council to meet on that day in said church, at half past 3 o'clock, to dissolve the relation existing between us.
GURDON W. NOYES.
NEW HAVEN, May 15th, 1861.

As usual in such cases, different persons would give different versions of the causes which led to this result. Perhaps the most impartial statement which can be had at this time, is the Report of the Standing Committee, submitted to the Church at a meeting held on the 24th of the same month, to consider the above communication. Said Committee consisted of Charles H. Warner, Dr. John Nicoll, and R. S. Pickett, elected members, and Deacons Minor and Horsfall, together with the Pastor, members *ex-officio*. Of the five lay members, three belonged to that wing of the Church which has since broken off from the main body, and two of them (Dr. Nicoll and Mr. Pickett) were among the warmest friends Mr. Noyes had in the Church. The Report of that Committee was as follows:—

Explanatory Statement from the Committee of the Church.
"It is well known to most of the members of the Church, that within the past year, and more particularly within the past six months, the attendance on our Sabbath services and the other regular weekly meetings of the Church, has seemed to be gradually diminishing. Notice has been taken of this by the Pastor and the Committee of the Church, and by other members. Conversation on the subject, and inquiry as to its cause, revealed the fact that many members of the Church and congregation were in the habit of frequently going to the meetings of other churches, and that a considerable number of the regular and constant attendants on the meetings of our own Church,—including those upon whose liberality the enterprise has mainly rested for its support,—were strongly impressed with the conviction that this enterprise could not be carried forward successfully under the ministrations of our present Pastor. This led to some informal consultations on the subject, which resulted in a communication of the facts, as they were then understood, to Mr. Noyes, by the Committee of the Church.

"While it was obviously impossible for Mr. Noyes to continue his labors with satisfaction under such circumstances, it was felt that a separation, if it must take place, should be made in a manner that would do least injury to our minister's reputation, and to the welfare and peace of the Church. In this point of view, it was considered better for Mr. Noyes that he should tender his resignation *before*, rather than *after* a public meeting for the discussion of the subject. Hence, no public meeting has before been called.

"It was also considered equitable that Mr. Noyes should receive satisfactory pecuniary compensation for the disadvantage to himself and family of leaving his charge under such circumstances; and arrangements have therefore been made, satisfactory to Mr. N., by which, in case his resignation is accepted, he is to receive a donation of $500."

After some discussion, the following resolution was adopted by the Church, with only five dissentients, including two who did not vote on either side.

"*Resolved*, That in accordance with the expressed desire of Rev. G. W. Noyes, we hereby accept his resignation as Pastor, while we regret that circumstances have made it appear necessary for him to leave us and sunder the ties of pleasant and profitable intercourse which, for a period of seven years, most of us have enjoyed with him."

The Church also voted to unite with Mr. Noyes in calling an Ecclesiastical Council. Said Council was held in the South Church, June 3d, 1861; and comprised delegates from the Centre, North, Third, Chapel street, College street, and Yale College Church. The result was embodied in the following Resolutions, prepared by Rev. Dr. Dutton, and Rev. Messrs. Eustis and Fisher, which the Council adopted unanimously:—

"*Resolved*, That while, in compliance with his own decided wish, we consent to the separation of Mr. Noyes from his charge, we bear our united testimony to the ability, faithfulness and success, as a Pastor and preacher, which have characterized his labors in this place.

"*Resolved*, That we express our cordial interest in the welfare of this flock of Christ, and earnestly pray the Great Head of the Church to send them a successor to the Pastor they have lost, who shall build them up in the faith of the Gospel, and who shall fully and fearlessly declare and apply all its doctrines and precepts."

This united prayer of the Council, we may charitably believe, has been answered; if not exactly in the way intended,—in a much better way. As "successor to the Pastor we have lost," God has sent us a man who "builds up his people in the faith of the Gospel;" and who, if he does not preach or pray Abolitionism, and blood up to the horses' bridles, if necessary to accomplish that object, does preach and pray with the angel choir which heralded the infant Saviour, "Peace on earth, good will toward men." If he does not so "declare and apply all the doctrines and precepts of the Gospel" as to play into the hands of a political party; if he does not preach electioneering sermons on the Sabbath, just before a Presidential election; he does beat up recruits for the Captain of Salvation; he does electioneer for the King of kings. But the members of the Council appear not to have been satisfied with the manner in which their prayer was answered; else why, eighteen months afterwards, did nearly the same body of men, with some others added, attempt to reverse that answer, by silencing or displacing the aforesaid "successor?" But more of this in the sequel.

Mr. Noyes' "Farewell Sermon" was preached in the South Church, June 2, 1861, being the day before his resignation was to go into effect, and was soon after published. It was a sort of stern-chaser, discharged upon his people as he was about to leave them. He virtually admits the declining state of the Church and congregation, but attributes it mainly to the people themselves. He tells how many thousand calls he had made (4,449) during his connection with the South Church, how many prayers he had offered (1,000) in the course of those visits, and how many other good things he had done. He says,—" During the four years of colleagueship, *I* received to the Church one hundred by profession and forty-six by letter; and during the three years since, seventy-seven,—thirty-six by profession and forty-one by letter,—making a total of 223." If Dr. Stiles, in giving an account of his own ministry, should be equally grasping, there would be very little left for Mr. Noyes. He would say, as Mr. Noyes does,—" During the four years of colleagueship, *I* received to the Church one hundred by profession, and forty-six by letter." And on the same principle might he not add,—" *I* also sowed the seed, and, ere I left, saw the grain spring up, which was harvested by Mr. Noyes in the following June." If Dr. Stiles should say this,—which he would be far enough from doing,—how would it strike Mr. Noyes? Would he deem it quite fair and honorable for Dr. Stiles to set to his own account all the fruits of their joint labor "during the four years of colleagueship," and so leave nothing for Mr. Noyes as the result of his three years' labor, after the in-gathering above mentioned, except nine persons admitted by profession, (an average of three per annum,) and a less number by certificate than were dismissed during the same period? We simply ask the question, and according to the answer given, will be Mr. Noyes' verdict in his own case, with only this variation, that "during the four years of colleagueship," which were in fact but three years and a half, Dr. Stiles was the principal, and Mr. Noyes the assistant.

In dealing with *his people*, the author of the Sermon was much less exposed to be over-indulgent and partial, than in reviewing his own labors. Accordingly he proceeds to "reprove, rebuke and exhort" them, agreeably to the instructions of Paul to Timothy, specifying "three things," which he says "have already retarded the growth and success of the Church, and which, if not corrected, will work more unfavorably in the future." They are as follows :—

"1. There has been an erroneous idea of the Pastor's work. Too much has been laid upon and expected of him." Under this head he asks :—" Is it not a fact too patent to be questioned, that upon him was placed almost the entire burden of the Church's affairs? In addition to preaching and visiting, has he not had largely to sustain the Sabbath evening and weekly meetings, and even lead the singing? Has not the opinion found expression in word as well as deed, that he was expected so to preach as to fill the Church and keep up a continual revival? And by such an attitude would not he be disheartened and the Church paralyzed?"

If these questions are to be answered in the affirmative, as they are evidently intended to be, they add Mr. Noyes' testimony to that of the Committee as to the dilapidated spiritual condition of the Church and congregation at that period. It is worthy of remark, that the evil of which Mr. Noyes complains, has not always existed in the South Church. It was not so under Dr. Stiles—it is not so under Mr. Carroll. On the contrary, there are very few churches within our knowledge, where so large a proportion of the male members are ready to be called upon for exhortation or prayer. How is it in the "Fulton street Prayer Meetings," as they are called, which are now held every Sabbath evening in the Chapel? Is there any difficulty in finding laymen there who are willing to speak or pray? None whatever. Numerically the church is not quite so large as when Mr. Noyes left; and yet the attendance on these meetings is quadrupled, and the spirit of them excellent. How is this to be accounted for? It cannot be caused by the return of those "many members of the Church and congregation" who, under Mr. Noyes' administration, according to the Report of the Committee, "were in the habit of frequently going to the meetings of other churches,"—for they have not returned. On the contrary, almost all of them have left us for good. On the whole, we know not how to account for the different state of things in the same congregation under different ministers, except by attributing it, or much of it, directly or indirectly, to the ministers themselves. This is on the supposition that the complaint of Mr. Noyes on this head was well founded, which, to the extent indicated by his remarks, we must be permitted to doubt.

2. "A second element of weakness and injury to the Church, is the neglect of wise discipline."

Never until the preaching of this Sermon, did we hear it intimated that Mr. Noyes was more ready to administer "wise discipline" to delinquent members, than were the great majority of his Church. We had heard, that in regard to two Scotch people whom it was proposed to discipline on account of the sale and use of intoxicating liquors, Mr. Noyes objected to doing it *at that time*,* because, he said, the Scotch were clannish, and if some of them were offended, they might all be, and leave. [A Scotch minister was then preaching once or twice on the Sabbath in Dr. Cleaveland's Lecture Room, and some of our

---

* On inquiring of some who were then members of the Standing Committee, we learn that we were not misinformed; and that in the matter of discipline generally, Mr. Noyes was certainly not in advance of the other members of the Committee in his efforts to promote it. According to the rules of the Church, it is made the duty of the *Standing Committee* to "examine and report on all cases of discipline." If then the Standing Committee, (of which Mr. Noyes was ex-officio a member, and by position the leading member,) did not do their duty, why reproach *the Church* for the Committee's own neglect?

Scotch people were in the habit of attending.] In a few months after Mr. Noyes left us, these two persons were suspended from the privileges of the Church, and afterwards struck from the list of members; as were two other persons, for similar offences.

3. "A third hindrance to the Church, is the unprecedented assumption of the minority."

What that assumption is, or was, Mr. Noyes does not say in so many words, but leaves it to be inferred that the minority assumed to overrule the majority. He says, "The pastoral relation, left to the tender mercies of a minority, has no security whatever, and better never be formed. It can be sundered at the *capricious* or *malicious* beck of a single individual." Well, who were the minority in the South Church? Mr. Noyes' own friends and adherents. What is the proof that they were in the minority? Their votes; which on the resolution to accept his resignation, stood three or five* to seventy, as was testified by the Chairman of the South Church Committee before the Council which dismissed Mr. Noyes. But we do not believe that this minority, or any other minority, claimed to overrule the majority. If they did, we never heard of it until announced in Mr. Noyes' Farewell Sermon. It is too absurd a position for rational men to take. Undoubtedly the minority claimed a right to speak to

---

* There were three negative votes, and two persons did not vote.

their brethren on affairs of common interest, and to influence their votes if they could convince their judgments. But this, so far from being an "unprecedented assumption," is a universal and just claim. Yet it appears to be the only basis for the charge preferred by Mr. Noyes under this head ; for, in another place (p. 13) he says, "If the majority, after being teased and tormented by them [the minority] for a time, should yield to their unreasonable demands, his pleasant and useful relation to them would be broken up, and he set adrift, when he might have labored on successfully for years." So, after all, there is no assumption of power on the part of the minority ; they only "*t*ease and *t*orment :" just as a fly *t*eases and *t*orments an elephant, until at length the noble animal, overcome by its importunity, surrenders at discretion ; and thus the "small yet influential minority" becomes a majority. But to drop the figure,—we know of nothing to prevent a minority, however small, from endeavoring to bring the majority over to its views by sound argument or undeniable facts ; and if successful, the presumption is, that the minority were right, and the majority wrong. In the case before us, there was no necessity for such an effort : for no sooner had there been a comparison of views, than it was seen at once that a large majority were in favor of a change. And when the vote was taken on the acceptance of Mr. Noyes' resignation, it was, as we said before, all but unanimous. It was a perfectly free, fair and full vote of the

Church, and was unanimously sanctioned by a Council composed entirely of men in sympathy with Mr. Noyes on all the agitating questions of the day. There was every disposition on the part of his people, one and all, to make the separation as harmless as possible, both to his ministerial reputation and to his personal comfort. With this view they gave him $500, and it was in their hearts to increase the amount by voluntary contributions at a parting *soiree*, to be held in the Ladies' Parlor of the Chapel; and at the same time to put forth expressions of sentiment which would relieve the discomfort felt on all hands in sundering a relation so sacred and so long continued. Such a parting interview was proposed to Mr. Noyes through a Committee, but declined. He preferred a different course,—and hence these comments.

From what has been said, it appears that each of the three leading positions of the Sermon was founded in error. If not " *unprecedented* assumptions," they were nevertheless " assumptions," unsustained by substantial facts.

There is one good thing in the Sermon, where the preacher says to his people, " Kindly, yet earnestly do I counsel you to give to my successor your sympathy and coöperation, if you would have new and more glorious things done for you by his ministry." Some of us are trying to heed this wholesome counsel. The way the preacher's special friends have done it, is a caution.

Mr. Noyes had not been long disconnected from the South Church, before he received and accepted an invitation to the pastoral charge of a Church in Fair Haven, Conn., where he still continues his labors.

CHAPTER IV.

MINISTRY OF REV. MR. CARROLL.

After Mr. Noyes left the South Church, its pulpit continued vacant for about a year. In the course of that period, *forty-four* different clergymen occupied it successively, some of them very able men, including several pastors of churches. For a number of months, neither wing of the Church seemed disposed to make any movement towards the settlement of another minister. All knew that there was a lurking antagonism among the members, which would be likely to show itself whenever a suitable occasion should occur to bring it out. Some of them hoped that time would reconcile differences, and for *that* reason were willing to wait. At length, on the 24th of October, 1861, at a meeting of the Church, a proposition was made to invite Rev. J. PARSONS HOVEY, D. D., (since deceased,) of the Eleventh Presbyterian Church in New York, to become our Pastor; and on the following day, at an adjourned meeting of the Church, the motion was adopted. A large majority of the Church and Society were in his favor; but a few individuals objected, on the ground that he was disloyal, a pro-slavery man, and a Secessionist; or to that effect. The Church took the trouble to test the truthfulness of these allegations, by sending their two Deacons down to New York, to inquire into the facts.

The Deacons called upon Rev. Dr. Thompson, formerly of the Chapel Street Church in this city, Rev. Dr. Hatfield, Rev. Dr. Asa D. Smith, and Rev. Mr. Coe, of the Am. Home Missionary Society, all of them strong anti-slavery men, from whom, and from other sources, they learned that Rev. Dr. Hovey was one of the most estimable ministers in the city; that he was not a Secessionist, nor in any proper sense a pro-slavery man, nor disloyal to the government. And when another Committee of this Church and Society waited upon his Presbytery, to present our call, there was a general outburst of, "We cannot spare him;" "Nobody can fill his place;" "He is doing invaluable service where he is," &c., &c. His own Church also were in great alarm at the prospect of losing him; paid up the arrearages of his salary; offered him more; and by a strong Committee urged upon the Presbytery the absolute necessity of retaining him where he was, unless they were willing to see his large Church and Society, with its eleven hundred Sabbath scholars, broken up and disbanded. Accordingly the Presbytery passed a Resolution, requesting the South Church to desist from the further prosecution of the call. Dr. Hovey felt himself bound by the rules of the Presbyterian Church to abide by the decision of the Presbytery, and so the call was withdrawn. This was voted at a meeting of the South Church, Dec. 1, 1861.

The failure to secure the services of Dr. Hovey was a great disappointment to some of our members, who knew him personally, and who had hoped, from his kind and conciliatory bearing, long experience, and high qualifications, both as a Pastor and Preacher, that he would be able to unite the jarring elements of our Church and congregation, and thus prevent a rupture, which otherwise seemed inevitable. The Committee of Supply, consisting of Deacons Minor and Horsfall, had nearly exhausted the list of candidates, and no one of those who had been heard, appeared to be the man for us. In the case of one of them, a motion had been made to engage him as Stated Supply for one year, but the majority voted no.

Under these circumstances, on Sunday morning, December 29th, 1861, a young man made his appearance in our pulpit, who, until the day previous, was unknown, even by sight, to any person in the house; and who, in his turn, had never seen an individual belonging to the Church or congregation. It afterwards appeared that a clergyman in the interior had sent his name to our Committee of Supply, as one who might, perchance, be acceptable to us, and we to him. On the strength of this recommendation, the Committee had written to him, inviting him to preach one Sabbath : and here he was, a perfect stranger, in a strange pulpit, having never before been in New Haven. The first impression which he made upon the audience, was not entirely favorable. But he had not proceeded far, before what had seemed to be overaction, disappeared in the real warmth and energy of his discourse. His text was,—"Therefore the ungodly shall not stand in the judgment." Ps. 1 ; 5. It was a powerful and deeply impressive sermon. When the service was over, the general inquiry was, "Who is the preacher?" "Where is he from?" &c. It was soon learned that his name was CARROLL, and that he was a son of Rev. Daniel L. Carroll, D. D., the successor of Dr. Lyman Beecher, in Litchfield, Conn. A few of our members had sat under the preaching of Dr. Carroll, in Litchfield, and remembered him with the highest veneration and respect. In the afternoon, the young man preached from the text, "Then the king's countenance was changed, and his thoughts troubled him." Daniel 5; 6. This discourse was in no way inferior to the former. At the quarterly meeting of the Sabbath School on Sunday evening, he addressed the children, keeping them spell-bound for nearly an hour. The entire services of the day were full of interest, and a general desire was expressed to hear him again. Accordingly, the Committee of Supply invited him to occupy the pulpit on the following Sabbath, January 5, 1862, to which he consented. The morning of that day was our regular Communion season. Mr. Carroll administered the Sacrament, addressing the Church with much effect, from the words, "It is finished." In the afternoon he preached from the text, "But they constrained him, saying, Abide with us ; for it is toward evening, and the day is far spent." Luke 24 ; 29. In the evening, being the Monthly Missionary Concert, Mr. Carroll was present, and took part in the exercises. Although laboring under great physical weakness, few persons in the congregation were aware of it, and still fewer would have inferred it from any lack of energy or power in his performances. There was, however, a general desire to see and hear more of him, and a general feeling that we had at last found our man. The Committee, therefore, invited him to preach a third Sabbath; but he respectfully declined, remarking, that they had had a fair specimen of his preaching; that if he should preach a dozen times, he might not do any better, and he hoped he should not do worse. At a meeting of the Church on the following Friday evening, Jan. 10th, it was—

"*Voted*, That the Society be requested to extend a call to Rev. J. Halsted Carroll, to supply the pulpit and act as Pastor for the term of one year."

On the next day, Jan. 11th, 1862, the call was forwarded to Mr. Carroll, at Brooklyn, N. Y., and soon afterwards he signified his acceptance of the same, as follows:—

"BROOKLYN, N. Y., Jan. 17, 1862.

"DEAR BRETHREN:—

"After deliberate and prayerful consideration, I feel that duty directs me to the field of labor and love to which you, as a Church, have so unitedly and recently called me. * * * And now, as I accept your call, my fervent prayer to the Great Head of the Church, is one which I know will be endorsed and uttered by you, and the dear people of God you represent, that I may "come to you in the fullness of the blessing of the Gospel of Christ;" and when come, that I may "know nothing among you save Jesus Christ, and Him crucified."

"Affectionately yours, in the bonds of a common Lord,
J. HALSTED CARROLL.
Messrs. Thomas Horsfall and E. S. Minor, Committee."

This cheering intelligence was soon blighted by the receipt of a letter from Mrs. Carroll to one of the Deacons, stating, under date of Brooklyn, January 31st, that in consequence of Mr. Carroll's severe indisposition, his physicians had ordered him as far South as he could go, so as to enable him to escape the coming Spring here; and that the state of his health was such as would prevent his undertaking the duties of a charge for at least six months to come. It was, therefore, "with tearful regret, and yet with submission to the mysterious providence creating the necessity, that Mr. Carroll must, for your sakes, recall his acceptance, and thus release you from the obligations which his acceptance involved."

At a meeting of the Society's Committee, holden on the 1st of February, 1861, the above-mentioned letter was read and considered:—Whereupon, the following Resolution was unanimously adopted:—

"*Resolved*, That the Committee of the South Church Society have heard with deep regret the statements communicated by Mrs. Carroll, through Deacon Horsfall, with regard to the impaired health of her husband; and of the necessity imposed upon him by medical advice, to postpone all professional and pastoral labor for some months to come; and they sympathize deeply in the regrets expressed by Mr. and Mrs. C in his consequently being obliged to recall his acceptance of the engagement we had proffered him.

And that while this Committee regard his proposal to recall his acceptance, as highly honorable to Mr. Carroll, they earnestly request that he will allow the engagement to stand, with the hope that by the kind providence of God, at the end of six months, *if not before*, he may be able to assume the duties to which with such gratifying unanimity our people have called him."

This action of the Society's Committee having been communicated to the Church at a special meeting, held on the 2d of February, 1862, the latter body adopted the following resolution:

"*Resolved*, That this Church do hereby concur in the sentiments of the Society's Committee as embodied in the resolution just read; and would earnestly pray the great Head of the Church to have our Pastor elect in His holy keeping, and if it please Him, to restore him speedily to health, that we may enjoy the benefit of his labors."

The above resolutions were forwarded to Mr. Carroll by a Committee, and elicited the following reply:

BROOKLYN, N. Y., Feb. 12, 1862.

My very dear Brethren:

The minutes of the South Congregational Society's Committee, adopted at a meeting held Feb. 1st, together with the resolution endorsing them, passed by the Church on the following day, were received duly, and the generous request contained therein "to permit the engagement to stand," has been carefully and comprehensively considered in all its relations both to you and to myself.

The honor thus conferred is one which I sincerely appreciate, and cannot too highly estimate;—whilst the sweet sympathy tendered in this hour of sickness and despondency, and the manifestations of attachment evidenced, evoked the sweetest and most cordial reciprocity. Upon this deliberate re-expression of your choice of me as your minister, and upon the strength of the reciprocal love I bear you as a Church of Christ, I base my hearty acceptance of your renewed proposal :—feeling too, that the same Providence re-decides me which first led me to you, gave me a call from you, directed my affirmative answer, compelled afterwards the withdrawal of it, and now, by your recent action, permits and prompts my re-acceptance.

The interval of separation ere we expect to meet and mingle in endearing fellowship, I trust will be one of preparation and prayer on the part of both; preparation of mind and heart, that will but furnish more thoroughly for every good word and work, both preacher and people. My time shall be yours, spent with reference to you, though absent from you; whilst my heart is already yours, in all its warmest out-goings of Christian love.

Permitting me again to thank you for the honor, sympathy and attachment, manifested toward me in this renewal of your call, I close this my answer with a hope, and a prayer ;—the earnest hope that by the kind blessing of our dear God, I shall be entirely restored to wonted health and vigor at the expiration of the mentioned months,—and with the oft-repeated prayer that Jesus, the great Head of his Church, will give me multitudes of deathless souls as the seals of my ministry among you, to be set, at last, as polished jewels in His own radiant crown of rejoicing.

In the bonds of the Gospel, and in the sweet hope of heaven,

I remain, faithfully and affectionately,
J. HALSTED CARROLL.
To Messrs. T. Horsfall, E. S. Minor, and others, Committee.

This final acceptance, by Mr. Carroll, of the call which had been tendered him, was responded to in behalf of the Society's Committee as follows :

NEW HAVEN, Feb. 15, 1862.
Rev. J. HALSTED CARROLL,

My dear Brother :—Your letter of the 12th inst., addressed to the Committee of the South Church Society, was duly received, and laid before the Committee at a meeting held last evening; whereupon the following resolution was passed, which I am instructed to communicate to you, viz:

"*Resolved,* That the Committee have read with great satisfaction the letter from Rev. J. H. CARROLL, signifying his re-acceptance of the call extended to him by the Society's Committee and the Church; and they trust that a kind Providence will fulfill all the good wishes expressed therein, regarding his restored health and future usefulness among us."

With fraternal and Christian regards,
I remain, very truly yours,
E. S. MINOR,
Clerk of South Church Society's Committee.

In the three or four months which elapsed between Mr. Carroll's acceptance of the call, and the commencement of his labors as Stated Supply, there was ample time for any who doubted his antecedents, to inform themselves fully on that head. And we may here remark, that if certain individuals had made a tithe of the effort to acquaint themselves with his real history, which they did to discover some stain upon his character, or some delinquency in his life, they would have been more than satisfied, if any thing *good* could satisfy them. They would have found that he was the son of distinguished parents; that his father occupied positions of the highest eminence in his profession, and all with great acceptance and usefulness; first, as successor to Rev. Dr. Beecher, in Litchfield, Conn.; then as Pastor of the Presbyterian Church on Brooklyn Heights; then as President of Hampden Sidney College, Va.; and lastly as Pastor of the First Presbyterian Church in Northern Liberties, Philadelphia. To the last mentioned Church there were added during his ministry of five years and four months, 259 members, or an average of forty-eight per annum. Ill health at length compelled him to relinquish his charge, and after a few years of increasing illness, he departed this life at the age of fifty-five, with the words, "Christ is all my hope," upon his lips. The writer remembers him well, and can attest the truthfulness and fidelity of the following portrait, drawn by Rev. Thomas J. Shepherd, who now occupies the same pulpit which Dr. Carroll vacated in Philadelphia. He says:

"Dr. Carroll was largely endowed by nature and grace with the qualities which give success to the preacher and pastor. In person he was tall, slender, yet symmetrically formed. He had a complexion rather dark; an eye singularly fine and expressive; a countenance that easily took on a winning smile, or brightened into a glow of animation; and a voice, withal, of great compass and melody, modulated ever with an exquisite taste. In manners he was uncommonly bland, graceful, fascinating. He had the rare faculty of making himself equally agreeable to people of all ages and of all ranks.

"In native intellect and studious culture, he was undoubtedly superior to most men. He had in ample measure the intuitive power of reason, and the imperial power of imagination. In College and in Seminary he studied hard, too hard indeed for his physical strength, yet so successfully as to gift the workings of his mind with a prodigious force.

"In sensibility, moreover, he was quick, subtle, strong. He had a nervous organization which perhaps was too highly strung for the world's rough ways, but which made him keenly susceptible of affection, and enthusiastically ardent in attachment.

"He was, too, in executive talent, a more than ordinary man. He had the disposition as well as the ability to labor. He wrought his sermons with pains-taking fidelity, and with disciplined skill. He gave himself to the work of the ministry with a zeal and self-forgetfulness that revealed not more the sense of religious responsibility than the spirit of indomitable energy.

"And all these qualities, native and acquired, were under the control of a profoundly scriptural and eminently conservative piety. He loved truth, and sought it ever with an inextinguishable thirst. He loved the souls of men; and, so long as his strength lasted, sought their salvation with an indefatigable earnestness. He was, in a word, a noble example of the Christian man and the cultivated minister."

Such was the father of Rev. J. HALSTED CARROLL, the present minister of the South Church, New Haven. The latter was born in Brooklyn, N. Y.; made a profession of religion at the age of thirteen years; entered College before he was fourteen; and graduated at the University of Pennsylvania, in July, 1851. In the following year he entered Princeton Theological Seminary, and graduated in May, 1855. At the close of his second year of theological study, he was licensed by the Presbytery of Philadelphia to preach the Gospel; and on the 30th of May, 1855, (the year he left the Seminary,) he was ordained and installed by the Presbytery of New Brunswick, as Pastor of the Presbyterian Church in Jamesburg, New Jersey. The exercises of the occasion were opened with prayer by Rev. Dr. McDonald, of Princeton. Rev. Dr. Hall, of Trenton, preached the Sermon. Rev. Dr. Hodge, of Princeton, then stated who Mr. Carroll was, and what studies he had pursued, which he said had been entirely satisfactory to the Board of Directors of the Theological Seminary, and to the Presbytery. He next proposed a series of questions to the candidate, and also to the people, which were answered satisfactorily, and then calling the Presbytery around the candidate, who took a kneeling position, offered up an impressive prayer, while the Presbytery were laying their hands on the candidate's head. When the prayer was over, the candidate rose, and the several ministers present welcomed him as a member of their body. Rev. Professor Green, of Princeton, delivered the charge to the Pastor, and Rev. Dr. McDonald, the charge to the people. Rev. Dr. Hodge pronounced the benediction, and then called upon the members of the Church to come and greet their Pastor, which was done by a large number. The Church of Jamesburg, over which Mr. Carroll was thus installed, is near the preaching-ground of DAVID BRAINERD, and within a few miles of the Church where those holy men, the TENNANTS, labored with such wonderful zeal and success. In the midst of these associations, and stimulated by such examples, Mr. Carroll entered upon his labors, humbly desiring to emulate Brainerd's heart-wish,—"O that I was a flame of fire in the service of my God." Faithful labors, put forth in such a spirit, could hardly fail of producing a rich harvest. Accordingly, from the very beginning of his ministry, there was more or less seriousness among his people, and occasional conversions. In the course of the following year, (1856,) these cheering manifestations deepened into a powerful revival, which affected not only his own congregation in Jamesburg, but also the neighboring congregation of Manalapan, where he labored a part of the time. A brief account of this revival was published in the New York Observer by Mr. Carroll, under date of

"JAMESBURG, Dec. 11, 1856.

"Since it has pleased God most signally to bless my own and a neighboring Church, and indeed this whole section of his vineyard, with the special out-pouring of his Holy Spirit, I take the liberty of sending you a brief narrative of the state of religion here at the present time, knowing it will prove a matter of rejoicing to you, as well as to the hearts of your numerous Christian readers. During last Spring, my Church enjoyed a delightful revival of religion, the influence of which has continued, and been manifest, more or less, ever since. But it is within the past six weeks that indications of the *special* presence of the Spirit have been seen, and the effects of his presence felt. In this period, besides the usual prayer meeting, we have held two weekly services in the Church, so eager and earnest are the people to receive the word of life. Indeed, never in this community has there been such an intense and pervading interest on the subject of the soul's salvation, as now. Christians are awake, Elders are at work, meetings for prayer and inquiry literally thronged, and in going from house to house and from soul to soul, time and again is heard the cry, 'What must I do to be saved?' And so universally is the influence of the Spirit of God felt, that I have not found five out of the thousand and more different individuals whom I have addressed personally, who were not both willing and waiting to hear. With us, truly blessed is this scene and season. Of the ninety members received into our Communion during the past fifteen months, fifty-eight united on profession of their faith; and of the twenty-nine last Sabbath, twenty on profession. * * * * * * * *

"The revival in the neighboring Church (the Manalapan) is even of greater extent and interest, if possible. In the first place, it is a new Church: and in the second place, they have never had a Pastor. These two facts lend an unusual interest to their refreshing, to them so unspeakably precious. It was my privilege to officiate at their first Communion season, the first Sabbath of October last; and O what a day was that in their history,—memorable to saint and sinner. God was most sensibly and signally present in his sanctuary there, and has taken up his abode with them ever since, giving the same efficacy to the preached word, edifying his children, convicting and converting his foes. And here I would remark, that in both places and Churches, there were no means employed, or measures adopted, but the simple preaching of the way of salvation through the cross of Christ, and a meeting of inquiry to direct the penitent to the Lamb of God. * * * There have been, during the revival here, upwards of a hundred anxious ones in the inquiry meeting,—between sixty and seventy cases of hopeful conversion. Of this number, between forty and fifty will probably unite with the Manalapan Church, and the remainder with the neighboring sister Churches. Truly before they called, God answered; and the people with amazement exclaim, Behold what God hath wrought.

J. HALSTED CARROLL,
Pastor of Presb. Ch. of Jamesburg."

During this revival, the Professors at Princeton were often present and took part in the multiplied services; but no such assistance could relieve the *Pastor* from excessive labor, care and anxiety, in a period so critical to many of his people, and when the work of years was to be done in a few months or weeks. For a time, the stimulus of joy and hope, gratitude and love, sustained him, under toils and burdens which his delicate physical structure had not strength to endure; but at length his health gave way; hemorrhage of the lungs ensued; and there seemed no alternative but to resign his charge, and seek a milder climate, as well as a cessation from labor. To this necessity he finally yielded, asking and receiving a dismission from a people much beloved, and who loved him in return. The following resolution was unanimously adopted by his Church on the occasion of his leaving them:

"*Resolved*, That we do hereby publicly testify our gratitude to God that during Mr. Carroll's ministry here, his labors have been signally blest by the out-pouring of the Holy Spirit, and that from a small beginning we have been raised up to be a growing and prosperous Church."

A. J. McKELWAY, *Chairman*.
J. C. MAGEE, *Secretary*.
JAMESBURG, FEB. 1, 1858.

Soon after leaving Jamesburg, Mr. Carroll proceeded South, stopping at Aiken, S. C., a place of resort for invalids, including many from the North. He had intended to remain there but a short time, but finding his health improving, he occasionally preached, and with so much acceptance, that the good people of Aiken desired him to settle over them as Pastor. With this view a Presbyterian Church was organized there on the 28th and 29th of August, 1858, and not long after a convenient house of worship was erected. Here Mr. Carroll labored with great usefulness and success, for nearly two years.

He then asked a dismission, for the purpose of going to Europe, hoping to gain more perfect health and strength, as well as to see what was worth seeing in foreign lands, and especially to hear the distinguished preachers of England and Scotland, such as Guthrie, Spurgeon, Cummins, and others. On his leaving Aiken, the following preamble and resolutions were adopted by the Church:

"*May 4th*, 1860.—Whereas, the relation which has subsisted between the Aiken Presbyterian Church and the Rev. J. Halsted Carroll, having been dissolved by his voluntary resignation of the office which he has held for nearly two years,—it is fit and proper that some expression of our sentiments should be made and recorded on the occasion of his departure from this field of labor:—Be it therefore

"*Resolved*, That this Church and congregation entertain a very grateful sense of the valuable services rendered by Mr. Carroll in the founding and organization of our Church; of his zealous devotion to the promotion of our enterprise, and his successful efforts in raising the means for the construction of our house of worship; and that we shall also ever affectionately cherish the recollection of his sympathising attentions to the members of his flock, in their mingled experience of joys and sorrows, during the period of his pastorship.

"*Resolved*, That with the hope that the able and eloquent discourses which characterized his ministry amongst us, replete with the most orthodox views and pious exhortations, and which may well be compared to 'apples of gold in pictures of silver,' may prove as the good seed in the parable, and by the blessing God yield in due season a rich harvest of spiritual fruit, we tender to him our best wishes for his future happiness and prosperity.

"*Resolved*, That the above preamble and resolutions be entered on the Session books of our Church, and a copy of the same be forwarded by the Clerk of Session to Mr. Carroll.

W. P. FINLEY, *Clerk of Session.*"

Fortified with strong letters of commendation from some of the most distinguished Americans, to eminent men in Great Britain, France, Germany, and other countries of Europe, Mr. Carroll left the United States in the early part of 1860, and was absent about a year. It does not fall within the design of this sketch to give even an outline of his tour. Suffice it to say that he accomplished, even beyond his expectations, all the objects which he had in view; formed the acquaintance of many celebrated men, by all of whom, on the strength of his letters, he was cordially received; listened to the preaching of the principal pulpit orators of Europe; saw whatever he desired to see; and returned home with improved health, enlarged experience of men and things, and with a strong desire to enter anew upon his great work of trying to benefit and save lost men by the preaching the Gospel of Christ. For a few months after his return, he passed his time chiefly in Brooklyn and New York, preaching here and there as duty called, but without any regular charge, until he was invited to the South Church, New Haven.

And this brings us back to the point from which we digressed. He had accepted the call to said Church, but was obliged to postpone for a few months the fulfillment of his engagement, by reason of ill health. On the first Sabbath in June, 1862, being the 1st *day* of June, his people were made glad by seeing him in their pulpit, apparently in comfortable health, and ready to serve them for Christ's sake, in the new relation which had just been formed. His first sermon was from the text, "I ask, therefore, for what intent ye have sent for me," *Acts* 10 : 29. In the afternoon, "O son of man, I have set thee a watchman unto the house of Israel," &c., *Ezekiel* 33 : 7, 8, 9. Both were exceedingly appropriate and excellent discourses, and were listened to by profoundly attentive and deeply interested audiences. The subjects gave him opportunity to enlarge upon the reciprocal duties of ministers and people, and their responsibilities to each other and to God. The spirit of tender earnestness and faithfulness to the souls of men, which breathed through these introductory sermons, has characterized his preaching ever since. Not that he is always dwelling upon one theme,—far from it. On the contrary, VARIETY, both of subject and manner,—variety in the construction of his sermons, in the mode of presenting truth, and even in the order of exercises,* is a prominent feature of his ministry. From the wells of salvation he draws ample supplies for the diversified wants of the soul, without resorting to politics or shade-trees.

---

* Most commonly, at the close of his sermons on the Sabbath, he retires to his seat, while the choir, under the direction of their accomplished leader, Mr. Frank L. Martyn, strike up a verse or two of some appropriate hymn or other choice selection, adapted and designed to deepen the impression left by the sermon. The effect is often exceedingly fine; the singing being good,—unusually so, for a volunteer choir,—and the organ-playing, by Mr. Martyn, admirable. The benediction is then pronounced,—sometimes preceded by a few short petitions bearing immediately upon the subject of the discourse, and sometimes not.

His sermons are full of thought, legitimately derived from his texts, though often not lying on the surface, yet when suggested, so obviously comprehended within the scope of the passage, that the hearer wonders he never caught the idea before. There is withal a terseness and point to his discourses, and a beauty of language and imagery, which render it impossible to forget them. His descriptions of scenes and incidents are exceedingly graphic. His "Scripture characters," as presented in the Chapel on Sunday evenings for many months in succession, until superseded lately by the "Fulton street Prayer Meetings," we have never heard surpassed; so life-like, and so full of instruction. The attendance upon them was very large. To those who never heard Mr. Carroll preach, we may remark, that one half of the power of his discourses consists in the delivery. Sometimes they are written out in full, but more generally not; and in either case he is entirely independent of his manuscript, seldom even looking at it, but holding constant communication with his hearers, not only by his voice, but by his expressive features and appropriate action. His enunciation is remarkably distinct, his voice soft and clear, and his command of the audience such, that amidst the profound stillness of the house, he is heard in every portion of it, even when speaking not much above the tone of common conversation. This is partly owing to the admirable construction of the audience-room, in which the laws of acoustics are better consulted than in any other within our knowledge, and partly to the causes above mentioned, viz: clearness of enunciation and stillness of the house. The fact, however, that with so little strain upon his voice, he is heard with perfect ease and comfort on the part of his audience, is a great relief to him; and may account in a measure for his increased health and strength, notwithstanding his abundant labors,—having no facilities for exchanging, and generally preaching two sermons on the Sabbath, and sometimes a third in the evening. It is a common remark among his people, that he is constantly improving, both in matter and manner. There is one peculiarity in his manner which we must not omit to mention, viz: that it combines in about equal proportions, *gentleness* and *fire ;* two things theoretically inconsistent with each other, but practically exemplified in the South Church every Sabbath. As an extempore speaker especially, his powers are extraordinary. Take him when and where you will, on any subject, in the pulpit or on the platform or in the conference-room, he is always ready, and always good; seldom hesitating or recalling a word, but going on like a quiet, steady stream, supplied by never-failing springs, until he has occupied the time allotted him, or accomplished the end at which he aimed. His duties as minister of a large parish, (for he has much to do outside of the limits of his congregation proper, in visiting the sick, attending funerals, &c.,) are quite enough for any one man to perform; yet occasionally he steps beyond the exact limits of his profession, as at the Irish Relief meeting in Music Hall a year or two ago, where, for an hour or more, he electrified an immense audience, who responded with peal upon peal, and cheer upon cheer. On all such occasions he is "at home," knowing exactly where and how to strike the popular ear and heart. It is well that such extraordinary speaking talents are consecrated to "Christ and his cause," and not to the drama, or the bar, or politics, or the forum. New Haven may well be proud of such a minister, and such a man.

Mr. Carroll came here without any flourish of trumpets, or anything in the position or circumstances of his Church and congregation to give him consequence or bring him into notice. He was deliberately shunned by ministers of his own denomination, or rather, of the denomination to which his *Church* belonged, as if they thought they could extinguish his light by not recognizing its existence. Meanwhile the tongue of slander was secretly moving against him, and had the greater power for mischief because he was so little known in this community. Men professing the religion of Jesus, acted as if they thought they were doing God service by undermining the influence and impairing the usefulness of one of His faithful ambassadors. He, however, went on with his proper work, trusting in God to vindicate his reputation and prosper his labors. Nor did he trust in vain. God gave him many souls as seals of his ministry and crowns of his rejoicing. [For particulars see Catalogue at the close of this volume.] His congregations steadily increased, and have continued to increase, until now, on Sabbath afternoons at least, they are believed to be larger, on an average, than those of any other Church of the same denomination in the city. And this, notwithstanding the remoteness of his position from the centre of population. The same increase was and is seen in the Sabbath evening meetings, and in those held during the week. Many influential families from town have joined the congregation, taking slips, and otherwise identifying themselves with its interests. A more harmonious, prosperous and happy Church and congregation it would be difficult to find. Their minister is universally beloved by his people, as well as respected and honored. This makes his burdens light.

And here we must recall some circumstances which it would be more agreeable to omit, did they not occupy so prominent a place in our history, and were they not, in fact, a key to the prosperity which, under God, we now enjoy. Mr. Carroll had not been long in his present position, before it was discovered by a portion of his people that he did not ring the usual changes on the subject of slavery and the war. In short, he did not make politics a part of his religion. Of course, had he made any politics but *theirs* a part of his religion, it would have been an awful desecration of the pulpit and the Sabbath ; but *their* politics were an essential part of Christian ethics, and no minister who ignored them, could be a faithful ambassador of Christ. Accordingly they began to complain—of him and to him. And finding this unavailing, they sent him written remonstrances and arguments, designed to convince his understanding and rectify his judgment. Doubtless they were surprised to find him still insensible to the claims of duty as *they* understood it,—still blind to their view of the obligations of his sacred calling. When at length they despaired of bringing him out on these subjects,—when they saw that his own convictions of propriety and duty forbade it,—the next step was, to attempt to get rid of him. So they began to agitate for a change. But it was not until the 18th of February, 1863, that they had opportunity to show their strength. On that day was held a Church meeting, of which public notice had been given, for the special purpose of providing for the supply of the pulpit *after the termination of Mr. Carroll's year*, ending 1st of June following. It is not to be denied that there was some anxiety among the friends of Mr. Carroll, as to what would be the result. The lines were not so distinctly drawn among the members, at least in many cases, as they are at present. There were quite a number of *floaters*, standing upon our books as members, who very seldom attended our Church. They were truants under Mr. Noyes' administration, and equally so under Mr. Carroll's; but now they were all on hand, as in duty bound, to assist in determining the question who should be our next minister. After the meeting had been organized, a member moved the following resolutions, which were duly seconded:

Resolved, That with grateful acknowledgments to our Heavenly Father for the blessings he has bestowed and is still bestowing in connection with the labors of our beloved Pastor, Rev. J. Halsted Carroll, we hereby express our earnest desire for the continuance of those labors, and of the relations now existing between Mr. Carroll as Stated Supply, and this Church and Society, until the same shall be annulled or modified by the joint consent of the parties, to wit, this Church and Society on the one part, and Mr. Carroll on the other, or by the separate action of either of said parties, in which latter case it is the opinion of this Church that at least four months notice in writing, should be given by the party desiring a change, to the party not desiring it; with the single exception, that this condition should be waived in favor of Mr. Carroll, if at any time by reason of bodily infirmity he should be unable to perform the duties of his office.

Resolved, That if, to relieve himself from an amount of labor beyond his physical strength, Mr. Carroll should desire the coöperation of Rev. Myron Barrett as Associate Supply, and if the expense of the whole arrangement can be brought within the means at the disposal of the Society, this Church deem it very desirable that Mr. Barrett, (whose labors among us have been highly appreciated,) should be engaged as such Associate, until the 1st day of May, 1864, leaving any further arrangement with him beyond that date, to depend upon circumstances and the wishes of the parties.

Resolved, That these resolutions be communicated to the Ecclesiastical Society connected with this Church, at its meeting appointed to be held this evening.

New Haven, Feb. 18, 1863.

On the question of adopting these resolutions, a lively debate ensued,—most of those members who were opposed to Mr. Carroll, expressing their views in words. A few of his friends also spoke,—one of them as follows :

"I protest against the doctrine that because a man does not deny an accusation, he therefore admits it to be true. Why, according to this doctrine, a minister might spend half his time in vindicating himself against false accusations, and after all there would be "a few more left." I trust this Church will never have a minister who will spend his time so unprofitably.

"Besides, a minister's private judgment on public affairs is his own property: as much so as the private judgment of any other citizen is the property of that citizen. It is lodged in a sanctuary which no man has a right to invade. The owner of that sanctuary may open it, or not, as he pleases; but no one can force it open without being guilty of impertinence and oppression.

"If a minister cannot justly be required to *declare* his politics, much less can he be required to preach them. He has a right to preach them, if such be his convictions of duty, but he has an equal right to withhold them. In either case he is responsible to his Maker, and to his own conscience, for the course he pursues. He is also responsible to his people,—to this extent, that if they deem his course objectionable, and if that course is persisted in, they have a right, as individuals, to withdraw from his ministry; or as a Church and Society, to dissolve their connection with him, under proper forms, subject to all the obligations and conditions of his settlement. Thousands of Churches and religious Societies in this our land have been broken up or depleted by one or the other of these processes. We need not go beyond our own city to find an illustration. How else can the fact be accounted for, that the aggregate attendance upon Congregational Churches in this city has scarcely if at all increased within the last 25 or 30 years, although in the mean time the population of the city has increased three-fold? Within the same period, another denomination in this city, from whose pulpits, as a general remark, political topics are excluded, has greatly increased, both in the number of its churches, and in the aggregate attendance. Congregationalism had the ground, and would have kept it if there had been no drawback upon its administration.

"Now, to bring the subject home to ourselves,—we have a minister who does *not* deem it his duty to preach politics, but who does deem it his duty *not* to preach them. He prays for our country, our rulers, our civil institutions, our liberties, our officers and soldiers, especially the sick and wounded, but he does not cater to the appetites of politicians of any party. He pursues the one great object for which he was commissioned as an ambassador for Christ, leaving secular topics to secular days and secular men; or perchance to those ministers, if such there be, who desecrate the Sabbath and the pulpit by making both subservient to political ends. Whether Mr. Carroll remains with us for a longer or shorter period, there is no probability that he will change his course in this respect, as it is founded upon settled convictions of duty, and these cannot be yielded to friends or foes. Now suppose, to gratify a few of our members who require a different style of preaching and praying, we consent to give up our minister after his present engagement shall have expired—what then? Are we to have a man in his stead who will give us political preaching and praying? Is this Church to have *such* a man for its Pastor in place of Mr. Carroll? If it is, I greatly fear that our prosperity is near its end. But if the Church will regard itself as an organization for strictly religious purposes, everything will be likely to move on harmoniously and prosperously; for there appears to be no other subject of difference. On this basis all can meet, on equal terms, and work together for the common cause:—Parthians and Medes and Elamites, and the dwellers in Mesopotamia and in Judea and Cappadocia, in Pontus and Asia, Phrygia and Pamphylia, in Egypt and in the parts of Lybia about Cyrene, and strangers of Rome, Jews and Proselytes, Cretes and Arabians,—Democrats and Republicans, Abolitionists, Secessionists and Traitors. And the greater sinners they are, the more they need the pure Gospel of Christ, which is able to make them *all* wise unto salvation.

"It is worthy of remark, that the men who are loudest in their complaints against Mr. Carroll, are those who know least about him. How is it that men who have seldom if ever spoken with him, and have rarely heard him preach or pray, should understand his views, and also his character and history, so much better than we do, "who have been with him from the beginning," listened to all his sermons, —who have seen him in the prayer meeting and conference room times without number,—met him at the fireside, in the chamber of sickness, and in the home of sorrow,—in short, who have seen and heard him continually for the last nine months, in all the different phases of ministerial and pastoral life. Yet such men come to us at this late day, and tell us, in effect, that we have made a great mistake in the choice of our Pastor, and should by no means retain him longer than the period for which he is now engaged. Well, they are entitled to their opinion, and we to ours. We *know* what he is. We have listened to his heart-searching discourses, his thrilling appeals, his fervent prayers, and his faithful warnings. We have felt the breathings of his gentle spirit upon our hearts, and the Holy Spirit upon his own and upon ours. We have seen the effects of his ministry in greatly increased congregations on the Sabbath, in fully attended prayer meetings during the week, in a goodly number added to the Church or propounded for admission; in others still seeking the way of life; in a Sabbath School of 230 members actually attending; in a large and prosperous Sewing Society; and in a pervading religious interest, more or less apparent, throughout the congregation. And should he still "abide with us," assisted by Rev. Mr. Barrett, we may hope for yet greater things than these. God grant that it may be so; and that this Church and Society may not so undervalue their inestimable privileges, as to sell them for a mess of pottage."

At a late hour of the evening, the question was taken on the resolutions, and they were ADOPTED, by a vote of *fifty-one* to *twenty-two*. They were then communicated to the Ecclesiastical Society connected with the South Church, which met the same evening agreeably to public notice; whereupon the Society adopted the following resolution, with only one dissenting voice:

"*Resolved*, That the resolutions of the South Church, communicated to us by its Clerk, in regard to the future supply of the pulpit of that Church, are cordially approved by this Society, and that a Committee consisting of Deacon Thomas Horsfall, be instructed to endeavor to carry the proposed arrangement into effect."

It was carried into effect accordingly; and the same arrangement still continues. So far, it appears to be a very good arrangement; giving both to minister and people all the freedom of action they could desire, while yet it requires no periodical agitation, as in the case of ministers who are engaged from year to year. The result of the meeting was of course a disappointment to the opponents of Mr. Carroll, and soon after [in March, 1863] a number of them asked and received certificates of dismission,—some to particular churches,—while others took general letters, having reference, it was understood, to the formation of a new Church. The Clerk also resigned, [in April,] who, under the practice then existing, would have had a right, as he would doubtless have been disposed, to call as many Church meetings as the disaffected might desire. Some time previously the *Society* had been freed in a great measure from the elements of opposition, as appears from the all but unanimous vote above recorded. Thus far, the policy of the opposition had seemed to be, to desert the sinking ship, and leave that portion of the crew who remained, too weak, or too much disheartened, to carry her into port. But the effect was exactly the contrary. Both the Church and Society were cheered and encouraged by the absence of a power which, to a considerable extent, had been available only for mischief. True, there were individuals among the opposition, including one of the Deacons, who had performed their duties faithfully towards the Church and Society, *as they understood them ;* but others were a mere dead-weight, doing nothing towards the support of public worship, and seldom attending the religious exercises of the Church, though always on hand, or liable to be so, whenever there was any voting to be done.

In July [1863] a little incident occurred which promised for a time to give them considerable capital ; we allude to the *bell* affair. A few members who had before been wavering, seemed now to be with the opposition. The leaders of the movement took heart, and under the excitement of the hour, seemed really to hope to accomplish their object. Accordingly they got up a paper, with as many signatures as could be obtained, requesting the Clerk to call a meeting of the Church, in order to *consider the expediency of asking Mr. Carroll to resign.* But here a new difficulty presented itself. In place of the resigned Clerk, a successsor had been elected (Rev. Mr. Barrett) who was not in sympathy with the "movement" party. When therefore the disaffected members applied to him for the above object, he saw fit to exercise his discretion, under the advice of the

Standing Committee, by refusing to call the proposed meeting. This led to a further secession of disaffected members, (including the aforesaid Deacon,) who asked and received certificates of dismission—general letters—July 31st and August 4th. In a few days or weeks the bell excitement passed away; the old Church was there yet, and its minister also. He appeared to have no idea of leaving; it was impossible to get a Church meeting at that time; and if a Church meeting were held, especially after this latest secesssion, there would be no chance of *voting* him away. Under such circumstances, what was to be done? Clearly, they must give up in despair, or endeavor to retrieve their error. Somehow or other, they must get back into the garrison, where they could have more power over it than they could as mere outsiders and enemies. So they sought to return their certificates of dismission and resume their membership. But the Church (practically) said no; we have dismissed you at your own request; and now we must hold you to the bargain. We cannot receive you back. Here was a dilemma, to be sure; and it required all the wisdom of the wise and all the ingenuity of the sagacious, to tell them what to do. Various consultations were held with each other, and with friends in town. We were not there, but may safely infer what was the result of their deliberations, from the course subsequently pursued. Call a Council, they said; a Mutual Council, if the South Church will consent; if not, then an Ex-parte Council, which will answer just as well; for, in either case, they are sure to be condemned. If they consent to a Mutual Council, you will be restored to your rights as members, and, with such re-inforcements as you can get from other quarters, will soon be able to out-vote them. But if they refuse that bait, then do you call an *Ex-parte* Council, which will be still more sure to condemn them, as all the evidence, and all the pleas, and all the judges, will be on one side. Such a Council will doubtless *unchurch* the old concern, and either pronounce *you* the South Church instead of them, or assist you in building and organizing a *new* Church, where the "whole Gospel" shall be preached. So the disaffected members,—those who had asked and received letters of dismission and those who had not,—gravely applied to the South Church to join them in a Mutual Council. As they expected, the Church declined. Or rather, the Clerk, with the unanimous approval of the Standing Committee, refused to call a meeting of the Church to consider the question; and the Church, at their annual meeting a short time afterwards, (Nov. 24, 1863,) passed a resolution approving the action of the Committee, and declaring that in future "the power to call a Church meeting for business, shall rest in the Church Committee together with the Clerk." Thus the way was prepared for the calling of an *Ex-parte* Council.

During all these agitations, which were aimed chiefly against Mr. Carroll, in the hope of either driving or mortifying him away, he maintained a calmness of demeanor and a steadiness of purpose, which even his opponents cannot fail to respect. Such moral heroism, lodged in such a delicate physical structure, (or any other,) is rarely to be met with. But all these troubles are now over; even his enemies are at peace with him. At least they are comparatively silent, while his friends, and the community generally, honor and applaud him. We doubt if to-day there is a more popular minister in New Haven. Certainly there is no one whom the public manifest a greater desire to hear.

CHAPTER V.

THE EX-PARTE COUNCIL.

The following is a copy of the letter missive by which the Ex-parte Council was convened:

"The Majority of the Brotherhood of the South Congregational Church in New Haven, to the Congregational Church in ———.

"Brethren: We having been deprived by usurped authority of the rights which belong to a Congregational Church, and having stated our grievances in a memorial, asking for a Mutual Council, which memorial was rejected by those who have assumed the power of government in this Church, do therefore invite you to be present by your pastor and delegate in an Ecclesiastical Council, at the Orange street Chapel in New Haven, on Monday the 21st inst., at 4 P. M., for the purpose of considering the difficulties existing in this Church as exhibited in our memorial and in the action thereupon, and of advising us concerning our rights and our duty.

E. S. MINOR,
JOHN NICOLL,
AMOS SMITH,
G. H. BUTRICKS, } *Committee.*
WM. C. SCOBIE,
ROBERT DYAS,
GEORGE S. MINOR.

New Haven, Dec. 12, 1863.

The Council accordingly met at the time and place above mentioned, and was organized by the choice of Rev. Wm. T. Eustis, as Scribe, and Rev. Joseph Eldridge, D. D., as Moderator. There were present from the

First Church, Hartford—Rev. Joel Hawes, D. D., Pastor; Hon. William W. Ellsworth, Delegate.
First Church, New Haven—Rev. Leonard Bacon, D. D., Pastor; Rev. Chauncey Goodrich, Delegate.
Church in Norfolk—Rev. Joseph Eldridge, Pastor; Brother Robbins Battell, Delegate.
North Church, New Haven—Rev. S. W. S. Dutton, Pastor.
Church in Wallingford—Rev. Edwin R. Gilbert, Pastor; Deacon John Atwater, Delegate.
Broadway Church, Norwich—Rev. C. P. Gulliver, Pastor.
Chapel Street Church, New Haven—Rev. Wm. T. Eustis, Pastor; Deacon Smith Merwin, Delegate.
Third Church, New Haven—Hon. John Woodruff, Delegate.
Church in Greenwich—Brother Allen Howe, Delegate.
Church in Bristol—Deacon William Day, Delegate.
Church in Essex—Rev. James A. Gallup, Pastor; Deacon Charles H. Hubbard, Delegate.
Church in Theological Institute—Rev. E. A. Lawrence, Delegate.

The South Church, having had no agency in getting up this Council, and having declined to recognize it in any way, or even to present their records, as requested by the Council, cannot be presumed to know what occurred there during its three days sittings, commencing December 21st, 1863, and ending December 23d, except so far as the same has been revealed or indicated by the published Result of Council, which is as follows:

RESULT OF THE COUNCIL,

Called by " the Majority of the Brethren of the South Congregational Church, New Haven."

This Council has been convened by certain brethren styling themselves "the majority of the brethren of the South Congregational Church in New Haven," and complaining that they "have been deprived of the rights which belong to brethren in a Congregational Church." Whether they are, or are not, entitled to the rights of a majority, is a question upon which we are not called to express an opinion, for it is not material to any of the issues involved in their complaint. These brethren, twenty or more in number, have addressed the Church in a memorial asking for a mutual council to consider certain matters by which they are aggrieved, and their request has been denied. Their right, therefore, of obtaining advice from neighbor Churches through an *ex-parte* council, in conformity with a reasonable and long established usage of the New England Churches, cannot be disputed.

First of all, this Council has made a communication to the Church through its Clerk and Standing Committee, and also to the Rev. J. Halsted Carroll, as another party interested in the matters referred to us, inviting them to appear and offer any explanations which they may desire to make concerning the transactions complained of. But these invitations have been explicitly declined. We are sorry to add, that we have been denied all access to the records of the Church, and that the complainants have not been able to obtain authenticated copies of the records, which they desired to present for our consideration.

Having carefully considered the documents submitted to us in behalf of the complainants by their committee, and having heard such testimony as they, in the disadvantageous circumstances in which they are placed, have been able to adduce, we find the following matters of fact:

I. The Church in question was instituted as a Congregational Church, with the advice and approbation of a council of Congregational Churches, and the complainants became members of it, in the warranted expectation that they were to enjoy all the rights belonging to the brethren of a Congregational Church, according to the principles and usages of the New England Churches.

II. The Rev. J. Halsted Carroll commenced his labors at the South Church in December, 1861, being invited by the Society's Committee to officiate as a candidate. He was soon afterwards employed by concurrent votes of the

Church and Society to supply the pulpit for a year. Before the termination of the year, a meeting of the Church was held to consider the question of a more permanent settlement of Mr. Carroll in the work of the ministry there. An arrangement was made, purporting to be between the Church and Society as one party, and Mr. Carroll as the other party, by which he was to remain in the work of the ministry among them indefinitely, and which could be terminated only when either party should give four months notice of a desire for the termination.

III. In that meeting the majority of the male members present voted against the proposed arrangement, but their votes were overruled by counting the votes of female members.

IV. The aforesaid arrangement having been made, Mr. Carroll assumed the title and authority of "Pastor of the South Church," subscribing official papers in that character, being habitually spoken of among the members of the Church, and in Church meetings, by that official title, and being frequently announced to the public as Pastor of that Church.

V. Certain members of the Church, fourteen in number, being dissatisfied with the ministry of Mr. Carroll, and desiring that notice might be duly given to him for the termination of the arrangement, presented to the Clerk of the Church their written request for a Church meeting, which request was refused by the Clerk and Standing Committee.

VI. Afterwards the same brethren and others, twenty in all, addressed their memorial to the Church, stating distinctly the grounds of their dissatisfaction with these proceedings and with the ministry of Mr. Carroll, and asking for a Council of Churches, to be mutually agreed upon, who should advise with the Church and the complainants. The Clerk, to whose hands the memorial was committed, refused, by the advice of the Standing Committee, to lay it before the Church.

VII. Between the time when the request was made for a Church meeting and the time of preparing the memorial, some of the complainants asked and received letters of commendation, in the ordinary form, by which their membership in the Church would be terminated whenever they might become members of other churches. But in the memorial those brethren gave notice to the Church that, upon mature deliberation, they had relinquished their intention of connecting themselves with other churches; and they remained, in the language of the testimonials which had been given them, "members of the South Congregational Church."

VIII. The reply which the Clerk, by the direction of the Standing Committee, returned to the signers of the memorial, was addressed "To Amos Smith, G. H. Butricks, and as many other signers of the above-named request as are still recognized members of the Church;" the said Clerk and Committee thereby assuming to exclude from membership those signers who held at that moment the written testimonials of the Church to their good and regular standing.

IX. At the annual meeting of the Church, held on the evening of November 24, 1863, Mr. Carroll, acting as moderator, denied to the members above mentioned the right of voting, or of speaking in defence of their right to vote; and that denial was approved by the meeting. The same meeting ratified all the doings of the Committee, including their suppression of the memorial.

X. The reasons for the dissatisfaction with the ministry of Mr. Carroll, presented to us by the complainants, and sustained by such evidence as the nature of this investigation has made practicable, are the following:

1. They had, at the time of his settlement, no proper evidence that he was an ordained minister of the Gospel in regular communion with the Congregational churches and ministers of Connecticut, or with any evangelical denomination.

2. Under his ministry there has been in the public worship of that Church, and in the lessons from the pulpit, no utterance of sympathy with our country in its struggle for unity and life; no expression of loyal desire for the success of the Government, or the defeat of the rebellion; no word implying that the attempts of the rebels to subvert by force the Government ordained by God in this land, is criminal;

no recognition of the righteousness of the cause in which sons and brothers of the complainants, some of them members of the same Church, are offering their lives.

3. In the pulpit and in private conversation he has characterized the action of the Government as tyrannical and unjust, and has implied that the attempt of the Government to maintain itself by force against the rebellion, is criminal; and when members of the Church have courteously inquired of him concerning his views, that they might know whether he had been misunderstood on these points, he has refused to give any satisfactory answer.

4. He has borne no testimony against the wicked doctrine of these times, that it is right for white men to make slaves of black men; but on the contrary, he has used his influence to suppress in the meetings of the Church all allusion to the injustice of slavery.

5. He has by his private and public influence brought certain young persons of the congregation into open sympathy with the existing rebellion.

These being the facts as we find them, our judgment is,

First. It is a distinctive and cardinal principle of our New England Congregationalism, that no person shall be invested with the pastoral office in any Church, otherwise than by the advice and consent of neighboring churches represented in a council; that a minority, however humble, objecting to the person chosen by the majority of the Church, may have full opportunity to present the reasons for their dissent before the council convened for the purpose of ordaining or installing him; and that no man can be imposed upon them as their pastor, unless their objections, after a fair hearing and consideration, are removed or overruled by the council.

Second. Mr. Carroll is not, in the proper use of language, pastor of the South Congregational Church in New Haven, nor is he "Acting Pastor," as that term is defined by the General Association of Connecticut. Any assumption of the title of pastor on his part is unwarranted, and the arrangements and proceedings by which he has been invested with the powers of a pastor in that Church, without the intervention of a council of neighboring churches to inquire into his qualifications for that office, are a contempt put upon the principle of communion of churches, and a violation of the rights of the complainants.

Third. The voting of women in the Church, by which, in the settlement of Mr. Carroll, the majority of the brethren was overruled, is contrary to the Scriptures (I. Cor. xix. 34; I. Tim. xi. 12) and contrary to the usages and principles of the New England churches, and invalidates the act of a majority, which was made such by these votes.

Fourth. The refusal of the Clerk and Standing Committee to call a meeting of the Church at the written request of fourteen brethren, (who were nearly one-third of the brotherhood), for the express purpose of requesting Mr. Carroll to resign his place, as provided for by the arrangement under which he was settled, was not only a violation of the compact, by which the question of his retirement is made at all times a proper question for consideration in the Church, whether with or without charges against his official character; but was a gross usurpation on the part of the Clerk and Committee, alike hostile to the rights of the members and destructive of the organization of a Congregational Church; and the refusal of the same functionaries to present a respectful memorial from twenty members to the Church, was a similar irregularity and wrong. The ratification of these proceedings by the annual Church meeting may justly be regarded as an additional grievance.

Fifth. The brethren who had received letters of dismission, but who, in a formal communication to the Church, had announced their purpose not to connect themselves with other churches, but to retain their membership in the South Church, were unjustly excluded from participation in the annual meeting of that Church. The decision of the moderator, Mr. Carroll, that they were not members, and the confirmation of that decision by the meeting, can not but be condemned as an arbitrary and unjust proceeding. Those brethren are still, according to the purport of the testimonials which they had received, members of the South Church in regular standing.

Sixth. The reasons for dissatisfaction with the **ministry** of Mr. Carroll, as alleged and proved by the complainants, **are** valid.

1. It is a sufficient reason for dissatisfaction with his ministry, that he was employed by the Church and Society without exhibiting any proper and adequate proof of his regular standing in the ministry.

2. The sympathy of Mr. Carroll with the existing rebellion, exhibited as it has been, not only negatively by his not saying the things which he ought to have said, but positively, by saying what he ought not to have said against the Government, and against the struggle of the nation to defend itself, and to perpetuate the inheritance it has received from God; his personal influence in the congregation, "leading captive" unthinking and unstable persons into outspoken sympathy with the most stupendous crime recorded in history since Christ was crucified, and his silence in regard to the atrocious heresy, religious and ethical, now so widely maintained, that it is right for white men to make slaves of black men, being made more significant by his endeavors to suppress in the Church all allusions to so great a wickedness, are sufficient grounds for formal charges against him; and being proved on trial, are sufficient for his condemnation, if there be any ecclesiastical body to which he is responsible.

Such being the facts, and our judgment upon them, we are prepared to answer the questions which the complainants have proposed to us for our advice:

First. In consideration of the facts which have appeared before this Council, and which we have already recited, we advise the complainants that the South Congregational Church, so called, ought not to be recognized any longer as a Congregational Church, and as a Council we advise the Churches which we represent, and all other Churches of our communion, to withhold from that Church those acts of mutual recognition and fellowship which are customary among Congregational Churches, and which are the form of their unity as an ecclesiastical commonwealth.

Second. We advise the complainants, and as many other members of that Church as may associate with them, to withdraw from their present relations to it. And we authorize our Moderator and Scribe to give to them, collectively or individually, in our behalf, letters certifying their regular standing as professed followers of Christ in full communion with the Congregational Churches of Connecticut, and commending them to any Church with which they may choose to connect themselves, or to any ecclesiastical council which may be convened for the purpose of recognizing the formation of a new Church. The question whether they shall proceed to constitute a new Church in the south part of the city of New Haven, is a question to be determined partly by local considerations, with which they, and the members of the other Churches here, are better acquainted than this Council can be. Yet we cannot refrain from saying that, for the sake of patriotism and of pure and undefiled religion, there ought to be among the growing population of that quarter a truly Congregational Church, from which the sympathies of patriotic Christian souls may freely go up to God on the wings of prayer and praise, and in which the whole counsel of God, "revealed from heaven against all ungodliness and unrighteousness of men who hold the truth in unrighteousness," shall be preached plainly and unswervingly.

REV. JOSEPH ELDRIDGE,
Moderator.

W. T. EUSTIS, Scribe.

REPLY OF THE SOUTH CHURCH
To the late Ecclesiastical Council.

The following reply of the Standing Committee of the South Congregational Church, to the action of the *Ex-parte* Council recently held in this city, was submitted to said Church on Friday evening, Jan. 1st, 1864, and by the Church was UNANIMOUSLY approved, and ordered to be published.

WHEREAS, an *Ex-parte* Council, representing twelve of the two hundred and twenty-two consociated Congregational Churches in this State, has been lately held in New Haven, at the request of twenty petitioners, now or recently connected with the South Congregational Church, for the professed purpose of advising them "concerning their rights and their duty;" and whereas, in advising *them*, said Council have sat in judgment on this entire Church and upon our ministers; and, whereas, the Council has given to the public its proceedings and result, which result has been telegraphed throughout the country; we owe it to ourselves, as a Church, to Rev. Mr. Carroll, as our minister, and to truth and justice, that the *facts* in the case be stated and published through the same channels.

As this Council has seen fit to vindicate its decision to the public, however degrading to a Church judicatory we feel such an appeal to be, we are compelled to suffer in silence, or respond before the same tribunal.

The petitioners for the Council, members of the South Congregational Church, ARE NOT, as they claim to be, "a majority of the Brethren" of said Church.

When the Council was convoked, we had forty-seven male members, not including those who had taken letters of dismission. [See Church records.] Of this forty-seven, but fifteen, including absent members, were petitioners for the Council.

The distinction indicated by the term "Brethren" in connection with voting, has never been sanctioned by any resolution or vote of the South Church. The right of voting by females has never been denied by the Church, and the exercise of this right obtained and was practiced prior to the Rev. Mr. Carroll's coming among us. It has simply been continued, not inaugurated, during his administration. In the early part of 1861, the vote of the Church on the question of accepting Rev. Mr. Noyes' resignation, (as was testified before the Council then held,) stood,— Yeas 70, Noes 5; total 75; which is a much larger number than there ever were, of males only, in the South Church. All this exposes the groundlessness of the assumption that this practice was introduced for the purpose of "imposing" Rev. Mr. Carroll upon this Church. The minority of the Church, as well as the majority, have exercised this right from that time to the present. At a meeting of the Church, Feb. 18th, 1863, on the question of inviting Rev. Mr. Carroll to continue his labors among us as Stated Supply, females as well as males voted, without objection on the part of the Chairman, E. S. Minor, then a Deacon of the Church, and since one of the petitioners for the Council. If this was "contrary to the usages and principles of the New England Churches," why did he not interpose his authority as Chairman, to prevent its exercise; and why did no other member raise a question of order as to the propriety of such a proceeding? When for the first time this distinction was recorded on the Church books in these words—"the majority of the Brethren voting in the negative,"—it was in violation of the judgment of the Church as to the rights of members, as is shown by the fact that soon after the interpolation was discovered, the Church by a unanimous vote, adopted the following resolution:

"WHEREAS, At a meeting of this Church held Feb. 18, 1863, a vote was passed to invite the Rev. J. Halsted Carroll to continue his ministerial labors with this Church, said vote being recorded fifty-one yeas and twenty-two nays, with these words added, 'a majority of the brethren voting in the negative:' and whereas, this Church has never made any distinction in its membership in regard to voting; and whereas, said vote was taken by *ballot*, with no official announcement or knowledge as to the vote of any member; therefore, voted, that the former Clerk of this Church, John Nicoll, M.D., is guilty of tampering with the records, and is hereby censured for such conduct by this Church."

But passing this, what evidence did the petitioners give the Council, or has the Council given the public, that they, the petitioners, were what they claimed to be, viz: "*a majority of the brethren*" even. It is found in the caption and first paragraph of the "Result," which we quote:

"*Result of the Council called by 'the majority of the Brethren of the South Congregational Church, New Haven.'*

"This Council has been convened by certain brethren styling themselves "the majority of the brethren of the South Congregational Church in New Haven," and complaining that they "have been deprived of the rights which belong to brethren of a Congregational

Church." Whether they are or are not entitled to the rights of a majority, is a question upon which we are not called to express an opinion, for it is not material to any of the issues involved in their complaint. These brethren, twenty or more in number, have addressed the Church in a memorial asking for a Mutual Council to consider certain matters by which they are aggrieved, and their request has been denied. Their right, therefore, of obtaining advice from neighbor Churches through an *Ex-parte* Council, in conformity with a reasonable and long established usage of the New England Churches, cannot be disputed."

The evidence furnished to substantiate this claim, is three-fold: (*a*) an assertion of it: "Result of the Council called by '*the Majority of the Brethren:*'" (*b*) a modification of it: "This Council has been convened by certain brethren '*styling themselves* a majority;'" (*c*) a partial abandonment of it: "Whether they are, or are not, entitled to the rights of a majority, is a question upon which we are not called to express an opinion; for it is not material to any of the issues involved in their complaint." The Council may regard the question of majority or minority as immaterial; but for important reasons, it is a point not only upon which an intelligent and unprejudiced opinion should have been formed and expressed, but formally *decided;* for, with this claim undecided, how was it possible that the Council should know what case was before them? And is this an unimportant point in the estimate of a Church Court, to know who are the parties before them? And yet this can only be settled when this claim is settled. If these petitioners, members of our Church, be a majority, then is the Council dealing with our Church; and in this case, because the Church has convened them and asked for advice. If, on the other hand, these "Brethren" be a minority, then are the Council dealing only with a few individuals asking for advice, and should confine their action to them. They have nothing to do with our Church—they have no jurisdiction over us—unless we, as a Church, asked for the Council, or consented to become a party to it. We say that this is the only way in which they could have any legitimate right to discuss and decide upon our affairs; for, we are an *Independent* Congregational Church, neither associated nor consociated, and as an independent Church, which we are and always have been, we are in this case no more amenable to this Council, uncalled by us, than a Baptist, Methodist, or Episcopal Church would be. And the same obtains in the case of our minister, Rev. Mr. Carroll. He is not a member of the Association or Consociation; but an Old School Presbyterian clergyman, "responsible" to his own brethren, and none other,—an ecclesiastical body which we regard as entirely "evangelical." Did both Church and minister, or either of them, call and ask advice from this Council? Neither did. We neither asked advice, nor needed it; for, the greater part of the minority having absented themselves from our services for some time past, we have been during this period a united and prosperous Church,—have had no difficulties to harmonize, no grievances to complain of.

The vote of sixty-one members ratifying the action of the Standing Committee in declining even to become parties to this Council, was unanimous.—This being so, by what authority has this Council, representing twelve out of two hundred and twenty-two Consociated Churches in this State, arraigned, tried, condemned, and attempted to "excommunicate" us? Who made them judges and rulers over us, an independent Church, and over our minister, who belongs to another denomination? It is simply impertinence and usurpation.

"The right of obtaining advice from neighbor Churches through an *Ex-parte* Council in conformity with a reasonable and long established usage of the New England Churches, cannot be disputed." We do not dispute it. But when called upon by others to advise *them*, (which advice was conveyed in a single sentence,) we do deny that it was either necessary or right for the Council, upon a whole Church, a Church over which they had no jurisdiction, and upon Ex-parte statements, to pronounce anathemas, and even attempt to assassinate the character of its minister. And however much "in conformity with a reasonable (!) and long established usage of the New England Churches," it is in manifest *non*-conformity with simple Christian courtesy, and "contrary to the Scriptures." 1 Peter, iv: 15; 2 Thess., iii, 11.

That the South Church was not before the Council, will appear from the fact that we had at the date it was called, one hundred and fifty-two members, (not including those who had taken letters of dismission.) Of these one hundred and fifty-two members not dismissed, forty-seven are males; of these forty-seven males not dismissed, only fifteen signed the petition for the Council,—the other five not being recognized as members by this Church, which as an independent body, has alone the right to determine who are its members and who are not. Are fifteen a majority of forty-seven? Are twenty, "styling themselves a majority of the brethren," a majority of fifty-three? which is our number of males if we include, as they do, the five petitioners dismissed, and one dismissed who is not a petitioner? No! And yet they ought to have known that they were not a majority, and might have known it had they used the proper means, and thus have saved themselves this exposure.

Thus the petitioners, members of this Church, were not what they claimed to be, a majority of the brethren, much less of the membership, of the Church.

"First of all, this Council has made a communication to the Church through its clerk and standing committee, and also to the Rev. J. Halsted Carroll as another party interested in the matters referred to us, inviting them to appear and offer any explanations which they may desire to make concerning the transactions complained of. But these invitations have been explicitly declined. We are sorry to add, we have been denied all access to the records of the Church, and that the complainants have not been able to obtain authentic copies of the records, which they desired to present for our consideration."

Two facts are here stated: "1. Rev. Mr. Carroll 'declined' to appear, and the records were 'denied.'" *Reasons*:— Rev. Mr. Carroll declined because he failed to see any jurisdiction over him by said Council, not being a member of the Association, nor a minister of their denomination, but a Presbyterian clergyman. The church declined sending its records or "authenticated copies" of the same, because it had decided by a **unanimous vote, (61,)** as stated above, not to become a party **to the Council.** It should be remarked, however, that **those of the** *petitioners* who **had not been dismissed, had free access to** the records; **one of whom (G. H. Butricks,) took extracts therefrom. Having declined to appear** before **the Council, how could we be expected to present our records, or authenticated copies thereof, and thus take away the ex-parte character of the Council !**

"Having carefully considered the documents submitted to us in behalf of the complainants by their Committee, and having heard such testimony as they in the disadvantageous circumstances in which they are placed have been able to adduce, we find the following matters of fact :

"1. The Church in question was instituted as a Congregational Church, with the advice and approbation of a council of Congregational Churches, and the complainants became members of it, in the warranted expectation that they were to enjoy all the rights belonging to the brethren of a Congregational Church, according to the principles and usages of the New England Churches."

True, it was organized as a Congregational Church ; but never having been associated or consociated, we are an *Independent* Congregational Church,—and as such, claim the right to regulate our own affairs.

Several of the petitioners, one of them a Deacon, (E. S. Minor,) organized with us, and assisted in making our rules, and in creating and sanctioning our customs. Such being the case, what reason have they now to complain of those rules and customs ?

Among these rules and customs, is the right of all members to vote. This right was acquiesced in and practically approved by the minority, in common with the majority, at the meeting in February last, already referred to—Deacon E. S. Minor, one of the petitioners, in the chair.

This right is further sustained by the action of the Church in all cases of the admission of members, and has been, from the organization of the Church to this day. In every such case, after the assent of the member or members to the covenant, the minister, speaking in behalf of the

Church, and all the members rising in token of approval, says:—"Then doth this Church affectionately receive you to its membership and welcome you to all the privileges, labors and blessings, of the Household of Faith." "Thus you are admitted to this Church, and have a right to all its privileges." "Then are you." Who? "Male members?" "Adult male members?" "Brethren?" No! You who take this covenant. Adults and youth, parents and children, male and female, *all* recommended by the Committee and received by the Church. "You are"—what? "admitted to this Church, and have a right to all its privileges." One of the privileges conferred upon *all* who take our covenant, is voting; and as an Independent Church, we claim the right of deciding not only who are our members and who are not, but also what are the privileges of our own Church conferred *by* the Church upon its members.

"II. The Rev. J. Halsted Carroll commenced his labors at the South Church in December, 1861, being invited by the Society's Committee to officiate as a candidate. He was soon afterwards employed by concurrent votes of the Church and Society to supply the pulpit for a year. Before the termination of the year, a meeting of the Church was held to consider the question of a more permanent settlement of Mr. Carroll in the work of the ministry there. An arrangement was made, purporting to be between the Church and Society as one party, and Mr. Carroll as the other party, by which he was to remain in the work of the ministry among them indefinitely, and which could be terminated only when either party should give four months notice of a desire for the termination."

Such an arrangement not only "purported" to be made, but was made. Is there anything peculiar in this relation of Rev. Mr. Carroll to the South Church? It is the same relation Rev. Dr. Stiles sustained to this Church, and Rev. Gurdon W. Noyes, during the early part of his ministry, except the "four months' notice," which made it apparently a more permanent relation than that of the present incumbent. Why, then, should this be cited as a grievance, or as something wrong on the part of people or minister?

That nothing of a permanent or pastoral relation was

secured by this arrangement, is admitted by the complainants themselves; for they say, "it could be terminated at anytime by giving four months' previous notice."

"III. In that meeting a majority of the male members present voted against the proposed arrangement, but their votes were overruled by counting the votes of female members."

How did the council obtain this information? If from the clerk, (Dr. Nicoll,) how did *he* obtain it? If from the other petitioners, or any of them, how did *they* obtain it?—*the vote being taken* (on motion of the clerk) *by* "*secret ballot.*"

"IV. The aforesaid arrangement having been made, Mr Carroll assumed the title and authority of "Pastor of the South Church" subscribing official papers in that character, being habitually spoken of among the members of the Church, and in Church meetings, by that official title, and being announced frequently to the public as Pastor of the Church."

If the charge is, that Mr. Carroll assumed the title and authority of *installed* Pastor, we deny it.—We have called him Pastor among ourselves and in Church meetings, and announced him so to the public: but so have several of the petitioners. On one occasion, three of *them*, with others, addressed him as "Pastor," in a formal letter, expressing the "great pleasure and profit with which they had listened to his Thanksgiving sermon on the claims of our country on Christians," and asking a copy for publication. The late Superintendent of the Sunday School, (Geo. S. Minor,) one of the petitioners, often announced him as Pastor. At quarterly and anniversary meetings of the Sunday School in the Church, how familiar these words from his lips—"We will now listen to our Pastor." When thus "called" and "announced" by us and them, were any of us deceived, or did we or *they* intend to deceive others? No more did he, in "subscribing" himself "Pastor," deceive or attempt to deceive others. The offense charged here, is about as formidable as that of addressing a man by the title of Esq., who is not an Esq., who himself knows he is not an Esq., and who is known not to be an **Esq.** by the party who addresses him thus. If the fact of *our* addressing Mr. Carroll as Pastor, be proof of *his* assuming the title and authority of Pastor, why were not his predecessors, while they sustained the same relation to this Church that he does, guilty of the same offence when addressed and even spoken of in print by the same title. (See Catalogue of South Church, E. S. Minor chairman of publishing committee.)

"V. Certain members of the Church, fourteen in number, being dissatisfied with the ministry of Mr. Carroll, and desiring that notice might be duly given to him for the termination of the arrangement, presented to the Clerk of the Church their written request for a Church meeting, which request was refused by the Clerk and Standing Committee.

"VI. Afterwards the same brethren and others, twenty in all, addressed their memorial to the Church, stating distinctly the grounds of their dissatisfaction with these proceedings and with the ministry of Mr. Carroll, and asking for a Council of the Churches, to be mutually agreed upon, who should advise with the Church and the complainants. The Clerk, to whose hands the memorial was committed, refused, by the advice of the Standing Committee, to lay it before the Church."

They did refuse. And why? (1.) Because this very question about the continuance of Rev. Mr. Carroll's labors among us, had been discussed at great length at a Church meeting specially called for that purpose, not long before, and had been decided in favor of such continuance by a vote of fifty-one to twenty-two. (2.) Because the regular annual meeting of the Church must be held in the ensuing month of November, when this whole subject could be re-discussed and re-decided.

We admit that the literality of the rule* requires the Clerk

---

* NOTE BY THE AUTHOR OF SOUTH CHURCH HISTORY.—After all, there was no such rule. It is not among the printed "Standing Rules" of the Church, where the duties of the Clerk are defined, nor in the manuscript records, nor any where else. The most that can truly be said is, that there *was* such a *usage;* but even this was not uniform

to call a meeting of the Church whenever requested by a certain number of members. But can it be supposed that in adopting such a rule, the Church intended to make itself liable to be called together every month, week, or day, at the pleasure of the requisite number of petitioners, and thus be kept in a state of constant agitation? If not, a reasonable discretionary power must be vested somewhere to prevent this abuse; and where better than in the Standing Committee. This discretionary power our Standing Committee exercised in the case before us, and their action was unanimously approved by the Church. And yet, for this irregularity principally—for this refusal under these circumstances—we are judged by Council as no longer " to be recognized as a Congregational Church;" and they feel constrained " to advise their Churches to withhold from us acts of recognition and fellowship, customary among New England Churches."

"VII. Between the time when the request was made for a Church meeting and the time of preparing the memorial, some of the complainants asked and received letters of commendation, in the ordinary form, by which their membership in the Church would be terminated whenever they might become members of other Churches. But in the memorial those brethren gave notice to the Church, that upon mature deliberation they had relinquished their intention of connecting themselves with other Churches; and they remained, in the language of the testimonials which had been given them, 'members of the South Congregational Church.'"

Answer.—"Members of the South Congregational Church." Why did the Council omit the next clause? viz: "and are hereby dismissed at their own request." The fact that those brethren gave notice to the Church that " they had relinquished their intention of connecting themselves with

---

nor well defined. Very often Church meetings were called by a simple announcement from the pulpit, without the intervention of the Clerk at all. There is *now* a recorded Rule, adopted at the annual meeting of the Church, Nov. 24, 1863, as follows:

"*Voted*, That the power to call a Church meeting for business, shall rest in the Church Committee, together with the Clerk."

other Churches," did not make them remain, "in the language of the testimonials," "members of the South Congregational Church,"* but members "dismissed." Besides, a simple "notification" to us, by those dismissed, "that they did not intend to present their certificates to *other* Churches," did not release them from the necessity of presenting them to *our* Church for re-admission; for our custom and usage is, and ever has been, when members hold certificates from us which have not been presented elsewhere, if such parties desire to return to us, their certificates must be acted upon by the Church. This was, and is, our custom. Have any of the petitioners holding certificates of dismission from us, conformed to our custom in this matter? No. They have never returned their certificates to the Church, but still retain them, claiming full membership, while carrying about with them the testimonials that they are dismissed from us. Why, then, should we make them exceptions to our rule? Why should we recognize them as in full membership upon a "notification," when others have never been so recognized in like circumstances? Are we, as a Church, bound by this, their new

---

* NOTE BY THE AUTHOR OF SOUTH CHURCH HISTORY.—The argument drawn from the language of the certificates of dismission, is just as good and no better than would be that of an officer who had been dismissed from the service of the United States by a Court Martial, but who should claim that by the very language of that order, he still held his position in the regiment. We will suppose the order to read as follows:

"*Decision of Court Martial, No.* 52.—Ordered, that A. B., First Lieutenant of Company H, ninety-eleventh regiment U. S. Artillery, be, and he is hereby, dismissed from the service in disgrace."

If such an officer should appeal to the language of the order, in proof that he had *not* been dismissed, who could gain-say his plea? Does not the order itself speak of him expressly as "First Lieutenant of Company H, ninety-eleventh regiment of U. S. Artillery?" How then can he be otherwise. If the Court Martial which dismissed him, is not good authority in his favor, who or what is? And yet this flimsy argument is endorsed by the Council!

claim? Further, this custom has recently been recognized and ratified by the formal action of our Church at its last annual meeting. It was decided in the case of George S. Minor,* claiming this right for the first time in our history,

---

* NOTE BY THE AUTHOR OF SOUTH CHURCH HISTORY.—That he intended to ask for an absolute dismission, is evident from the language of his application, as follows:

"NEW HAVEN, July 19, 1863.
" To the Clerk of the South Congregational Church.—
"*Dear Sir:* Feeling it a duty to dissolve my connection with this Church, I respectfully ask through you, of them, a letter of dismission, with a certificate of Christian character, and recommendation to any Church of Christ to which by God I may be directed to hold fellowship and communion.
Very respectfully,
GEORGE S. MINOR."

We have before us the requests of several other persons who applied for general letters of dismission about the same time with the above. The following is a copy of Deacon Minor's application.

"NEW HAVEN, July 22, 1863.
" To the South Congregational Church.—
"*Dear Brethren:*—Feeling that I cannot with satisfaction to myself and advantage to the Church, retain connection with it while under its present circumstances, I respectfully ask for a letter of dismission and recommendation to whatever Church I may wish to connect myself.
Respectfully yours,
E. S. MINOR."

After reading these requests, and others like them, can there be a doubt what was the intention and wish of the applicants? They felt it a "duty" to separate themselves from the South Church and the South Church granted their request. Neither party, it is safe to say, had *at that time* the slightest idea of any further ecclesiastical connection with each other. If Paul and Barnabas, after "shaking off the dust of their feet against" the sinners of Antioch, had subsequently returned and claimed it as their property, and demanded to have it put back upon their feet, the Antiochans would have been hardly more surprised than were the South Church people at the claim of their dismissed members to to be still members of that Church in full, entitled to speak and vote in their meetings, the same as if they had not been dismissed. And yet the Council sustains this claim.

by a vote of sixty-one to one, (see Church records,) that those members who had taken letters of dismission, though not presented to other Churches, while entitled to "occasional communion," are not entitled to vote; and as an independent Church we have the right not only to make our own rules for our government, but the right of interpreting them also. This rule and interpretation is not unusual. It is endorsed by Dr. Dwight, President of Yale College, (see 4 vol. Theo. p. 320,) where the fact is stated that "Persons are not unfrequently dismissed from particular Churches in good standing and with full recommendation of their Christian character. These persons are certainly not members of any particular Church or Churches, until they are severally united to other Churches in form. It is plain that they can act no where as members of the Church of Christ, except in what is called occasional communion." Again, this rule of ours is not "contrary to the principles and usages of the New England Churches," if the Center Church, of which Rev. Dr. Bacon is pastor, conforms to those "principles and usages." Among the standing rules of that Church we find the following:

"Every member of this Church shall be considered as under the watch, care and discipline of this Church, until he shall have been regularly dismissed from his connection with it by a vote of this Church."

This clearly implies that *when* regularly dismissed by a vote of the church, he is no longer under its watch, care and discipline. Would a person having been thus dismissed—not even under its "watch, care and discipline,"—be still considered a member of that Church, and entitled to vote on questions before it? And this is the case of the complainants before the Council against the South Church. They have been "regularly dismissed by a vote of the Church," and have received letters certifying that fact; therefore, according to the decision of our Church, they are no longer members of it in such a sense as to be entitled to vote. Wherein, then, does our course differ from what necessarily would be the course of the Center Church under similar circumstances? And yet that Church is a constituent part of a Council which condemns us for the same action its own rule requires.

"VIII. The reply which the Clerk, by the direction of the Standing Committee, returned to the signers of the memorial, was addressed 'To Amos Smith, G. H. Butricks, and as many other signers of the above named request as are still recognized members of the Church;' the said Clerk and Committee thereby assuming to exclude from membership those signers who held at that moment the written testimonials of the Church to their good and regular standing."

And why should they not exclude them? They had been regularly dismissed by a vote of the Church, and neither the Clerk nor Standing Committee, nor both together, had power to reinstate them. The Church only could do this. The case of Amos Smith, one of the petitioners, illustrates this point. Some years since, having taken a letter of dismission, he did not present it to any other Church, but on his return to this city, he expressed a desire to renew his former connection with this Church, and was received accordingly by a vote of the Church, to which he returned his certificate of dismission.

"IX. At the annual meeting of the Church, held in the evening of Nov. 24, '63, Mr. Carroll, acting as moderator, denied to the members above mentioned the right of voting, or of speaking in defense of their right to vote; and that denial was approved by the meeting. The same meeting ratified all the doings of the Committee, including their suppression of the memorial."

Only one of the persons alluded to, (Geo. S. Minor,) was present at the annual meeting, and as he was not recognized by the custom and rule of the Church as a member, of course he could not be allowed to take part in the proceedings.

"X. The reasons for the dissatisfaction with the ministry of Mr. Carroll, presented to us by the complainants, and sustained by such evidence as the nature of this investigation has made practicable, are the following:

"1. They had, at the time of his settlement, no proper evidence that he was an ordained minister of the Gospel in regular communion with the Congregational Churches and ministers of Connecticut, or with any evangelical denomination."

Why did the complainants have no proper evidence that Mr. Carroll was a minister in regular communion with any evangelical denomination? Simply because the complainants, for reasons best known to themselves, never asked him, or they would have had proper evidence that he was an ordained Minister of the Gospel in regular communion with the Old School Presbyterian denomination,—a graduate of Princeton Theological Seminary in the class of 1855, ordained and installed in the Presbyterian Church at Jamesburg, N. J., May 30th, in the same year, by the Presbytery of New Brunswick. Rev. Dr. Hall, of Trenton, N. J., preached the sermon; Rev. Dr. Hodge, of Princeton, N. J., proposed the constitutional questions; Rev. Prof. Green, of Princeton, delivered the charge to the Pastor; and Rev. Dr. McDonald, of Princeton, delivered the charge to the people. [See records and roll of the New Brunswick Presbytery.]

"2. Under his ministry, there has been in the public worship of that Church, and in the lessons from the pulpit, no utterance of sympathy with our country in its struggle for unity and life; no expression of loyal desire for the success of the Government, or the defeat of the rebellion; no word implying that the attempt of the rebels to subvert by force the Government ordained by God in this land, is criminal; no recognition of the righteousness of the cause in which sons and brothers of the complainants, some of them members of the same Church, are offering their lives."

Is it not extraordinary that under such influences the friends of Mr. Carroll in the South Church and congregation have sent quite as many men to engage in the service of their country as have the petitioners and their friends in the same Church and congregation? At least thirteen of the former class are or have been in that service by voluntary enlistment—most of them for a period of three years. Is it not strange that the Council should make such statements as those above quoted, in the face of such facts as we have presented, and of such "utterances" as are expressed in the subjoined extract of a letter dated Nov. 3d, 1862, from Mr. Carroll to Mr. E. S. Minor, one of the petitioners to the Council, who, at the above-mentioned date, was a deacon in this Church. This letter has been in his possession more than a year:

"I pray for our *rulers*. This I do every Sabbath; that God would endue them with his Holy Spirit; give them wisdom from above, which is alone profitable to direct; crown with His blessing and success their every effort which shall secure the real good of the land, thereby effecting His own purposes in it and concerning it, and redeeming them thus from narrow, groveling views. I pray for the *soldiers;* this I do every Sabbath; that God would encamp round about them; that he would preserve them in body and soul, in health and morals, in all their interests for time and eternity; and for their families and friends as well; and for *Peace,* in God's own way, (and His ways are not our ways;) for *Peace* in God's way of thinking—purposely, therefore, 'shutting out of view the great principles *we* think involved,' (inasmuch as God's thoughts are not as our thoughts;) for *Peace,* which if God sends, must be righteous and 'free from crime.' I pray for the *country;* I do this every Sabbath; that God would pity her and interpose in her behalf, so that she may no longer be made one vast Golgotha, but the land of Immanuel. It is not enough that I thus recognize Government as an institution of God, and the 'powers that be, as ordained of God,'—no! but because in holiest approach unto the Most High, I do not advocate a certain policy;—because before the throne of God I do not intone the Shibboleth of a party."

"3. In the pulpit and in private conversation he has characterized the action of the Government as tyrannical and unjust, and has implied that the attempt of the Government to maintain itself by force against the rebellion, is criminal; and when members of the church have courteously inquired of him concerning his views, that they might know whether he had been misunderstood on these points, he has refused to give any satisfactory answer."

Mr. Carroll has characterized a certain action of the Government as "tyrannical and unjust." This Mr. Carroll did. How, and when? It was in connection with the case of John Nicoll, M.D., one of the petitioners, then an officer and member of our Church, and about the time when he was summarily taken to Fort Lafayette. His home was broken—his practice interrupted—his reputation as an honest man suffering—his character as a Christian clouded—and believing him innocent, with no opportunity to prove it, and thus save himself and family—it was under *these circumstances* and in *his case,* that Mr. Carroll said the action of the Government was "tyrannical and unjust," and "in the pulpit" prayed for his speedy deliverance and return. And when he did return, *he* prayed what Mr. *Carroll* had said, *and more;* that they might be put out of power. Proof—an entire prayer meeting. Now, which was most "disloyal;" to say what Mr. Carroll said, or to pray what Dr. Nicoll prayed? And yet the one who prayed thus in our meeting, is one of the aggrieved "brethren" before the Council, whose patriotism and piety are shocked by Mr. Carroll's prayers.

"4. He has borne no testimony against the wicked doctrine of these times, that it is right for white men to make slaves of black men; but on the contrary, he has used his influence to suppress in the meetings of the Church all allusions to the injustice of slavery."

True, Mr. Carroll does not preach or pray abolitionism, or any other "ism."

If he has used his influence to suppress "in the meetings of the Church all allusions to the injustice of slavery," he has not been very successful, at least in the case of several of the petitioners.

"5. He has by his private and public influence brought certain young persons of the congregation into open sympathy with the existing rebellion."

Who these "certain young persons of the congregation" are, as a Church we do not know; and if there be any, Mr. C. could not have made them such. Even the petitioners virtually confess this; for they assert that "when members of the Church have *courteously* inquired of him concerning his views, that they might know whether he had been misunderstood on these points, he has refused to give any satisfactory answer." The question may fairly be raised, whether, instead of being brought to that position through the influence of Mr. Carroll, it has not been caused by the indiscreet zeal of parents and friends.

JUDGMENT OF THE COUNCIL.

"These being the facts (!) as we find them," say the Council, "our judgment is," [here follow six conclusions, based upon the alleged facts.] To answer the conclusions in detail, would be to answer the "facts" over again. This we need not do. We will, however, say a few words on two of the conclusions, in addition to what has been said above on the same topics.

"Second. Mr. Carroll is not, in the proper use of language, pastor of the South Congregational Church in New Haven, nor is he 'Acting Pastor,' as that term is defined by the General Association of Connecticut. Any assumption of the title of pastor on his part is unwarranted, and the arrangements and proceedings by which he has been invested with the powers of a pastor in that Church, without the intervention of a council of neighboring churches to inquire into his qualifications for that office, are a contempt put upon the principle of communion of churches, and a violation of the rights of the complainants."

The last Annual Report of the General Association of Connecticut, in its tabular statements, p. 83, has the following entry opposite South Church:

"J. Halsted Carroll, (A. p.)" Acting Pastor.

If, however, the Council rest their assertion upon a report submitted by Dr. Bacon "*for examination*," and contained in said Annual Report, Mr. Carroll is neither "Acting Pastor," "Pastor," nor "Stated Preacher" of this Church, nor indeed sustains any relation to it, but "*may reasonably be regarded with suspicion.*" Suspicion? Why? Simply because Mr. Carroll "insists upon retaining his Church relation and clerical connection" "with his own ecclesiastical body."

"Third. The voting of women in the Church, by which, in the settlement of Mr. Carroll, the majority of the brethren was overruled, is contrary to the Scriptures (I. Cor. xix. 34; I. Tim. xi. 12;) and contrary to the usages and principles of the New England Churches, and invalidates the act of a majority, which was made such by these votes."

The assertion here is, that it is wrong for women to vote: (1) Because "contrary to the Scriptures." There are no such "Scriptures" as those above-quoted, nor any others denying the right of women to vote in Churches. (2) "Because contrary to the usages and principles of the New England Churches." But not to those of *our independent Church*. (3) That it "invalidates the act of a majority." It might so in a consociated Church, but not in ours, which being an independent Church, has a right to establish its own rules as well in regard to voting as to other things.

ADVICE OF THE COUNCIL.

"First. In consideration of the facts which have appeared before this Council, and which we have already recited, we advise the complainants that the South Congregational Church, so called, ought not to be recognized any longer as a Congregational Church, and as a Council we advise the Churches which we represent, and all other Churches of our communion, to withhold from that Church those acts of mutual recognition and fellowship which are customary among Congregational Churches, and which are the form of their unity as an ecclesiastical commonwealth."

Thus far in our history, acts of "recognition and fellowship" toward us on the part of the Churches represented in the Council, have been few and far between. Whether the action of Council will make them fewer hereafter, remains to be seen. At present we are unable to appreciate our loss.

"Secondly. We advise the complainants, and as many other members of that Church as may associate with them, to withdraw from their present relations to it. And we authorize our Moderator and Scribe to give to them, collectively or individually, in our behalf, letters certifying their regular standing as professed followers of Christ in full communion with the Congregational Churches of Connecticut, and commending them to any Church with which they may choose to connect themselves, or to any ecclesiastical Council which may be convened for the purpose of recognizing the formation of a new Church. The question whether they shall proceed to constitute a new Church in the south part of the city of New Haven, is a question to be determined partly by local considerations, with which they, and the members of the other Churches here, are better acquainted than this Council can be. Yet we cannot refrain from saying, that for the sake of patriotism and of pure and undefiled religion, there ought to be among the growing population of that quarter a truly Congregational Church, from which the sympathies of patriotic Christian souls may freely go up to God on the wings of prayer and praise, and in which the whole counsel of God, "revealed from heaven against all ungodliness and unrighteousness of men who hold the truth in unrighteousness," shall be preached plainly and unswervingly.

"Signed in behalf and by direction of the Council.
"REV. JOSEPH ELDRIDGE, Moderator.
"REV. W. T. EUSTIS, Scribe."

In this second and last paragraph of advice, the Council recommend (1) that the complainants and such as sympathize with them, "withdraw from their present relations" to us. In this recommendation we cordially concur. (2) A modest intimation that they proceed to constitute a new Church in the south (this) part of the city. Reasons,—considerations of "patriotism" and of "pure and undefiled religion." If "pure and undefiled religion before God and the Father" is this, "to visit the widow and fatherless in their affliction, and to keep ourselves unspotted from the world," this we have humbly tried to do, not only positively but negatively; our Church, by refusing to convert itself into a political machine, and our minister, by refusing to preach or pray politics.

In what respect are the patriotism and piety of the proposed new Church to differ from ours, as above described? But without pressing this question, we are inclined to hope that the recommendation of the Council to build a new Church will also be complied with, and that the old and wealthy Churches here will give it a liberal support.

It is likewise insinuated against Rev. Mr. Carroll, that he has been unfaithful as a minister, "*failing to declare the whole counsel of God.*" What is the evidence the Council furnish the public upon which they made, and made public, this fearful charge against Mr. Carroll, as recreant to his official duties and faithless as a minister of God? None whatever. And they not only pronounce sentence upon him on the strength of *ex-parte* statements, but upon him, though beyond their jurisdiction, and amenable to another denomination. But the best refutation of this slander is the simple record of his ministry. What is the record of the year just closed, from January, 1863, to January, 1864? Our congregations on the Sabbath, and at weekly meetings, have never before been uniformly so large, in our history of eleven years, except during a short period under the ministry of Rev. Dr. Stiles; while the additions to our Church membership have been 43—a larger number than in any year of the previous nine years. Comparing this accession with that of other Churches during the year 1862, as recorded in the minutes of the General Association of Connecticut, we find more fruits from his labors, and larger accessions of members, than in the ministry and Churches represented in the Council who condemned him and us as unfaithful. Of the 284 Congregational Churches in the State, (222 consociated, and 62 independent,) only *two* had so large an accession.

If these be indications of infidelity to duty and to God, we pray they may abound; that as a Church we may be "steadfast, unmovable, always abounding in the work of the Lord;" and that as a minister, Mr. Carroll may continue to refuse to promulgate for doctrines of Christ "the commandments of men," and may continue to know nothing among *us* save Jesus Christ and Him crucified.

NEW HAVEN, January 1, 1864.

(Signed) THOMAS HORSFALL,
NICHOLAS COUNTRYMAN,
CHARLES H. WARNER,
CHAS. F. HOTCHKISS,
JOHN H. LEEDS,
} Standing Committee.

MYRON BARRETT, Stated Clerk.

THE EX-PARTE COUNCIL.   133

At a meeting of the South Congregational Church, held in their Chapel on the evening of January 1, 1864, the above Reply was read, and the following resolution, offered by Mr. Edwin W. Treat, was UNANIMOUSLY adopted:

Resolved, That the Report of the Standing Committee just read, in reply to the Ecclesiastical Council recently held in this city, be approved by this Church, and published.

THOS. HORSFALL,
Clerk of the Meeting.

The above documents were published in the New Haven papers,—the former near the close of 1863, and the latter on the 2d of January, 1864. They were followed by others, which are here subjoined:

REJOINDER
To the "Reply of the South Church."

The *Standing Committee* of the South Church, in their reply to the Result of the Ecclesiastical Council recently convened at the request of certain petitioners in this city, have undertaken to bring charges against the body of the complainants and against individual members by name.

The petitioners desire to state, that in their action they have been influenced only by a *sense of duty*. On consulting as to the best means of providing a place of worship more congenial to their views of duty, they were advised that a Council convened to form a new Church, would have as one of its first duties, to inquire into the reasons for their leaving the South Church, and that to call a *Mutual Council* where both parties might represent their case, was the most suitable course to be taken in pursuance of their object. No other course, therefore, seemed open to them, but the one they have taken.

The petitioners, of course, are not to be held responsible for the action and finding of the Council, yet the unanimous judgment of the men who constituted that body, representing Churches in every part of the State, will scarcely be over-ruled in the opinion of thoughtful and impartial minds, by the assertions of those who refused to submit the case to a tribunal, half of whose members they were at liberty to select.

The petitioners did not claim before the Council that the names signed to the Memorial *were* a majority of the brethren of the Church, but that they *represented* a majority of them. This claim was grounded on the following facts, viz:—Mr. Carroll's official returns to the General Association of Connecticut, state the number of *male* members, January 1st, 1863, to be 44. The petitioners knew of but six *male* members who had since been received up to the date of their memorial, making the whole number 50; six or more had been dismissed and united with other Churches within the same period, leaving the number of *male* members at 44,—and they know that 26, including the memorialists, sympathized with them. If then, the official returns to the Association were correct, the number the petitioners claimed to represent, was a MAJORITY.

It may be proper to add a word to illustrate the views of some of the members of the *Standing Committee* as to the treatment which an *unquestioned* majority might expect to receive from the "*ruling powers*" of this Church. One of the petitioners in conversation with a member of the Committee, declared his belief, that if a Church meeting was called, and the subject fairly considered of requesting Mr. Carroll to tender his resignation, two to one would be in favor of the motion; and furthermore he offered if his statement was doubted, to give the names of those who he had reason to believe would vote for it.

The reply was in substance, that it would make no difference if even *three fourths* of the members were in favor of the motion; so long as *Mr. Hallock wished* Mr. Carroll to stay, he *would stay*, and they could not help themselves. It has been often admitted by members of the Committee and others, that while the Church is sustained as it now is, *almost entirely* by the contributions of *one man*, his wishes would have paramount weight, and the self-governing power of the Church be virtually abrogated.

It is said that "those of the petitioners who had not been dismissed, had free access to the records." In reply to this, one of the petitioners who has *not* been dismissed, affirms that he applied for an inspection of the records and was denied by the Clerk.

One of the petitioners is informed for the *first* time by this document, that censure has been passed upon him by the Church; which it is understood was voted at the *close* of the *prayer meeting Dec. 29th*, 1863, (barely in time to be *used* in the reply of the Committee of the Church,) and without any summons to the accused, who was condemned without a hearing. Considering that this brother is one of those who received letters of dismission and over whom this Church has declared itself to have no control, it must be acknowledged that their action in the case vindicates the position which they claim for themselves, of being an "*Independent Congregational Church*."

This brother would state that the fact which he noted in the records, was derived from the *public* declarations of a majority of the brethren in the meeting, both as it respected their opinion, and their votes; and it being the duty of the Clerk to note *all* matters of interest to the Church, this fact was duly recorded.

In relation to one of the special grievances of the petitioners, the deprivation of their rights by the Committee,— the latter justify their action in refusing to call a Church meeting upon the request of a sufficient number of members, by the assertion, that the subject of Mr. Carroll's ministrations over the Church had been sufficiently discussed at a recent Church meeting, and "the annual meeting must be held in the *ensuing month of November*," when the whole matter could be rediscussed and redecided. In reply the petitioners would state that Rev. Mr. Carroll is settled for an indefinite period, and in order to dismiss him it is required that four months notice be given, and this was their object in requesting the meeting. It was nearly *four* months before the "*annual meeting*" to which they refer, would be held. It is true that the subject had been discussed at a previous meeting and declared to be settled by a decisive vote, but in the mean time matters had assumed a different aspect. Mr. Carroll's summary silencing of the bell while ringing for the victory at Vicksburg, had induced many who had before been his supporters, to believe that he was not a loyal man, and they were ready to unite in the call for his dismissal. It was under these circumstances that the Standing Committee assumed their "discretionary powers," and standing between Mr. Carroll and the Church, refused to allow the latter to pronounce its judgment, which it is nearly certain would have condemned him. But the Committee went further than this. The petitioners addressed a respectful memorial to the Church (in the customary form) requesting them to unite in calling a Mutual Council to advise in regard to our respective duties. This memorial the Committee *suppressed*,--refusing to allow it to come before the Church for their decision. In this they claim they exercised a reasonable discretionary power, which must be vested somewhere to prevent the constant agitation of the Church. The rule of the Church under which this Committee are appointed, and act, makes no mention of such discretionary power, but on the contrary implicitly forbids it by prescribing their special duties, and ends by stating that they shall attend to such other matters as may be referred to them by the Church. As the call for a meeting, and the memorial, had never been referred to them by the Church, it is clear that they had no discretionary power in the matter, but assumed a power without right or authority.

Upon the question of female voting—

The Committee say "that the right of voting by females has never been denied by the Church." Very true; neither has the right been affirmed by the Church, which would seem necessary, as the custom of Congregational Churches forbids the practice. It was the usual practice in the Church to vote by raising of hands, excepting in the case of officers who were elected by ballot, and female votes were rarely offered or counted. No instance is known in which females voted by ballot previous to the meeting when Mr. Carroll was settled by female votes. At that meeting some of the females had such an expansive idea of their rights that they not only voted themselves, but also deposited votes for absent friends, thereby showing what irregularities are likely to prevail on exciting occasions, if the practice of female voting obtains.

But the Committee have endeavored to strengthen their position by an argument from the covenant, which as they claim, by giving every member all the privileges of the Church, must necessarily give to females the right of voting. This argument proves, if anything, that females have the right of being appointed deacons, acting upon Committees, the right of discussion in business meetings, and of prayer and exhortation in prayer meetings. The right of performing these actions is granted by the covenant as well as the right to vote, and has never been denied by the Church. We hardly think the Committee would be prepared to follow out this argument to its logical conclusion.

Mr. Carroll's "utterances" in a certain letter addressed to one of the petitioners, are brought forward in this reply, to disprove the imputation of his disloyalty. As it is implied that this letter was withheld from the Council, it is due to this brother, as well as to Mr. Carroll, to state that Mr. Carroll's WHOLE LETTER WAS READ TO THE COUNCIL, and he has received all the advantage he could derive from having these utterances of his laid before them.

That the public may understand the reasonableness of the demand which the petitioners make in relation to this point, the following extract from the rejoinder to Mr. Carroll's letter is here given.

"I know of no one in our Church who desires to have 'party politics' either preached or prayed in the pulpit. I know of no one who wishes the 'Shibboleth of a party intoned in prayer,' but I do know of MANY whose LOYAL, not PARTIZAN, feelings crave at least this concession, viz: a decisive REPROBATION of the rebellion, and a decisive APPROBATION of the Government in its efforts to maintain its own integrity.

"They crave an ADMISSION that the cause to which their fathers, sons, and husbands, and brothers have freely devoted their lives, is a JUST and WORTHY cause. I do not see how this can be construed into PARTIZAN politics, unless the partizans are SECESSIONISTS on the one hand and LOY-

ALISTS on the other; for men of all the late acknowledged parties, and religionists of every persuasion, ARE FOUND UNITED ON THIS PLATFORM. Neither do I know or believe that this concession to the feelings of our members would give offense to any one, or produce any division among our people."

What is there in this demand that is either unreasonable or unchristian?

The petitioners would also reaffirm what has been sustained by the signatures of some forty names of persons who are or have been members of the South Church, that "it is not known to us that either in preaching, prayer or conversation, Mr. Carroll has ever admitted that the rebellion of the South against the Government of the United States is CRIMINAL, or that he has ever expressed a wish or a prayer for the SUCCESS of our armies over the rebels, or for the re-establishment of the Union over the rebellious States, or that he has ever expressed in public a word of thanksgiving for any victories or successes obtained by our armies. Is there another minister of any denomination in this city or in the State, of whom this can be said?

Allusion is made to disloyal sentiments said to have been uttered in prayer by one of the petitioners who had been unjustly imprisoned in Fort Lafayette.

It is true that Dr. Nicoll, while smarting under the wrong inflicted by an abuse of power, the proper use of which he has never questioned, did pray that those who trifled with and misused the power with which they were entrusted by God, might be removed from places of authority; and it is also true, (which the Standing Committee neglected to mention,) that in the same prayer he did earnestly pray for the overthrow of the rebellion, and for the freedom of the oppressed.

This reply intimates that in but one instance Mr. Carroll has characterized the action of the Government as "tyrannical and unjust."

It was stated before the Council, that at the breaking out of the rebellion his outspoken sympathy with the traitors compelled him to leave a hotel in a neighboring city, because the guests would not endure the presence of one so disloyal.

It was also stated that he had declared in effect, that were it not for personal considerations, he would go south of Mason and Dixon's line and share the fortune of the rebellion, with which cause he was one at heart.

Has Mr. Carroll forgotten the language he used in public prayer on the morning of the Lord's Day when the news came of the battle before Fredericksburg? Certainly those well-considered sentences condemning the war can not have slipped his memory, since he expressed to one of our number a regret that he was absent, and did not hear the "TALL PRAYING" in the forenoon.

In the matter of loyalty claimed for the friends of Mr. Carroll—this has not been denied. It is the persistent efforts and determination of a few who hold the power, to foist and fix in the pastorate of the Church a man whom they believe to be disloyal, of which the petitioners complain. Of the soldiers who have gone from the Church into the army, we know of but one or two who have ever acknowledged that they had received a word of sympathy and encouragement from Mr. Carroll, in regard to their DUTIES AS SOLDIERS. Will the congregation ever forget the deep disappointment that was felt at the character of the services when soldiers from the 15th Regiment were present, by special invitation, to hear their minister's parting counsel?

The Standing Committee claim that, under the ministrations of Mr. Carroll, the congregation has been larger than before; while the additions to the Church, within the year just closed, have been forty-three—"a larger number than in any year of the previous nine years."

To this it may be replied, that at least SEVENTY members, including the petitioners, have left during the year, or are ready to leave the Church when another place of worship shall be provided, because of their dislike to Mr. Carroll's ministrations: and that in the year 1857 the number of members admitted to the Church was forty-seven.

It may be stated for the information of those interested in our object, that already a larger sum has been pledged by persons in the vicinity of the South Church to support the preaching of the Gospel, in case a new Church is formed, than has ever been raised in one year by that Church for the same purpose, aside from the contributions of one individual; and that if those who are friendly to their object will provide them with a suitable building, the petitioners will have no occasion to depend upon the contributions of the old and wealthy Churches.

Whether in view of the foregoing facts the complainants were wrong in asking to be heard IN THE CHURCH; and when that was forbidden, in a PRIVATE CONFERENCE; and when that was declined, in seeking for a MUTUAL COUNCIL; and when that was denied, in calling for an *Ex-parte* COUNCIL—the public will determine.

IN BEHALF OF THE PETITIONERS.

SOUTH CHURCH,—AGAIN.

REMARKS ON THE "REJOINDER."

MESSRS. EDITORS:—As the Standing Committee of the South Church have not seen fit to reply to the "Rejoinder" of the petitioners for an Ex-parte Council, and as the petitioners might deem themselves slighted if their production was wholly passed over in silence, permit a member of said Church, not belonging to the Standing Committee, to offer a few words by way of comment. He will be best understood by quoting brief extracts from the "Rejoinder," and then adding his own remarks. The petitioners say:

> "On consulting as to the best means of providing a place of worship more congenial to their views of duty, they were advised that a Council convened to form a new Church, would have, as one of its first duties, to inquire into the reasons for their leaving the South Church."

So this Ex parte Council was itself the result of *counsel;* and, although called ostensibly to consider the expediency of forming a new Church, was mainly designed, at least by the "advisers," for another purpose, viz: to get a dig at the South Church. [We had no doubt that such was the fact, but did not expect the petitioners to confess it.] Accordingly the discussion and finding of the Council in regard to the South Church occupy almost the whole extent of their "Result," as given to the public, while in regard to the formation of a new Church they have said very little, and *that* little of a very indefinite character. Who these "advisers" were, may be safely inferred from an inspection of the roll of Council. That several of them had long been aching for a chance to whip the South Church into their Abolition traces, was well understood by members of that Church; who, while they would do nothing intentionally to invite or provoke such interference, were not disposed to purchase exemption therefrom by the surrender of their just rights as an Independent Congregational Church. But leaving what we have further to say on the subject of the Council, and of Councils generally, to the closing part of this article, we pass to another extract from the petitioners' Rejoinder:

"The petitioners of course, are not to be held responsible for the action and finding of the Council."

Why not? Was not the Council a thing of their own creating? Did not its decisions rest mainly on their own assertions? To this extent they *are* responsible for "the finding and action of the Council;" and they will not be permitted to escape from that responsibility by throwing the whole burden upon the shoulders of men who have as much as they can carry, with all the help the petitioners can give them. Do the petitioners mean to repudiate the action of their own Council? Besides the slur above indicated, one of them has applied to the South Church for a letter of dismission and received it, since the meeting of the Council, notwithstanding the generous offer of the latter body to give them letters of its own, thus usurping or superseding the powers of the Church in that matter. But it seems that at least ONE of the petitioners prefers to receive his credentials from the Church, although resting under the ban of the Council, rather than from the Council itself. We commend the wisdom of his course.

"The petitioners did not claim before the Council that the names signed to the Memorial *were* a majority of the brethren of the Church, but that they *represented* a majority of them."

Hear the Council on this head:

"This Council has been convened by certain brethren *styling* THEM-SELVES the majority of the brethren of the South Congregational Church in New Haven."

Which shall we believe,—the petitioners?—or the Council?

"This claim [of a majority of the male members] was grounded on the following facts, viz:—Mr. Carroll's official returns to the General Association of Connecticut, state the number of *male* members, January 1st, 1863, to be 44. The petitioners knew of but six *male* members who had since been received up to the date of their memorial, making the whole number 50; six or more had been dismissed and united with other Churches within the same period, leaving the number of *male* members at 44,—and they know that 26, including the memorialists, sympathized with them."

"Mr. Carroll's official returns." These returns were furnished to Mr. Carroll by Deacon Minor, who is therefore responsible for their correctness. They state the number of *male* members of the South Church on the 1st of January, 1863, at 44. The petitioners say they "knew of but six *male* members who had since been received, up to the date of their memorial."* Now, the fact is, that *twelve* male members had since been received, viz:—On the 4th of January, 2; 1st of March, 4; 3d of May, 4; 5th of July, 2. Total, 12.† This shows how careless the petitioners are about their figures. They count but six when there are twelve. Add 12 to 44, and it makes 56, instead of 50, does it not? From 56, then, deduct 6 who they say had been dismissed and united with other Churches, (we know of but

---

* Following the petitioners, we shall hereafter speak of the memorial as if dated at the time it was presented; say about the last of October. Strictly speaking, it is not dated at all. But the Clerk's reply to it is dated Nov. 3d.

† The names are before us, and can easily be had by the petitioners, if wanted.

five who had united with other Churches,—certainly there were not *more* than six,) and it leaves 50 male members at the date of the memorial. Of these they claim 26,—the least possible majority,—*including six sympathisers*. These sympathisers, we suspect, are a very uncertain reliance; for, if it had been possible by solicitations and entreaties to get their names upon the memorial, we need not say that it would have been done. Now, if a single individual of the six claimed as sympathisers, is not so in fact, then, according to their own showing, after correcting a single blunder as above, (which they cannot and will not deny to be such,) they have NOT a majority of the brethren, and do not even REPRESENT a majority. Observe further, that among the signers and sympathisers are included six who had been dismissed from the Church by general letter. Deduct these from the whole number of male members (50) as above, at the date of the memorial, and also from the 26 claimed by the petitioners, and it leaves 20 signers and sympathisers, out of a total of 44 male members; being three less than a majority. We have thus carried out the calculation of the petitioners, after making the single correction above mentioned—from which it appears that in order to show even the smallest possible majority, they are obliged to assume: 1st, That there were only 44 male members on the 1st of January, 1863, which is contrary to the fact. 2d, That members dismissed by general letter are still members in full, and entitled to the privilege of voting; which is contrary to the fact, at least in the South Church. 3d, That six members sympathize with the petitioners who cannot be induced to sign their paper. 4th, In order to make these assumptions available to their purpose, they are obliged further to assume that only male members have a right to vote; which is contrary to the fact, at least in the South Church. Upon the validity of these assumptions, all of which are fallacious, rests the only shadow of a claim which the petitioners had, to represent the South Church before the Council.

A careful examination of the records shows that instead of 44 male members on the 1st of January, 1863, as reported by Deacon Minor to Mr. Carroll, and by the latter to the General Association of Connecticut, there were in fact

FIFTY male members at that date, EXCLUSIVE of two, who, with their families, had been for a considerable period absent from the city, and whose present residence was, and is, to the Church unknown. Between the 1st of January, 1863, and the date of the petitioners' memorial, TWELVE male members were added by letter or profession, and SIXTEEN dismissed, viz: 5 by letter to other Churches, 8 by general letter, 1 by discipline, and 2 by death. Leaving at the date of the memorial, FORTY-SIX male members, exclusive of the two above mentioned. If these two were included, it would make 48. But call it 46. Of the eight dismissed by general letter, five are signers of the memorial; two are doubtless included among the "sympathizers;" and one is understood to have joined another Church. Deduct the first seven of these eight from the 26 signers and sympathizers claimed by the petitioners, (for in all their calculations they include the general letter men,) and it leaves them but 19. That is, they do not even claim more than 19 signers and sympathizers, out of the 46 male members above stated;—the other seven of their number consisting of men who had been dismissed by general letter, and who therefore were no longer reckoned as members by the Church. If, however, these were included as members, it would increase the number of male members to 53 at the date of the memorial. Twenty-six is not a majority of 53; neither is 19 a majority of 46. Take it which way they will, therefore; include the general letter men, or exclude them; and count in for the petitioners all the sympathizers they claim; still they fall short of a majority of the *male* members. Hence it appears—

1. That the petitioners to the Council, 20 in number, are not what they "STYLED THEMSELVES," according to the published declaration of that body, "the majority of the brethren of the South Congregational Church in New Haven."

2. That they do NOT "REPRESENT" a majority of the brethren.

3. That they and all the "sympathizers" they claim, are not TOGETHER a majority of the brethren of the South Church.

4. And admitting that they were, it would amount to nothing in a Church where there is no CASTE, but where ALL the members, 150 to 160 in number, are by covenant and usage entitled to vote; and where, since the last "secession" of disaffected members, 31st of July last, there has been almost perfect unanimity; not five votes having been given at any Church meeting, since that date, in opposition to the views of Mr. Carroll and his friends. In one of those meetings the number of votes was between 60 and 70.

GOSSIP.

The conversation alleged in the Rejoinder to have taken place between one of the petitioners and a member of the Standing Committee of the South Church, is not recognized by *any* member of that Committee as an actual occurrence. One of them remembers the conversation which he supposes is alluded to, but denies that it is correctly reported, even "in substance." He is represented to have said, in substance:

"It would make no difference if even *three-fourths* of the members were in favor of the motion; so long as *Mr. Hallock wished* Mr. Carroll to stay, he *would stay*, and they could not help themselves. It has been often admitted by members of the Committee and others, that while the Church is sustained as it now is, *almost entirely* by the contributions of *one man*, his wishes would have paramount weight, and the self-governing power of the Church be virtually abrogated."

The smallest proportionate majority *ever* given for Mr. Carroll, by the South Church, was on the 18th of February last, when there were 51 votes in his favor, and 22 against him, as announced at the time by the chairman, Dea. Minor. The way to test the truth of the "three-fourths" statement, is, to get such a majority, or any majority at all. There is no chance to test it, so long as the petitioners and their sympathizers can muster only 22 votes against 51. They will not pretend that a majority *vote* of the Church was ever overruled, or attempted to be overruled, by Mr. Hallock. Perhaps their meaning is, that a majority vote is sure to be given in accordance with his wishes. But how are his wishes ascertained when he does not express them, as is often the case? It would be more correct to say he is sure to sustain the will of the majority. Happily, an accordance of views has commonly existed between him and a majority of the Church, but not always. How about that "majority of the brethren" claimed by the petitioners on the occasion above alluded to? So there was a *little* independence left at that date, although confined to the petitioners and those who "sympathized" with them! When the last of them has withdrawn, agreeably to the advice of their own Council, all independence of opinion and of action will have gone with them, no doubt! In other words, the Church will be united.

"One of the petitioners is informed for the *first* time, by this document, that censure has been passed upon him by the Church, which it is understood was voted at the *close* of the *prayer meeting*, Dec. 29th, 1863, (barely in time to be *used* in the reply of the Committee of the Church,) and without any summons to the accused, who was condemned without a hearing. Considering that this brother is one of those who received letters of dismission, and over whom this Church has declared itself to have no control, it must be acknowledged that their action in the case vindicates the position which they claim for themselves, of being an '*Independent Congregational Church*.'"

The censure passed upon the late Clerk, Dr. Nicoll, for tampering with the records, was in perfect accordance with the position maintained by the Church as to members dismissed from it without as yet being connected with any other Church, viz: that although such persons are not entitled to the full rights of membership, yet the Church can exercise a watch and discipline over them until received into some other Church. By what authority, then, do the petitioners assert that "this Church has declared itself to have no control over those who have received letters of dismission?" When did they make such a declaration? Never.

"This brother would state that the fact which he noted in the records was derived from the *public* declarations of a majority of the brethren in their meeting, both as it respected their opinion and their votes, and it being the duty of the Clerk to note *all* matters of interest to the Church, this fact was duly recorded."

We rather wish that "this brother" had been called before the Church, as it would then have been practically shown whether he held himself amenable to its jurisdiction, or whether he claimed the right of speaking and voting in its meetings, WITHOUT being subject to its watch, care and discipline. However, both the Church and the public now know what would have been his defense, viz: that he made the entry complained of, on the strength of "the public declarations of a majority of the brethren in the meeting, both as it respected their opinion and their votes." Does he mean to say that "a majority of the brethren in the meeting" spoke in the meeting against the continuance of Mr. Carroll, and declared that they should vote against him? If so, it looks like a previously contrived plan to accomplish an object. He first moves, and gains assent from an unsuspecting majority, that the vote be taken by "secret ballot;" and then, in his own "secret" way, claims to have ascertained that "a majority of THE BRETHREN" voted in the negative; and so enters it upon the official records of the Church. No opportunity was given to the majority to challenge the statement; confessedly it was not founded upon any actual vote; it was not declared by the chairman or by any body else before the Church—but rested, and still rests, upon the naked assertion of the then Clerk, Dr. Nicoll. A prudent man would not have voluntarily placed himself in a position where his integrity or accuracy would be so liable to be called in question, without any visible means of substantiating his statement, which, even if correct, he had no right to enter upon the records of the Church, as it made a distinction which the Church had never authorized, between the votes of members, and because such a stealthy mode of obtaining results, would, if tolerated, expose the Church, or any other body of persons where it was practiced, to the most enormous abuses.

"Mr. Carroll's summary silencing of the bell while ringing for the victory at Vicksburg, had induced many who had before been his supporters, to believe that he was not a loyal man, and they were ready to unite in the call for his dismissal. It was under these circumstances that the Standing Committee assumed their 'discretionary powers' and standing between Mr. Carroll and the Church, refused to allow the latter to pronounce its judgment, which it is nearly certain would have condemned him."

If this is a correct statement, it proves that the occasion alluded to was exactly the time when any discretionary power which the Standing Committee possessed, should be exercised, to prevent hasty and injudicious action. The incident about the bell (which was subsequently explained to the satisfaction of a great majority of the Church,) was seized upon by those who had previously sought to displace Mr. Carroll, but had signally failed, as an encouragement to renew the onset, hoping, under the excitement and misapprehension of the moment, to accomplish their object. Had they succeeded, it is now certain that they would have precipitated a course of action which a great majority of the members in their calmer moments would have deeply regretted; for, in every subsequent as well as previous meeting of the Church, Mr. Carroll has been sustained by a triumphant majority. Not sustained in the matter of the bell, for THAT as a distinct issue has never come before them; but sustained in his general course, as a most faithful, talented, and eminently useful minister of Christ, whom they desire to have for THEIR spiritual teacher and guide, in preference to any other clergyman within their knowledge. Therefore we say that if, at the moment of the bell excitement, the Church would have been "ready to unite in the call for his dismissal," as alleged by the petitioners, the Clerk and Standing Committee did them an invaluable service by refusing to call them together at that time.

"The Committee say 'that the right of voting by females has never been denied by the Church.' Very true; neither has the right been affirmed by the Church, which would seem necessary, as the custom of Congregational Churches forbids the practice."

This is falling from high ground. Before, the practice was contrary to the *Scriptures;* now it is contrary to *cus-*

tom. Whose custom? "Of Congregational Churches;" but not of the South Church, as an independent body. And do the petitioners pretend that among all the 284 Congregational Churches in this State, the custom in regard to female voting is uniform? Is it so in all the Churches represented in the late Ex-parte Council? If we are rightly informed, two Churches at least, of the twelve represented in said Council, practice female voting, at least sometimes. We refer to the Chapel-street Church, of which the Scribe of the Council, Rev. Mr. Eustis, is Pastor, and to the North Church, of which Rev. Dr. Dutton is Pastor. We have it from one who was present at the meeting which called Rev. Mr. Eustis, that female members voted for him as Pastor. Why then may not females in the South Church vote for Rev. Mr. Carroll as Stated Supply? Also in the North Church, at a meeting subsequent to the one called for the purpose of repairing the organ, when it was suggested that the organ at the other end of the Church needed to be repaired, or replaced by another, there was a general rally of the Church members, male and female, and by their joint vote it was decided to retain their Pastor.* As to the Chapel-street Church, we can hardly be mistaken when we find the statement confirmed by so good an authority as Rev. Dr. Dutton, one of the members of the late Ex-parte Council. In a letter, dated May, 1856, he wrote as follows: "The Chapel-street Church, in one instance of electing Pastor, received the votes of females; and also have done the same in the election of Deacons." In another part of the same letter Dr. Dutton wrote: "From the NATURE OF A CHURCH, as composed of renewed persons, and as having power of self-government, I do not think any argument can be drawn against the voting of females, but the contrary." This is sensible talk—pity he should talk differently in 1863-4. Another gentleman writes thus, under date of the 13th inst.: "I was present at a meeting to give Mr. Eustis a call, at which Deacon W. rose and sug-

---

* NOTE BY THE AUTHOR OF SOUTH CHURCH HISTORY.—This information, although derived from a member of the North Church who was present at said meeting and voted, proved to be incorrect.

gested that he would like to know how those present regarded Mr. Eustis,—whether they would like to have him for minister. ALL that were present and disposed, threw in a vote." The same thing occurred in the College-street Church, if we are correctly informed, at a meeting for the election of pastor a few days ago,—since the holding of the Council. Nor are these the only exceptions to the "custom" referred to, among the Congregational Churches of Connecticut. Indeed we KNOW that in some others it is customary for females as well as males to rise, in token of assent to the reception of members into the Church, after the latter have taken the covenant. Raising the whole person is as truly voting as if only a hand were raised, and makes as much noise. If the "silence" text forbids the latter, then, A FORTIORI, it forbids the former. But it does neither. Nor any more does it forbid women's voting by ballot. Without quoting further precedents at this time, we should like to ask how and why it is so much worse for the South Church to do a certain specified act, than for the Chapel or North or any other Congregational Church to do the same; and whether it is BECOMING for one Church to assist in excommunicating another, for doing what it does itself. As the South Church is now the aggrieved party, why should it not proceed to convene a Council, ostensibly to consider its own grievances, but really to get the Chapel-street and North Churches excommunicated, for violating "the principles and usages customary among the New England Churches?" And why should not Mr. Carroll assemble the Presbytery to which he belongs, and cause to be arraigned before it the several ministers who were members of the late Council, and if they neglect to appear, have them pronounced NOT ORDAINED, because they failed to give to the Presbytery "proper evidence of their ordination" as clergymen in regular communion with the Presbyterian body, or with any other "evangelical denomination?" and then TELEGRAPH IT AS A FACT all over the land. Again we ask, why not?

"It was the usual practice in the South Church to vote by raising of hands, excepting in the case of officers who were elected by ballot, and female votes were rarely offered or counted."

They were sometimes, then,—when the females chose to vote? Exactly. This was and is our custom.

"No instance is known in which females voted by ballot previous to the meeting when Mr. Carroll was settled by female votes."

No one said they did. No one said that the vote on accepting Rev. Mr. Noyes' resignation was by ballot;— whether the 70 for accepting it and the five for rejecting it, voted by raising the hand or by ballot; but, that they enjoyed the right of VOTING, and did vote; and if entitled to vote, (which the petitioners now admit,) they could vote either way. It is the right, not the mode, which is claimed, and the former includes the latter.

"This argument [from the Covenant,] proves, if any thing, that females have the right of being appointed deacons, acting upon committees, the right of discussion in business meetings, and of prayer and exhortation in prayer meetings."

Begging pardon, this does not follow. The covenant does not authorize what the Scriptures forbid. The Scriptures forbid females becoming deacons. Acts, vi., 3. "Look ye out among you seven MEN." The Scriptures forbid females to become exhorters in meeting. 1. Tim. ii. 10, 11. The privileges conferred by the covenant upon ALL who take it, are limited by the Scriptures. Female members who take it, take it with this limitation, of course. While not permitted to become deacons, or to exhort, they ARE entitled to all the privileges of membership not forbidden by the Scriptures. Voting is one of them. No where is it forbidden in the sacred volume. We judge that the Standing Committee ARE "prepared to follow out this argument to its logical conclusion."

MR. CARROLL'S LOYALTY.

A considerable portion of the petitioners' Rejoinder is occupied with the question of Mr. Carroll's LOYALTY. There are several kinds of loyalty in this country at the present time,—some good, and some not so good. In order to know whether a man is loyal or not, it is necessary to ascertain which kind of loyalty is intended. One kind blows its own trumpet, while it looks out for fat contracts, custom-house pickings, or any other chance to serve its country by filling its own pocket. Another kind, which is perhaps the most common of all, would, if analyzed, yield about the following results: abolitionism, 23; sectionalism, (the same which existed before the present war began,—not to say, which fomented and precipitated the war,) 27; patriotism, 2; self-righteousness, 6; real benevolence, 1; party animosity, 10; intolerance, 13; dish-water, 4; shoddy, 9; other ingredients too subtle to be easily ascertained, 5. Total, 100. It is admitted that IN THIS SENSE of the word, Mr. Carroll is not as loyal as he might be. And if on that account he was waited on by a mob some two or three years ago in his native city, Brooklyn, it is nothing more than has happened to many of the purest patriots in the land. During the war of 1812, Gen. Lingan, of Baltimore, was killed by a mob. Even abolitionists have sometimes been complimented in that way. The Apostle Paul encountered one at Ephesus. Mobs only disgrace the parties concerned in them, or who set them on; NOT the objects of their hatred.

When the petitioners are obliged to resort to an alleged remark "stated" to have been made some where to somebody at some time or other, by Mr. Carroll, to the effect that, "were it not for personal considerations, he would go south of Mason and Dixon's line and share the fortune of the rebellion," it shows how hard up they are for evidence to impeach his loyalty. They are however kind enough to say, "In the matter of loyalty claimed for the FRIENDS of Mr. Carroll—this has not been denied." Well; 130 of these loyal "friends," in their letter to Mr. Carroll accompanying a New Year's Gift of $500, say,—"WE ARE WITNESSES of the gross injustice of the imputations attempted to be cast upon your fidelity to the Government under which we live. On nearly if not quite every Sabbath since you came among us, you have prayed for our country, its rulers, its officers and soldiers, the sick and wounded, the dying and bereaved; that the crushing sorrows which rest upon us may be overruled for the highest good of our whole nation, and the glory of God; and that in His own time and way He will stay the torrents of blood and tears which are flowing all over the land, and grant us a righteous Peace." And again,—"We never heard a word from your lips which by any fair construction of language could be made to imply a lack of real patriotism, or any thing inconsistent with a faithful allegiance to the Government of your country."

" Has Mr. Carroll forgotten the language he used in public prayer on the morning of the Lord's Day when news came of the battle before Fredericksburg ? "

If Mr. Carroll has forgotten that prayer, his people have not. Whether it was "tall" or short, it was one of the most solemn and earnest prayers that we ever listened to; melting an entire audience, except, of course, the petitioners and their "sympathizers," whose lively imaginations pictured images of disloyalty where nothing of the kind existed. On the following Sabbath he delivered a deeply interesting address on the character and life of Thomas E. Barrett, one of his members, who fell in that battle; describing him as a real patriot, who went forth not for any selfish or sinister purpose, but honestly to serve his country.

As to that ever memorable sermon to the 15th regiment upon their "duties as soldiers" to their country and to Christ, the immense audience who listened to it, filling the entire church, were held in breathless silence and riveted attention, and none were more moved than the soldiers themselves, several of whom have written home about that very discourse, the memory of which strengthened them in the front of the battle. Would that it might be repeated by our Pastor—speaking not, as one of our former ministers did, to *empty pews*, SUPPOSED *to be filled with soldiers*, but to actual soldiers, either in his Church or at the Hospital, where he has always officiated with the utmost pleasure to himself and to those whom he addressed

"In the year 1857 the number of members admitted to the [South] Church was forty-seven."

There must be some mistake here, as the number of persons admitted in 1857 was only sixteen. Probably the year 1858 is intended; but even in that year, according to the Church records, only 42 were admitted, and according to the tabular statement in the Congregational Quarterly, 43. The number *might have* been 47, or even greater, speaking after the manner of men, but for the fact that at the most interesting period of the revival, our then minister was absent from his charge for nearly a month, on a preaching expedition to the West. While the South Church, under the faithful labors of its pastors, has, with the blessing of God, received in the year 1863 about as many members as it did in the memorable year before mentioned, (the year of the great revival throughout the land,) most other Churches have languished. Indeed, for the last five years, the statistics of the Churches generally, so far as we have had opportunity to examine them, show but a melancholy record. The last report (1863) of the General Association of Connecticut contains a paper by Rev. Dr. Cleaveland, of this city, which says:—"In 1859, one hundred and ten Churches, with 14,184 members, gained not one from the world. In 1860, one hundred and thirty-six Churches, with 19,323 members, were alike fruitless. In 1861, one hundred and forty-six Churches—more than half our whole number—with 19,685 members, received not one by profession." It further appears from the same document, that in 1859, 1860 and 1861, the aggregate number of members admitted by profession into all the Congregational Churches of Connecticut, was 597 less than the number of deaths. The statistics of the years 1862 and 1863 are not presented in the same way, but we doubt if they will prove any more favorable. Indeed, we expect they will show a further diminution. Dr. Cleaveland barely hints at what may be one of the causes of this declension, when he says, "It becomes us to be on our guard lest any of the great doctrines of grace which in all ages have been the wisdom and power of God unto salvation, should be eclipsed by nearer, but infinitely less important objects."

"At least SEVENTY members, including the petitioners, have left [the South Church] during the year, or are ready to leave the Church when another place of worship shall be provided, because of their dislike to Mr. Carroll's ministrations."

We have learned to be somewhat distrustful of the calculations of the petitioners. Thus far they have done the Church no harm, but good, by leaving it. Notwithstanding secessions, the number of members is larger than when Mr. Carroll first came among us. The audiences are also larger. They are larger since the holding of the Council than before. What the petitioners and their "sympathizers" may be able to accomplish HEREAFTER, of course we do not know. But, at present, we feel no uneasiness about it. We only hope they will be as comfortable and happy in their new relations as we are in ours. It is the general feeling among the members, that the prospects of the Church were never better. Now that Mr. Carroll has declined the call to New York, we all breathe more freely, and expect to prosper greatly, if his life and health are spared, and if God continues to bless his labors among us.

"Already a larger sum has been pledged by persons in the vicinity of the South Church to support the preaching of the Gospel, in case a new Church is formed, than has ever been raised in one year by that Church for the same purpose, aside from the contributions of one individual."

In a paragraph quoted above, the petitioners speak of the Church as "sustained * * * ALMOST ENTIRELY by the contributions of ONE MAN," and complain of the influence thereby exerted by him. As the petitioners and their sympathizers appear to have a plenty of money, the question is, why they did not curtail this one man's power, by taking upon themselves a larger portion of the burden which gave him that power. It will not answer to say that they do not like Mr. Carroll; for he has been with us but about twenty months, and his predecessor, during the latter part of his ministry at least, was in full sympathy with the petitioners on the topics of which they now complain. Why did not the "seventy" pour forth their offerings liberally to sustain Mr. Noyes? Why leave the burden of supporting public worship under his ministrations, as well as Mr. Carroll's, almost entirely to "one man?" That one man, we dare say, would at any time have been willing to have his influence curtailed in such a way. He simply paid what no one else did, or offered to pay. As however the petitioners, with all their ability, have, by their own showing, done "almost" nothing towards the support of the enterprise, might it not have been as well, (if they were dissatisfied with a minister whom they had more agency in procuring than the "one man" had,) to withdraw quietly to other Churches, as to get up an Ex-parte Council and excommunicate or attempt to excommunicate the whole concern? However, if they are satisfied with the result, we are. But before parting, we will just quote an extract of a letter from a Congregational minister in the interior of the State, which we hope they will duly ponder. In feeling and judgment at least, we suspect he is one of many. He says, "If Congregationalism is right, your Church, as respects the management of its own affairs, is eminently right. If Congregationalism is right, your Church is not only right, but prospered because it is right. Your practice is in harmony with common sense. Your reply to the Ex-parte Council is conclusive. According to your rules, or custom, each member has equal rights with every other member in strictly Church meetings, and of course may vote. In these particulars you are on the rock. Unless I sadly mistake, yours is a model Congregational Church. I admire your manner of doing things. I pity the Ex-parte Council. Of course they will not confess it, but they must be ashamed of their officiousness as respects your affairs. Since writing the above, I have read the Rejoinder. If there was no more to be said, it had better not have been said; for, in the light of brother C.'s friends' reply, what they say is not very creditable to them."

In conclusion, we append the following extracts from an article in the Congregational Quarterly for January, 1860, on the "Authority of Councils," written by one of the Editors, Rev. ALONZO H. QUINT. If we rightly understand the positions of the writer, they accord much more nearly with the views of the South Church on the points he discusses, than with the ACTION of the Ex-parte Council recently held in this city.

EXTRACTS FROM THE CONGREGATIONAL QUARTERLY, JAN., 1860.

"Whenever perplexity arises in the administration of Congregational Church policy, it is either because its principles are misunderstood, or because, when understood, they are not observed with Christian manliness and fidelity by its adherents. When practical confusions arise in the workings of Councils—Councils stepping out of their legitimate work—Councils called to override Councils—Councils arrayed against Councils,—we believe that it is because the fundamental principles which are their basis, are forgotten. Though loth, as we are, to admit that want of principle ever enters, we must confess that our policy is evidently intended, by its reliance only on moral power, for people in a high state of grace, and that that grace is not always found."

"To remedy the want of grace is not in our power. To do what little in us lies to explain some features of Councils—especially under the rather general title above, we are glad to attempt."

"What the authority of Councils is, depends entirely on our essential principles. These are two-fold: first, the entire sufficiency of every Church, in and of itself, for all purposes of government and discipline; and, secondly, the obligations growing out of the fellowship of Churches, as such, to each other, and especially in all matters concerning the general welfare. When these principles are followed, there is no practical difficulty as to the proper occasions for, or the proper work of, Councils. It is to these principles that we look, to find how Councils come into being,—their prerogatives while in being,—and the force of their decisions."

"1. THEIR COMING INTO BEING."

"Councils cannot come into being except a Church be directly concerned in the matter for consideration. Individuals cannot, for their own matters, summon a Council; a Church must be a party in inviting,—the apparent exception of Ex-parte Councils called by aggrieved individuals being no real exception, as the individual must complain of some CHURCH action, and bases his call upon the fact that the Church of which he complains, OUGHT to have been a party, but has UNREASONABLY refused. An individual complaining of another individual, a party in a Church complaining of an opposing party, dissatisfied members complaining of a pastor,—cannot call a Council. There must have been some distinct CHURCH action, of which complaint is made. Thus, if an individual complaining of another, wishes for a Council, he must first bring the complaint formally before the Church; if the Church do not remedy his grievance, he has no resource unless the Church do in some way deprive him of his rights; and even these rights cannot come before a Council by his demand, unless the rights affected concern his relations of fellowship with the Churches at large."

"While this is the case in matters concerning which there is agreement, an idea sometimes prevails that Councils have appellate jurisdiction in all matters of Church action with which parties are dissatisfied. But this is a mistake."

"They have no supervisory power over the internal affairs of a Church; that Church is, on Congregational principles, entirely sufficient to take care of its own affairs. The 'Churches consulting' control THEIR FELLOWSHIP, but not the action of the particular Church."

"The well known Council called by the aggrieved members of the Church of the Puritans, New York, erred, or rather their officers did, on this very point; they declared the action of the Church to be null and void, which they had no business or power to do; they could only say that THEY were willing to fellowship these brethren notwithstanding the Church action, and advise Churches to receive them even without the letters which had been, as they said, unjustly withheld. We remember an Ex-parte Council, which aggrieved persons who had been admonished without trial, as they said, had called, (after endeavoring to obtain a mutual one, in vain;) the admonition had left the parties still in regular standing. The Council in proceeding to organize, and censure the Church, went beyond their province, and were guilty of a gross usurpation, as well as impertinence. It was alleged that the Church had violated Congregational order—which may have been the case; but that gave the neighboring Churches no right to interfere, unless the case was so marked as to have justly required withdrawal of fellowship from that Church. The dissatisfied members could take letters; if these were denied, they could then have asked for a Council—on that point. If the action of a Church stops within itself; that is, if the effect of it does not impair the regular standing of the aggrieved, the latter have no claim for a Council, nor has any Council a right to interfere."

"The principle then is, 'neighbor Churches' have a right to expect to be called together on all matters relating to the general welfare; they have a right to act when a party invites them who is aggrieved by Church action IN SUCH A MANNER AS DESTROYS HIS FELLOWSHIP WITH THOSE OTHER CHURCHES; and they may convene when invited by any Church which wants "light and peace." But they have no right to demand a voice in the internal affairs of any Church, and no power whatever to supervise them. They control the fellowship of the Churches, but not the action of any Church in its own matters. The remembrance of this simple principle would sweep away half our Councils, and all of those which have become an offense in the nostrils of the community. Invited Churches ought never to accept an invitation to INTERFERE WITH THE BUSINESS OF A CHURCH WHICH DOES NOT CONCERN THEM. We have never yet seen more than ONE Ex-parte Council which was not an impertinence."

II. PREROGATIVES OF A COUNCIL IN BEING.

"The Council will find not only its CHARACTER in the letters missive, but the Council is LIMITED IN ITS ACTION to the subject matter of the letters missive."

"The object alleged in the letters missive, is the sole one which the Council is competent to consider. The reason is obvious. Deriving all power in this particular case from the letters missive, they can no more go beyond, than the government of our country can exercise powers not delegated to it by the Constitution. Nor would it be proper, on the one hand, that delegates asked for a special purpose, should act for another; nor, on the other hand, that an inviting party having secured a Council, should use it for purposes not previously mentioned. Called together for one thing, they have no right to do another.

"We are aware that this rule is frequently transgressed. Many Councils have seemed to regard themselves irresponsible, and as being put in charge of the Churches at large. It seems to be felt by some men "dressed in a little brief authority," that under the high sounding title of COUNCIL they are endowed with great prerogatives. Whereas they are like courts martial in respect to their object; limited to the precise work for which they are summoned. For example: a Council is called for organizing a new Church, for the alleged reason that great want of harmony exists in another in the same town; it is then perfectly competent for the Council to inquire as to the alleged dissensions, and whether they are such as to furnish good reasons for advising a new organization, and whether they are irremovable; but they have no right to proceed to an investigation into the merits or demerits of the dissensions,—because the parties are not before them; and if THEY were, the CASE is not."

"Having carefully and prayerfully examined into the subject matter, the Council have power to embody its opinion upon that matter, AND NO OTHER, in a 'result of Council,' which is to be signed by the Moderator and Scribe, and be formally communicated to the parties concerned."

"The Congregational doctrine of the authority of Councils therefore is this: Councils come into being by the call of parties inviting. They have power to organize; power to examine credentials; with no power to enlarge or diminish their number; power to examine the subject specified in the letters missive, but no other subject; power to hear evidence; power to deliberate on the proper course to be taken in reference to that subject; power to advise the parties inviting them, what to do in the matter, with no power to direct or order any particular course, or to reverse individual Church action; AND, WITH POWER TO PRAY A GOOD DEAL MORE FOR DIVINE ASSISTANCE THAN MANY COUNCILS DO, they have power to dissolve."

"Their only power is reason. So far as they have any authority, it is through their piety, their integrity, their manliness and their common sense. For, 'the decree of a Council,' well says Richard Mather, 'hath so much force as there is force in the reason of it.'"

Alas! then, for the force of the decree of the Council recently held in reference to the affairs of the South Church in New Haven.

A MEMBER.

MISSTATEMENT OF FACTS
IN THE DEFENSE OF THE SOUTH CHURCH.

That the public may learn what reliance is to be placed upon the statement of facts by the defenders of the South Church and of their officiating Pastor, I would draw attention to the assertions of the communication from "A Member," in respect to the voting of females, in the Chapel street Church when the present Pastor was called; and in the North Church, when a resolution of confidence in the Rev. Dr. Dutton was passed. IN NEITHER OF THESE CASES WAS THERE A VOTE CAST BY A FEMALE, NOR WAS THERE ONE PRESENT.

When Mr. Eustis had received a call from the brotherhood of the Church, and from the Society, he preached to the congregation, and at his request, after a Tuesday evening lecture, there was an informal expression, by those present, of their desire in respect to his acceptance of the call, which had already been tendered. At that meeting the proposition was made, not as the blundering informant of the writer states, by Deacon W., who was not Deacon until ten years afterward but by an OPPONENT of the Pastor elect, that the ladies should express their wishes. This was consented to; and this informal expression of opinion, though of course never put upon record, was reported to Mr. Eustis.

Dr. Dutton has no recollection of writing any such letter as the writer professes to quote from. If any such letter exists, he would like to see it, for he is confident that the extract quoted does injustice to his sentiments. If he made any such statements in respect to the Chapel street Church, they were founded on a mistake; and he knows that the allegation that women have ever voted in the North Church is utterly untrue.

The South Church has, therefore, among Congregational Churches in this city, the peculiar claim to the title of a "WOMAN'S RIGHTS" Church, and deserves by this radicalism to be ranked with the Church in New York City, over which Dr. Cheever presides.

One word in addition. Those who read the result of the late Council, will remember that it was in three parts; first, a statement of facts; secondly, a declaration of principles in the Congregational Order; and thirdly, advice to the parties calling the Council.

The voluminous replies have not DENIED ONE OF THE FACTS—not even so much as to show, what a word of his might have done, that THE REV. MR. CARROLL BELIEVES THAT THIS REBELLION IN BEHALF OF SLAVERY IS WICKED.

THE APOLOGISTS have avowed that the South Church is not governed by the principles affirmed in the Result, which is precisely what the Council adjudged. They therefore cannot demur at being declared not a Congregational Church, but an INDEPENDENT Church, OUTSIDE of our order; although to obtain a respectable standing, they procured at the start, recognition by a Council; intending, as it would appear, to break their pledge of walking in the Congregational order, so soon as it might seem convenient.

Whenever they DENY the FACTS affirmed in the result, with proper evidence; or AVOW the PRINCIPLES of Congregationalism, as set forth in our standards, and authorized by the Scriptures, they will be entitled to a respectful hearing.

A MEMBER OF THE EX-PARTE COUNCIL.

REV. DR. DUTTON'S LETTER ON FEMALE VOTING.

Messrs. Editors:

In a communication which you published last Wednesday, "A Member of the Ex-parte Council" said, in reference to Dr. Dutton's letter of 1856, from which I had previously quoted, "Dr. Dutton has no recollection of writing any such letter as the writer [myself] professes to quote from. If any such letter exists, he would like to see it; for he is confident that the extract quoted does injustice to his sentiments." Others besides himself "would like to see it," and I am happy in being able to gratify both him and them, as well as to relieve the incredulity of "A Member of the Ex-parte Council," who pretty clearly intimates that in "*professing* to quote from" such a letter, I was humbugging the public. I now publish it entire, except the postscript, which relates to other matters. If Dr. Dutton still doubts the existence of "any such letter," he can see the *original*, in his own hand-writing, by calling at No. 240 State street, main floor. The following is a copy of it:

"NEW HAVEN, *May* 3, 1856.

"DEAR BROTHER: I received yours this afternoon, and reply at once.

"I suppose it is not the *general* custom in our N. E. Congregational Churches, for females to vote in Church meetings, either for officers, or on other occasions, yet it is sometimes done. The Chapel-street Church, in one instance of electing Pastor, received the votes of female members, and also have done the same in the election of deacons. The Congregational Church in Milbury has in some instances had voting by females.

"I believe among the Baptist Churches, (which are strictly congregational,) the female members generally vote.

"I have not the 'Practical Church Member' at hand, but I have no doubt that Mr. Mitchell (who is quite a conservative man,) would say that the brotherhood (the male members,) should do the voting, and that that is the meaning of the passage to which you refer

"From the *nature of a Church*, as composed of renewed persons, and as having power of self-government, I do not think any argument can be drawn against the voting of females, but rather the contrary, for they are members of the Church. The argument, i. e., against female voting, is from *the general customs of society*, founded as those customs are supposed and claimed to be, on the differing natures of males and females. The argument is, that the custom of non-voting and non-speaking in public by females, which prevails outside of the Church, should prevail in the Church.

"To my mind the argument is not very strong. And, as custom is not universally against female voting, if I was pastor of a Church in which females had been accustomed to vote, I should not endeavor to break it up, unless there was a general disposition to dispense with it. I should not make a contest against it.

"Yours truly and in haste,
S. W. S. DUTTON."

What Dr. Dutton in 1856 said he *would* do in a supposed case, Rev. Mr. Carroll *has done*. When the latter took charge of the South Church, 1st June, 1862, he found that "females had been accustomed to vote" there, and did "not endeavor to break it [the practice] up,"—there not being "a general disposition to dispense with it." Yet for taking exactly the course which Dr. Dutton said *he* would take in similar circumstances,—for this among other things,—the latter assists in excluding Mr. Carroll and his Church from fellowship with other Congregational Churches.

Another curiosity is revealed in this letter, viz: the basis of "the argument against female voting." The Ex-parte Council objected to such voting as contrary to the Scriptures and Congregational usage. The petitioners, in their Rejoinder, drop the Scripture argument, and mention only "the custom of Congregational Churches." But Dr. Dutton, in the above letter, mentions neither of these bases, but only "the general customs of society," "*outside of the Church.*" For not conforming to the world in this particular,—for this, among other things,—he assists in cutting off the South Church from its fellowship with other Congregational Churches. Well may he say, "To my mind the argument is not very strong;" that is, the argument from the general customs of society.

Dr. D. well remarks, that against female voting no argument can be drawn "from *the nature of a Church*, as composed of renewed persons, and as having the power of self-government," "but rather the contrary; for they are members of the Church." Yes; they are members of the Church, as much as men are; and *therefore* have a right to all the privileges of members,—subject of course to any restrictions contained in the Scriptures; but voting is not one of them.

Dr. D. gives us some further information as to the prevalence of female voting. Besides the Chapel-street Church in some instances, he mentions another Congregational Church, where, in 1856, such voting was sometimes practiced; and expresses his belief that "among the Baptist Churches, (which are strictly congregational,) the female members generally vote." We were aware that in Presbyterian Churches voting by females was not unusual, but were not so well informed concerning the Baptists. As the Methodists allow females to pray and exhort in their meetings, voting by females would follow as a matter of course. One would think that a custom so extensively prevalent in Christian Churches of different denominations, might be tolerated in the South Church by other Churches of the same order; or at least, not be made a basis of excommunication. And here allow me to copy a paragraph of a letter from the gentlemen to whom the above letter of Dr. Dutton's was addressed; dated Jan. 27, 1864:

"At the time of Rev. Mr. Eustis's call to the Chapel-street Church, I remember being present at a week-day evening religious meeting in the Lecture Room of the Church edifice, when, at the close of said meeting, Dea. Whittlesey (now Deacon.*) did then and there rise, before

---

* NOTE BY A MEMBER OF SOUTH CHURCH.—"A Member of the Ex-parte Council" makes a great ado because our "blundering inform-

any one else, and propose, in a neat little speech, informal action by way of determining how many then present would like Mr. Eustis for Pastor. Suffice it to say, *all present felt at perfect liberty to vote, and all who chose, did vote on the occasion.*"*

"A Member of the Ex-parte Council" is pleased to say that the voluminous replies to the Result of said Council "have not DENIED ONE OF THE FACTS." That is true: the South Church people never deny *facts*. Noah Webster says, "To deny a fact knowingly, is to lie." [See the word "fact" in quarto editions.] But the South Church people *have* denied or disproved many of the *statements* of the Council and of the petitioners, either in terms or in effect. In short, if ever the under-pinning was effectually knocked out from beneath an *imposing* structure, it has been done in the present instance.

A MEMBER OF SOUTH CHURCH.

The above are the principal documents which have heretofore been published in relation to the Ex-parte Council. And now the question may be asked, especially by persons at a distance, "What, after a year's experience, has been the effect of the action of that

---

ant," as he calls him, gives Deacon Whittlesey his present title. Why should he not? He was writing in 1864 of an event which took place some years previously. So likewise he gives Dr. Dutton his present title, although he might not have received it prior to 1856. If our informant had said *Mr.* Whittlesey and *Mr.* Dutton, the same facility of censure which in one case calls him a "blundering informant," would most likely have been offended by his rudeness.

* This statement, taken in connection with a paragraph quoted in my last from "A Member of the Ex-parte Council," together with my comments thereon, sets the matter of female voting in the Chapel-street Church, on the occasion alluded to, in a clear light.

body upon the South Church, and upon other interests?" We answer:

1. It has freed the South Church from all disturbing elements, leaving it united and harmonious in all matters pertaining to its common welfare as a Church of Christ.

2. By so doing, it has provided a pleasant religious home for many families heretofore connected with Churches represented in the Council, (as well as others,) who had long been deprived of the privileges of the sanctuary, except on the condition of exposing themselves to an installment of politics or war, along with or in place of, what they came to hear.

3. While the action of the Council has doubtless prevented some members of sister Churches from joining us, by a knowledge of the fact that they could not obtain certificates of dismission for that purpose, others have come to us notwithstanding that impediment; offering themselves for examination by our Standing Committee, as in the case of new members, and thus being admitted on profession of their faith. In a few cases we have reason to believe that individuals have joined us *because*, as they said, they did not wish to belong to Churches which denied to a sister Church, as good as themselves, the common courtesies of Christian recognition and fellowship. The whole number admitted to the South Church during the calendar year 1864, which covers the period since the action of the Council, is 25.

4. In some cases the action of Council has pre-

vented members of the South Church from joining other Churches. One case in particular is before our minds, where an exemplary member asked and received a certificate to another Congregational Church, near which she resides, but finding she could not be admitted on the strength of that certificate, unless endorsed by the Scribe of the Council, she returned it to the South Church, and was received back into our fold in the usual way. She is still a member.

5. The action of the Council has established the *independence* of the South Church beyond dispute. This position it intended to occupy from the first. But experience has taught us that by the simple act of assisting in the organization of our Church, as requested by its first members, and by a few subsequent acts of intervention *when invited by us,* the denomination claims to have got us within its meshes, insomuch that any half a dozen of its ministers, by calling themselves a Council, can regulate our affairs *without our consent and against our remonstrances,* even to the extent of transferring our members to other Churches. As much as this is exemplified in the action of late Ex-parte Council. The South Church repelled the interference, and thus brought the Council to an acknowledgement of its independence, by withdrawing fellowship from it, and advising other Congregational Churches to do the same. It is now, in theory at least, i. e., in *their* theory, further off from other Congregational Churches, than if it were a Baptist, Methodist, or an Episcopal Church.

To Churches of either of these denominations, the Churches represented in the Ex-parte Council and others of the same class, would recommend any of their members who wished to join them,—but not to the South *Congregational* Church. Their ministers, too, would on fit occasions exchange pulpits with ministers of either of those denominations,—but not with the minister of the South *Congregational* Church.

6. The action of the Council, so far from establishing a non-intercourse between the South Church and the members of other Congregational Churches, has had exactly the opposite effect. We do not now refer to the numerous families, recently belonging to other congregations, who have taken slips in the South Church, but to the many *visitors,* from all the other Churches, who come occasionally, and some of them frequently, (and they are always welcome,) to hear the proscribed minister. If they could hear him sometimes in their own Churches, it might satisfy their curiosity, or whatever motive impels them to hear him; but as they can not, their only alternative is, to go and hear him in his own Church, where they are pretty sure to find *him,* and not some stranger, in the pulpit.

7. The action of the Council, by placing us outside of the pale of Congregational Churches, has placed us within easy communication with Churches of other evangelical denominations. Accordingly, many persons from all those denominations are frequently found in our audiences, and feel themselves all the more at

home because they are in no other fold but Christ's. They know that the South Church can have no denominational ends to answer,—no ambition to gratify except in doing good,—that it welcomes with equal cordiality good men and women of whatever Christian name,—and that they are safe *there* from the agitations and storms which beset most other Christian organizations. We speak of the South Church as it now is, and not as it was before the action of the Ex-parte Council.

8. The aggregate effect of all these influences is, to place the South Church on a far more substantial basis than ever before; to enlarge its congregations; to increase its revenue; to bind its members together in strong bonds of Christian fellowship; in short, to make them an eminently united and happy people, whose God is the Lord. If these things are so, it is plain that whoever else may have cause to regret the action of the Council, the South Church has none.

9. Even if the Council could build a Chinese wall between their own Churches and the South Church, the latter would still have scope enough in the "wide, wide world," from which to obtain recruits to its ranks, and all the better for being compelled to obtain them, to a large extent, from the enemy's kingdom, rather than from other Churches. A change of members from one Church to another is rarely of any great advantage to the cause of Christ; but when converts are gained from the ranks of sin, and become shining lights, *that* is a change which makes angels

rejoice. Well, this field of the world is still open to the South Church, and is likely to continue so. There is no repulsion here, except from Satan and his emissaries, but the Spirit and the Bride say come, and whosoever will, let him come.

10. We are not aware that the action of the Council has conferred any real benefit upon those who invoked its aid. It has separated them from their pleasant religious home, where they had their full share of influence and of privilege, as well as abundant opportunities of usefulness,—*without* providing them with any other. They are now scattered into different Churches, mostly at inconvenient distances from their residences. If this was what they wanted, they had only to ask letters of dismission and recommendation, in order to secure the accomplishment of their wishes. But many of them preferred to go without leave,—thus unnecessarily disregarding our Standing Rules, to which they were voluntary parties. The consequence was, that, with the help of the Scribe of the Ex-parte Council, they were nominally members of *two* Churches at the same time, for a period of about three months. At the annual meeting of the South Church, Nov. 22, 1864, they were all taken at their word, or rather, at their act, (except one or two who had been transferred by the Scribe of the Ex-parte Council, contrary to their own wishes,) and dismissed, *from that date,* "in the same sense as if they had asked and received from us letters of dismission and recommendation in the usual

form." [For particulars, see Catalogue at the close of this volume.] There *was* an effort to raise money and build a Church for the seceders, but it appears to have fallen through. The following are the proceedings of a meeting held on the 26th January, a year ago, " by the advice of the Pastors of the Congregational Churches of the city."

CIRCULAR.

At a meeting of gentlemen, convened by the advice of the Pastors of the Congregational Churches in this city, at the Lecture Room of Dr. Cleaveland's Church, on Tuesday evening, Jan. 26, 1864, Thomas R. Trowbridge, Esq., in the Chair, and Edwin Marble, Esq., Secretary, a statement was made by Dea. E. S. Minor with regard to the need of a new Congregational Church edifice in the south part of the city. He stated that about *forty* families and some *seventy* Church members are desirous, as soon as a place of worship is provided, to unite in the organization of a new Church and a Sabbath School. He had received, already, pledges from persons in that vicinity of more than $1,000, as their annual contribution for supporting public worship, and he believed if a Church was provided, that they would be able to maintain Christian worship and a Sabbath School, without further extraneous aid. A place of worship is needed that will seat about four hundred persons, with a room for smaller meetings, (as Sabbath School, prayer meetings, and for a Ladies' Society.) It is estimated that $12,000 will be wanted to provide land and a building suitable for these objects.

Remarks were offered by various gentlemen present, and a resolution adopted approving of the object. A committee was appointed to confer with the gentlemen representing this enterprise, and to advise and aid them in the accomplishment of their plans. The said committe having met with these gentlemen, and having made inquiry with regard to the parties they represented, as to their character and their ability to sustain and carry forward the enterprise, adopted the following

MINUTE.

The committee to whom was referred the matter of advising with regard to the enterprise of forming a new Congregational Church in the south part of the city, having conferred with the gentlemen representing this enterprise, are of the opinion that it is deserving of public encouragement, and that the estimated outlay of $12,000 is a suitable sum to be invested for an eligible lot and house of worship for their purposes.

The committee recommend that subscriptions for the aforesaid object be made to trustees, under whose direction the lot shall be purchased, and the house built, and in whom the property shall be vested for a term of *ten* years, when, if the enterprise has proved successful, it shall be made over to the Ecclesiastical Society then existing.

They further recommend that the condition of these subscriptions shall be, that the property, when obtained, shall be secured, so as to *remain free from all incumbrance* for the use of a Church and Society in *full and regular fellowship with the Congregational Churches of Connecticut;* and if, by any reason, this enterprise fail of its object, the trustees of this property shall be authorized and required to sell the same, and use the proceeds for the purpose of religious missions in this city, in connection with the Congregational order.

The committee further recommend that payment of these subscriptions be made at the call of the trustees, and in such installments as they may consider desirable.

(Signed) THOMAS R. TROWBRIDGE,
EDWIN MARBLE,
ALFRED WALKER,
SIDNEY M. STONE,
} Committee.

N. B.—The following gentlemen have (by request) consented to act as trustees of the funds subscribed for the above mentioned object, viz :

> ALFRED WALKER, Esq.
> EDWIN MARBLE, Esq.
> MORRIS TYLER, Esq.
> MATTHEW G. ELLIOTT, Esq.

On the 11th of February, 1864, a gentleman of the above named Committee inquired of the principal proprietor of the South Church property, whether it could be bought. The answer was in the negative. The next day, to guard against misconception or misconstruction, the following *written* reply was addressed to the gentleman proposing the inquiry :

> NEW HAVEN, *Feb.* 12, 1864.
>
> DEAR SIR : Your inquiry yesterday in regard to the South Church property was so unexpected that I scarcely knew how to answer, except by a plain negative. Permit me now to say that it is about the last thing I should think of selling—especially at this time, when all our incumbrances are removed, and when our prospects of great usefulness and success are more cheering than ever before. I might be willing to *exchange*, on fair terms, for the North or Center Church,—as a very considerable percentage of our immense congregations on Sabbath afternoons and evenings, come from the central parts of the city, or beyond—but this, I suppose, would not answer your purpose. On the whole, I think the South Church people and those of the North and Center Churches, will be best accommodated by a *conservative* policy—each retaining their own, and exercising toward each other as much charity as is consistent with poor human nature, even when partially sanctified. No more excommunications, if you please.
>
> Truly yours,
> GERARD HALLOCK.

On the 24th of the same month, a copy of the Circular was addressed to the present writer by the Collecting Agent, accompanied with a courteous note, inviting him to head the subscription list; an honor which he felt obliged to decline. The following is his reply:

NEW HAVEN, *Feb.* 27, 1864.

Rev. and Dear Sir:

Your favor of the 24th inst. is at hand, inviting me to head the subscription for building a new Congregational Church in the southwestern part of the city, "say with $1,000 or $2,000, or whatever sum may seem right" to me. While I sincerely desire that the secessionists from the South Church may be provided with a suitable place of worship elsewhere, and thus have no excuse for returning to the fold from which they have voluntarily strayed, I doubt the expediency of placing in the van of the movement a member of an excommunicated Church,—excommunicated too by the same Ex-parte Council which recommended the establishment of this opposition line. Would not an enterprise so led, "be justly regarded with suspicion," and perhaps be viewed as merely another "land speculation?" It strikes me that it would be better for the members of the wealthy old Churches represented in said Council, to put their shoulders to the wheel, and see what they can accomplish. Should it prove too much for them, and should I have any thing to spare after seeing the South Church established on a permanent, self-supporting basis, I can then, if I find no better use for the money, take hold and help.

In the meantime, I am

Very truly yours,
GERARD HALLOCK.

We have heard but little said about the project recently, and are inclined to think it has been abandoned, at least for the present. If, however, it should be carried into effect, it would have no perceptible bearing upon the interests of the South Church and people, who are now so well adjusted on the principle of elective affinity, that no antagonistic establishment would have any attractions for them. In order to make any impression upon the South Church, the leaders of the new movement must find a man for their pulpit, not only of equal talents with Mr. Carroll, and equal qualifications in other respects, but of *similar principles and views* as to the proper sphere of pulpit ministrations. If they could induce Mr. Carroll himself to take the lead of their enterprise, and occupy their pulpit instead of that which he now fills so acceptably to his people, then indeed they might safely count upon a respectable stampede from the South Church, especially if the latter should supply his place with a minister of opposing views. But none of these contingencies are likely to happen at present.

CHAPTER VI.

MISCELLANEOUS.

NEW YEAR'S GREETINGS, *January*, 1864.—While the discussion about the Ex-parte Council was going forward in the newspapers, as recorded in the preceding chapter, the South Church people, desiring to express their undiminished confidence in their ministers, presented to Mr. Carroll the following Address, signed by more than a hundred and thirty members of his Church and congregation, together with a New Year's gift of five hundred dollars. To his associate, Rev. Myron Barrett, they presented a variety of good things, including a well filled purse, accompanied by an appropriate address from the Senior Deacon.

TO THE REV. J. HALSTED CARROLL:
Dear Pastor,—The undersigned members of the South Church and congregation desire to give you some token of our undiminished confidence in your fidelity to every important interest which falls within the range of your duties as a Christian minister, or as a citizen of our common country; and with this view we beg your acceptance of the enclosed $500 as a New Year's Gift. Most of us, you are aware, are in moderate circumstances pecuniarily,—otherwise we would make the sum correspond more nearly to the proportions of our affection and gratitude to our beloved *Pastor;* for such you are, practically and in effect, and such we will call you, even though masters in Israel should command us to hold our peace. Would to God that all

who are technically Pastors,—as you formerly were, and might be now if such had been your choice,—were as faithful in that relation, and in all other relations pertaining to the Christian ministry, as you have been to us. Then might they be as successful in winning souls to Christ, instead of occupying themselves with denunciations of yourself and us, on evidence avowedly ex-parte, gathered from a few disaffected members of this Church, some of whom have very seldom heard you preach or pray, while others are so deeply imbued with the *isms* of the day, that without an admixture of these ingredients, they cannot be satisfied with the preaching of the word, however faithfully dispensed, or with the incense of a pure offering, however fervently breathed into the ear of God. Did the venerable Doctors of Divinity expect, on a basis such as this, to rear a structure which would stand the test of impartial investigation by those who *know* the facts, and know them to differ widely, as a general remark, from the representations upon which the verdict of the Council was chiefly founded? Did it not also occur to their minds, that possibly an intelligent community might deem the judges and jury as objectionable as the witnesses? *They* too were ex-parte, selected by a party, and many of them so prejudiced against you, as from the day of your coming among us until now, to have withheld from you the courtesies, not to say civilities, usual among ministerial brethren, and even among gentlemen who are bound together by none but earthly ties. The very document which is the product of their three days' labor, betrays the bitterness of local, sectarian, and party animosity, to a degree which probably they were not themselves aware of, and which, to impartial minds, must afford convincing proof that a verdict from such a source, based upon such evidence, without a particle of rebutting testimony, or any plea in behalf of the accused, is entitled to no consideration in any quarter. Least of all will it have any weight with us, your Church and people, some of whom have listened to all, and most of us to nearly all, your pulpit performances since you first entered upon your labors as minister of the South Church. *We are witnesses* of the gross injustice of the imputations attempted to be cast upon your fidelity to the Government under which we live. On nearly if not quite every Sabbath since you came among us, you have prayed for our country, its rulers, its officers and soldiers, the sick and wounded, the dying and bereaved; that the crushing sorrows which rest upon us may be overruled for the highest good of our whole nation and the glory of God; and that in His own time and way He will stay the torrents of blood and tears which are flowing all over the land, and grant us a righteous PEACE. Undoubtedly there is a marked difference between the tone of your prayers on these topics and those of some of your ministerial brethren, (certainly there ought to be, if we know anything of the spirit of Christianity;) but we never heard a word from your lips which, by any fair construction of language, could be made to imply a lack of real patriotism, or anything inconsistent with a faithful allegiance to the Government of your country. Whether you approve of all the measures of the Administration or not, is another question—with which neither we nor your accusers have anything to do. There never was an Administration all of whose measures were approved by all the people, and we may safely say there never will be. According to the proverb, "Silence gives consent." But in your case, it is construed by your accusers as implying *dissent*. They demand that you *shall speak* on these topics. If you speak *their sentiments*, well and good. If the opposite sentiments, then of course you are "disloyal." If you are silent, you are "disloyal." A hard case for a minister of the Gospel who has so learned Christ that he deems it his duty to keep politics out of the pulpit. And here, we suspect, is the front of your offending. While you stand up in this pulpit from Sabbath to Sabbath, proclaiming the unadulterated truth of God to large and deeply interested audiences, and reaping from time to time the appropriate fruits of your labor, "you reproach us, also," some of the learned Doctors may say, and say it truly. But we thank God that He has sent us a minister who will not and cannot be made to follow their example in this particular. Truly you have been to us a minister of the Gospel, and not a political declaimer. The talents which God has given you, you have devoted to His service. We have seen you in the conference room, the prayer meeting, the chamber of sickness, the home of poverty, and the house of mourning; have known and shared your faithful, judicious, unremitting labors as a spiritual counsellor and guide; have admired the meekness with which you bore reproach and all manner of misrepresentation—when reviled, reviling not again; in short, following the example and teachings of your blessed Master, in this the most difficult, or one of the most difficult parts of the Christian life.

We have known your history—the honored son of a distinguished father, the late Rev. D. L. Carroll, D. D., whom several of us loved as our Pastor when settled in Litchfield, Conn., as the successor of Rev. Dr. Lyman Beecher,—of your graduating at the University of Pennsylvania before you were eighteen years of age, having already consecrated yourself and your all to Christ; of your graduating at Princeton Seminary, where you received your theological education; of your ordination to the ministerial office and installation as Pastor in 1855, by some of the most distinguished ministers of the Presbyterian Church; your great success as a minister of the Gospel, not only in New Jersey, where you were first settled and remained until excessive labors broke down your health, but wherever else you have statedly dispensed the Word of Life. Even in this South Church of New Haven, during a period of unusual spiritual dearth in the Churches generally throughout the land, the blessing of God has attended your labors and those of your worthy colleague, to a degree which calls for our united thanksgiving.

Our records show that the accessions to our Church membership within the past year, have been larger, except two, than in any of the 284 Churches in the State. Our congregations on the Sabbath and Sabbath evenings, and also on week-day evenings, have been, and still are, much larger than under any previous ministry, except for a short period during the incumbency of Rev. Dr. Stiles. And this notwithstanding the opposition of individuals within your own Church, and a much larger number out of it, culminating at last in the convocation and fizzle of the late

Ex-parte Council. Charity leads us to hope that much of this opposition is the result of ignorance; although ignorance is a poor excuse when the means of obtaining correct information are at hand; and prejudice is a poor excuse when based upon ignorance or misinformation which might have been avoided; much more if it be the offspring of sectarian exclusiveness, professional rivalry, party animosity, or an unwillingness to entertain strangers, which some doing, have entertained angels unawares.

Among the conclusions arrived at by the Council, this is one, viz: ",that the South Church, so called, ought to be recognized no longer as a Congregational Church." "No longer." They admit, then, that it has hitherto been a Congregational Church. One of two things follows: Either that this Ex-parte Council, representing a dozen Churches out of 200 or 300 in the State, claim and have exercised the power to put us out of the denomination; or else that, not claiming this power, they have gravely decided that we "ought not to be recognized"—as what we confessedly are. In other words, that the truth ought to be suppressed or ignored. If the latter be their meaning, it is in good keeping with the evidence, and with the avowedly ex-parte construction of the Council. If, on the other hand, they say they *have* power, and have exercised it to put us out of the Congregational Church, then of course, according to their own showing, they will have no more right *hereafter* to meddle with our affairs, than with those of a Baptist, Episcopal, or Methodist Church. This is some comfort; and if the few disaffected members who have not already left us, will do so, according to the advice of their own Council, we may confidently hope for a lasting PEACE; for there are no other elements of discord among us. Not that we are all agreed on all subjects, social, political, and economical; agricultural, mechanical and financial; but since by common consent and choice we leave all these matters outside the Church, they make and can make us no trouble as a Church of Christ. As to ecclesiastical interference unasked for by us, we shall henceforth stand where we intended to do from the first. We were organized simply as a Congregational Church. We were never connected with any Association or Consociation. Efforts have more than once been made to bring us into one or the other of these relations, but always without success. And now we see the wisdom of our choice. As an *Independent* Congregational Church, which we always have been and continue to be, we can manage our own affairs without troubling other Churches with our differences, if any we have, or having *their* differences thrust upon us. But although a Congregational Church, we are not sectarians. And here is another advantage of our position. We can listen to faithful preachers of other denominations with as much pleasure as if they bore our own name. It has so happened, or been so ordered, without any design of ours, that all our ministers have been Presbyterians, with the exception of Rev. Mr. Noyes during a part of his connection with us; and that, with the same exception during the latter part of his incumbency, they have all held the position of Stated Supply, and not of Pastor, technically so called. We were organized as a Church by a Congregational Council while under the charge of a Presbyterian Stated Supply, (Rev. Dr. Stiles,) and have continued under a Presbyterian Stated Supply, except as above, to the present day,—a period of more than eleven years. Yet on neither of these grounds have we ever encountered any interference or remonstrance from other Churches, until now. It is now discovered that *you* are not a Pastor! Why are you not? So far as this Church is concerned, the objection came from those, or some of them, who called this Ex-parte Council. And it was to secure their concurrence in the call, as well as to meet your own wishes, (which were known to some of us,) that you were invited as Stated Supply, and not as Pastor.

And now, in closing this letter, already too long, we desire to express our admiration of the moral heroism which has enabled you successfully to resist the manifold influences which have been brought to bear upon you, tending to swerve you from your one great purpose of "knowing nothing among us save Jesus Christ and him crucified." In one of your earliest discourses in this Church, you declared that such should be your aim, and nobly have you redeemed the pledge. We thank you for it, and God for sending us such a man. Go on, beloved Pastor, and He will bless you, if man do not. You have His promise, which cannot fail:—"Blessed are ye when men shall revile you and persecute you, and shall say all manner of evil against you *falsely*, for my sake." Matt. v. 12. History is full of examples which show that no strange thing has happened to you. Remember Luther, Bunyan, Whitefield, Paul, Jeremiah, and above all, Christ. The Clergy are often the greatest persecutors. Our own feeble support we pledge you; but *that* is a small matter compared with what you *apparently* lose. Fame, popularity, is a dazzling bait to a youthful mind, but *that* we cannot promise you in our retired locality, proscribed and maligned as we have been, in common with yourself. It is however within your grasp, if you will only consent to abandon your principles, and violate your convictions of duty. So your Divine Master was offered all the kingdoms of the world and the glory of them, if only He would fall down and worship the Devil. He successfully resisted the temptation, and so have you, through Him.—Large salaries are an attraction to most men, but we have no large salaries to offer. If we are rightly informed, a call has been placed in your hands from a Church in New York City, [they appear to have no trouble about your being an ordained minister,] with more than double the salary you are receiving from us. We see it stated in a New York paper, that another Church in New York was about to call you, when they learned that they had been anticipated by the first mentioned. And yet, notwithstanding these overtures, we expect, perhaps too confidently, that you will still "abide with us." We feel a bond of affection in our hearts which seems to make you our own. And we know that, to a delightful extent, the attachment is mutual. May the Lord bless you and keep you, and continue to bless us and this community through your instrumentality. Such is the earnest desire and prayer of your Church and people.

Signed by over 130 members of the Church and congregation.

NEW HAVEN, *January 1st*, 1864.

MR. CARROLL'S REPLY.—HONORS TO REV. MR. BARRETT.

From a New Haven paper, Jan. 30, 1864.

SOUTH CHURCH.

As the late Ex-parte Council have brought the South Church so prominently before the public, permit me to say that the week now closing has been a most interesting one to that Church and people. Not to speak of the very impressive services in the Church last Sabbath day, and in the Chapel in the evening, and the very large audiences who attended them, we had on Tuesday evening a noble gathering in the Chapel parlor, which covers nearly the entire area of that building, to listen to a Scripture exposition by Rev. Mr. Carroll, and then to hear his response to the letter of 130 of his people, accompanying their New Year's gift to him of $500. That large hall was crowded on the occasion, so that it was necessary to bring in benches. In connection with his response, they expected to learn his decision in reference to a call which had been extended to him by a Church in New York, and which, it had been reported that he was likely to accept. Great anxiety was felt by his people on this point; and on the whole, they were in such a state of mingled apprehension and hope, that when in his earnest eloquence he poured forth his warm heart in love and gratitude for the confidence and kindness they had manifested towards him, a large part of the audience were in tears, or struggling to restrain the outburst of their emotions. When he came to the subject of the call, and announced that after much prayerful deliberation, and not without some hesitation, he had *that day returned a negative answer* to the invitation, nothing but the sacredness of the place prevented a general explosion of rejoicing. At the close of the meeting half an hour or more was spent in mutual congratulations, before the audience could be willing to separate. It was an occasion long to be remembered; and was the more impressive because of the warm and generous sentiments expressed by our pastors towards each other, as well as towards their people.

Mr. Carroll, among other things, remarked that from the day they first met each other until now, there had never been a jar between them, even the slightest; and Mr. Barrett, (who has always seemed to enjoy the honors intended for Mr. Carroll as much as those received by himself,) said he heartily assented to the remark. Mr. Barrett, in addressing the people, said he had called upon most or all of them at different times, and had much enjoyed such opportunities—but now he was comfortably settled in his own home, and wanted they should call upon him. "We will," "we will," was heard from different parts of the room, and on Thursday evening following, sure enough they did come, bringing with them all manner of good things, besides what had been previously placed in the Chapel parlor, where it was deemed expedient by his friends to have the reception held, on account of the numbers who were expected to be present.

It was fortunate that they did so; for even that spacious room was filled with a united and happy people, rejoicing at this opportunity to express their kindly feelings toward one who has so endeared himself to our entire Church. A very bountiful and beautiful table was spread, loaded with substantials and confections, to which due respect was paid by all. After supper our worthy senior deacon, (God bless him!) accompanying the act with an apt and graceful address, presented Mr. Barrett with a PURSE on behalf of the people, in addition to the large supplies of commodities which had accumulated in other forms. Mr. B. responded in a most appropriate and happy manner. This called out other speakers—then an impromptu choir made sweet music —then a parting prayer and blessing. It was one of the pleasantest evenings in the history of our hearts and of our Church home. A MEMBER.

As the time drew near for the close of Rev. Mr. Barrett's labors among us, agreeably to the arrangement made with him twelve or fifteen months previously, the South Church people desired to give him some parting expression of their good will, and of the high esteem which they felt for him as a minister, and as a man. Such was the object of the interviews mentioned in the following extract :—

From a New Haven paper of April 2.

The young folks connected with the South Church, paid the Rev. Mr. Barrett, assistant Pastor, a surprise visit at his residence on Wednesday night last, notwithstanding the severe storm which prevailed at that time. After a cordial greeting all round by the Pastor and his excellent lady, the Rev. J. Halsted Carroll presented the following resolutions :—

At a meeting of the South Congregational Church, March 29th, 1864, it was unanimously

Resolved, That in parting with Rev. Myron Barrett, who for more than a year past has officiated in this Church as associate Pastor with Rev. Mr. Carroll, we desire to express to him our cordial affection, respect, and esteem, and our regret that we are no longer to enjoy the benefit of his faithful and most acceptable labors.

Resolved, That the harmony and good understanding which, without the slightest interruption, have uniformly existed between him and this Church, and also between him and Mr. Carroll, (who has so far recovered his health and strength, that he expects to be able, henceforth, to perform the full duties of his ministry,) are a subject of pleasant remembrance to us, and will add to the interest with which we shall ever follow him in his future course of usefulness, wherever in the Providence of God, his lot may be cast.

Resolved, That these resolutions be signed by the proper officers of this Church, and be communicated to Mr. Barrett as our parting salutation, with our best wishes for the prosperity and happiness of himself and family here and hereafter.

J. HALSTED CARROLL,
THOS. HORSFALL,
CHAS. H. WARNER,
NICHOLAS COUNTRYMAN,
C. F. HOTCHKISS,
JOHN H. LEEDS.

Mr. Barrett, with a heart overflowing with gratitude, responded in a few brief remarks, thanking Mr. Carroll and the Church, for this acknowledgement of his humble efforts in the past year. Mr. Frederick Willoughby then, in behalf of the young people, presented Mr. Barrett and lady with a beautiful photographic Album, nearly filled with pictures and "greenbacks," as a testimonial of their esteem, friendship and good will, towards one who had ever been their friend through weal or woe, in sunshine or darkness, and regretted exceedingly that they were called to part so soon. Mr. Barrett was so completely taken by surprise, that he was at a loss for words to thank his friends, but assured them, that though absent, they would not be forgotten. On Thursday evening the adult members of the Society presented Mrs. Barrett with a beautiful rosewood work box, filled with all the little trinkets which are so necessary and useful to a lady's work table. Mr. Barrett leaves many friends in this city who will always feel interested in his welfare.

STATE AND PROGRESS OF THE CHURCH.

At each annual meeting of the South Church, held in the month of November from year to year, a Report has been presented by a Committee previously appointed for the purpose, on the "State and Progress of the Church" during the twelve months immediately preceding. The first two of these Reports, viz., for the years 1853 and 1854, were given verbally, and therefore we are unable to quote any extracts therefrom. The same was the case with the Report of 1863. From those of the other nine years since the organization of the Church, we proceed to give extracts, more or less extended, as follows :—

YEAR ENDING NOVEMBER, 1855.

Lewis M. Mills and Thos. Horsfall, Committee.

During the past year, the number of those received into the Church, has been encouraging in no small degree, amounting to fifty-two, of whom thirty-four were by profession and eighteen by letter. The largest number received at any one communion was twenty-one.

The Gospel in its purity has been preached twice every Sabbath, the efficacy of which we trust may be seen in a great measure, from the fruits of holy living among the members of the Church, and in the deep interest manifested on the part of the impenitent, in the oft repeated inquiry, "What shall I do to be saved?" And the evening service, where a review of the great and important truths presented during the day from the pulpit, has been made, has had the tendency, in our opinion, to fix on the mind, and impress upon the heart and conscience, whatever has been presented in the public assembly. Thus has been afforded opportunity for self-application and self-examination, producing the peaceable fruits of righteousness.

At the close of the afternoon service, the Young Men's Prayer Meeting, numbering at times as high as three and thirty, and averaging about twenty, has been well sustained during the year, in which those who have just entered the Redeemer's service, have been gathering strength, and where, by their united prayers and exhortations, a unity of sympathy has sprung up, arming them with a moral power which has stood by them in their hours of temptation and trial, when engaged in the busy scenes of the world. In this meeting it is worthy of remark, that every one has felt it to be his duty to sustain the exercise. Every one has been at his post, and all have considered the time devoted to this hour, as consecrated and precious.

The Monthly Concert for the conversion of the world, has been sustained with great interest. Here, not only has the Church been ready to cry mightily unto God for the outpouring of His Spirit on the dark places of the earth, as our beloved Pastors have set forth the great wants of the dying nations, and held up the glorious promises for their redemption which draweth nigh,—but, according as God has prospered them, they have contributed of their substance, counting it all joy to be permitted to co-operate with the great God in the glorious plan of human Redemption.

Your Monthly Donations for this object have
amounted, during the year, to ....$ 205 89
For the Southern Aid Society, ...1,029 78
" " American Tract Society, ... 217 00
" " American Bible Society, ... 50 00
" " American and For. Christian Union, 100 00
" " American Home Miss. Soc., ... 66 09
" " City Mission, ... 33 74
" " Am. Seaman's Friend Soc., ... 31 50
" " Collections at Communion Service, . 53 00

Amounting in all to $1,787 00
besides what has been collected for the Sabbath School.

The Tuesday evening conference meetings have been occasions of the most intense interest; the number in attendance averaging about fifty. The exercises have been usually opened by one and sometimes by both of the Pastors, by remarks whose savor has been of life unto life, as we trust shall be evinced, when the great Book shall be opened. These occasions will long be remembered by many of those who during the past year met with that glorious change from darkness to light, and from Satan to God. Precious meetings these have been, brethren and sisters, in which we have gained new accessions to the throne of our Father. Their memory will ever be green, and the retrospect of them will summon up before our minds, seasons when our souls had a nearness to God, and a communion which was sweet.

YEAR ENDING NOVEMBER, 1856.

C. F. HOTCHKISS AND CHAS. H. WARNER, COMMITTEE.

The increase to the Church during the past year, by profession, is 16; being but about half the number of the year previous. The blessed influences of the Holy Spirit, to a greater or less degree, have ever attended the truth delivered to our congregation on the Sabbath by our Pastors; and it is worthy of remark that many of their extraordinary and earnest appeals have been sent home to the hearts of those who were *occasional* in their visits to our sanctuary; thus sowing the seed, to grow and ripen for the harvest at the Great Day. We may never gather them in this fold upon earth; we may never see them again here; but we may see them in the mansions of our blessed Saviour, and hear them tell that their acquaintance with the truths of the Gospel commenced in these temples consecrated to the service of God.

The Sunday evening meetings in the Chapel, where the subject matter of the day's service has been reviewed, have during the year been extremely well attended, and the opportunity to apply these great truths, has not, we trust, been in vain. The usual number in attendance, has been about 130 persons.

Connected with our Sabbath exercises, is another auxiliary in the cause, of no less importance. We allude to the meeting following the afternoon service, called the "Young Men's Prayer Meeting." This is held in the Chapel, and has been kept up ever since that building was completed. Here a feeling of brotherly love has been exhibited, well worthy the imitation of all our other organizations; for your Co mittee are constrained to say, that in this branch of the Church an earnestness in prayer, a freedom of exhortation, and an anxiety for the welfare of the Church, have been displayed, that will add great strength to the cause, and to the Church in its future history. The average number present at these meetings is 16.

The Tuesday evening prayer meetings held in this room, are among the most interesting, and as your Committee hope, profitable branches of the Church, both to its members and the strangers whom we often see in our circle. The Church is largely represented in these meetings, and it has uniformly been so during the year. The average attendance for the year has been 51. The largest number present at any time, was on the 26th of February, when the meeting numbered **74 persons.**

The Bible Class, under the instruction of brother Mills, has become a source of great interest to those who are connected with it.

Another auxiliary in the cause, is the Ladies' Sewing Society. Suffice it to say, that the efforts of the ladies have been signally comforting, not only to the poor in our neighborhood, but to destitute missionaries and their families at the West.

The Sabbath School, under the superintendence of brother Minor, numbers about 100; average attendance 80.

The records of the Secretary of the Church show the following contributions during the year, viz:

Foreign Missions,	$205 90
Am. Tract Society,	218 42
Sabbath School,	31 75
Am. Bible Society,	37 15
Am. and For. Christian Union,	92 07
City Mission,	35 56
Am. Home Missionary Society,	61 00
Am. Seamen's Friend Society,	36 00
Southern Aid Society,	1,000 00
	$1,717 85

The state of our finances is next in order, and is usually in all large bodies a matter of great importance. With us, our financial department seems to claim but little of our concern. We certainly have great cause for thankfulness that we are so comfortably situated, and that these blessings are so bountifully provided for us. The yearly expenses of our whole Church arrangements must, in the opinion of your Committee, be between $6,000 and $7,000; while our whole income proceeds from rents of slips, and cannot probably exceed $700.

YEAR ENDING NOVEMBER, 1857.

Thomas Horsfall, C. B. Foote, and Wm. M. Hubbard,
Committee.

We have been permitted, in the providence of God, to enjoy the labors of two ministers another year. They have labored faithfully for the upbuilding of the Church. We have had preached to us two sermons every Sabbath, and there has been a good attendance on these means of grace, not only by our own Church and congregation, but by strangers and members of other congregations in the city. The preaching of the Word has been owned and blessed of God in the conversion of sinners, and in the edifying, comforting and strengthening of his people. There have been added to the Church during the year, 13, viz: 8 by profession, and 5 by letter. Three have died. The whole number of Church members in good and regular standing is 180. You will perceive, brethren, that the number added to the Church this year is much smaller than in any previous year since the Church was organized. Your Committee are aware that the number of unconverted in the congregation has been smaller than in any former year. Yet if we had all been as faithful as our Pastors have been, we think the number of conversions would have been larger.

The religious exercises on Sabbath evening have been very well attended throughout the year, not only by our own Church and congregation, but by many whom we never see in the Church during the day. One of the most interesting features of these meetings is the large number of young persons who are present every Sabbath evening. Your Committee feel confident that the earnest, searching appeals made to them so often by our ministers, cannot be lost upon them.

The Monthly Concert of Prayer for the conversion of the world, has been very well attended. Also the Young Men's Prayer Meeting, held in the Chapel immediately after the afternoon service. The average number in attendance at the last mentioned meeting has averaged about 16. These meetings have been greatly blessed to all who have attended them.

The Sabbath School, it will be remembered, was brought nearer to our Church at the last annual meeting, by the adoption of a rule making it the duty of the Church to appoint a committee of three at the commencement of every quarter, for the purpose of visiting the families connected with the Church and congregation, and endeavoring to awaken an interest in the School on the part of parents, and to secure a more regular attendance of the children. Also to visit the School occasionally, and thus coöperate with the Superintendent, by every means in their power, to promote the welfare of the School. Your Committee feel no hesitation in saying that this rule has worked well. Very soon after the first committee commenced their labors, the School began to increase. The committee have been uniformly well received, and parents seemed ready and willing to coöperate with them in awakening on the part of children a new interest in the School. The number of scholars has increased during the year from 100 to 145. Average attendance about 90. Teachers, 19.

The Bible Class, under the instruction of brother Mills, has been well attended. The Class numbers about 20 at the present time. The average attendance is about 14. Four or five members of the Class have united with the Church this year.

The Tuesday evening prayer meeting has been well attended throughout the year, sometimes numbering between 60 and 70. Average attendance about 50. The brethren who have been called upon to lead us in prayer, have manifested a strong desire for a revival of religion in the Church, and the burden of their prayers has been, "O Lord, revive thy work." The exhortations of our Pastors have evidently been directed to the same object. Quite a number of families have been united to our congregation recently, and we find, on inquiry, that they are almost all of them unconverted. This teaches us, brethren, that our Lord and Master has work for us to do. Then let us pray on, brethren, not only in our social prayer meetings, but in our closets, and let the burden of our prayers still be, "O Lord, revive thy work."

YEAR ENDING NOVEMBER, 1858.

E. S. MINOR, C. H. WARNER, AND J. T. MIX, COMMITTEE.

On the 15th of last November, Rev. Dr. Stiles, who had been Stated Pastor of the Church from its organization in

1852, having been requested by the committee of the Southern Aid Society to devote his whole time to the interests of that Society, resigned his connection with this Church, that he might enter upon the wider sphere of usefulness which Providence had thus opened to his labors. * * * By the settlement of Rev. Mr. Noyes as Pastor of the Church, and the formation of an Ecclesiastical Society, our organization was completed according to the usages of our denomination. It was hoped that under such auspices, the Church and Society would develop what native strength they possessed, and more rapidly grow to the fulness and stature of a self-sustaining body. It is too soon now to speak with much confidence of the results of this step. The anticipations of the more sanguine have not perhaps been fully realized; yet it is believed there is a deeper sense of responsibility in regard to the maintenance of public worship, and a readier disposition to assume the duties it imposes, than was felt before.

The usual meetings for public and social worship have been regularly maintained. The attendance on Sabbath Day service has been somewhat increased. The Young Men's Prayer Meeting, held after the afternoon service on the Sabbath, has been changed in name, and in the character of its attendance. It is now maintained as a Young *People's* Prayer Meeting, and the attendance of both sexes is invited. The Sabbath School and Bible Class continue, as to numbers in attendance, very much as they were a year ago. The average attendance is 83, being seven less than was reported last year.

At the last annual meeting of the Church, there were reported 180 members, in good standing. During the past year, 28 have been admitted by profession, and 14 by letter. Eleven have been dismissed, and recommended to other Churches, leaving the net gain of the year 31, and making the present total 211.

The past year is one greatly distinguished in the history of the Church as a season of wide-spread and gracious revival of religion. Our Church has shared in the blessing. Such awakenings produce increased attention to the truth; illuminate darkened understandings; make tender, hard hearts; and by the gentle, yet powerful constrainments of Divine love, win reluctant souls to the love and obedience of the truth as it is in Jesus. Who has not asked himself, when witnessing these divine effects, if the Church could not evermore rejoice thus in the light and glory of Christ's salvation?—if the power of religion could not evermore be all-pervading in the family and the business walks of life, sanctifying the commonest duties, and inscribing " Holiness unto the Lord " upon the products of human skill and the gains of merchandise, making every form of employment a heart-service to God, and not to man? If such are our aspirations, they are the kindlings of the Divine Spirit. Let us carefully cherish them, and each in his particular sphere of duty, endeavor to fill out in his own life and by his performances, that idea of a perpetual revival with which God has inspired him.

YEAR ENDING NOVEMBER, 1859.

C. N. SHUMWAY, CHAIRMAN OF COMMITTEE.

The year now ended is the second of the pastorship of Rev. G. W. Noyes. His labors in the pulpit for the last year, have, it is believed, been performed with faithfulness and energy, and an earnest desire has been manifested in his sermons to bring the Church up to a higher standard of piety. His labors as Pastor are believed to have been rendered faithfully, and have been blessed to those who received them. The Sabbath day and evening services have, we think, been quite as well attended as during the preceding year. And this is true too, we think, of the Tuesday Evening Prayer Meeting and Young People's Prayer Meeting. The average attendance at the Sabbath School, as reported for the last quarter, was 115, with a total of 150; which is a larger number than has been reported for any preceding quarter. The Superintendent and Teachers, and all who have labored for the School, have well deserved the success which has crowned their self-denying labors. A Bible Class has met during the year, on Sabbath noons, and the most of the time has been well attended; but under the impression that it in some way interferes with the Sabbath School, it has been decided to abandon it. Those who have been connected with it, will, it is hoped, find places and work in the Sabbath School.

This is the second year of our organization as an Ecclesiastical Society, and we have reason to be gratified with its results. More money has been pledged for the support of the Gospel, by the rent of slips in the Church,* than in any former year.

The choir are deserving all praise for the time and labor they have expended, and for the success which has enabled them to make so interesting the choral services of the sanctuary.

There has been collected for benevolent purposes during the year, $1,115.83.

YEAR ENDING NOVEMBER, 1860.

Rufus S. Pickett, George S. Minor, and John W. Scofield, Committee.

The stated meetings of the Church have been the same as in former years. The attendance at the usual service on the Sabbath has increased somewhat, especially in the afternoon. Your Committee are not able to report an increased attendance at the Sabbath evening service, but are under the painful necessity of saying that it is somewhat less than formerly; which is a cause of discouragement to those who labor to sustain that meeting. The Young People's Prayer Meeting has been sustained with the usual interest; but we regret to say that a majority of the females who formerly attended it, have of late deserted it, which has reduced the attendance to an average of thirteen. The Church Prayer Meeting on Tuesday evening has been sustained with much interest. The largest num-

---

* Partly raised by subscription.—Ed.

ber present at any one of these meeting is 60; the average attendance, 38. The average attendance on the Sabbath School during the year is 114; and the whole number of names on the Secretary's book is nearly 200. These figures, compared with those of 1858, show a gain of over forty per cent.

YEAR ENDING NOVEMBER, 1861.

WM. C. SCOBIE, THOMAS E. BARRETT AND ALFRED W. MINOR, COMMITTEE.

Your Committee find themselves unable to present as favorable and cheering accounts as have been presented in former reports. The unhappy state of our country has perhaps been one prime cause of this; tending, as it does, to withdraw the minds of the Church from spiritual to temporal things, and consequently disturbing the harmony of purpose and unity among its members.

Some time in the month of May, our Pastor, Rev. G. W. Noyes, sent in his resignation, preached his farewell sermon on the 2d of June, and was dismissed on the 3d. Since then the pulpit has been filled by an irregular supply. During the past year the attendance upon the Sabbath services has been very irregular, the whole congregation at times numbering considerably less than one hundred, and that too, before Mr. Noyes was dismissed, and without any good reason why the attendance should not have been larger. The regular Sabbath evening meeting has throughout the year been sustained by a very few members of the Church; the numbers present being frequently too small to sustain the interest of the meeting. The young people have continued their meeting, with an average attendance fully equal to the standard of previous years. This meeting, which was established a few weeks before the formation of the *Church*, has been felt by those who have attended it, to be one of the pleasantest gatherings connected with the Church. Average attendance during the year, 14; being one more than the average of last year.

The regular weekly prayer meeting has been held every week but one throughout the year. The largest number present at any time was 44; the smallest, 9. Average, 25. The average attendance at the Sabbath School has been 115; one more than last year. By the report of the Ladies' Sewing Circle, we find that their income, and consequently their disbursements, have been considerably less than in any previous year.

Your Committee are not aware that there have been any hopeful conversions, or that there has been any particular religious interest, either in the Church or congregation. There has been but one addition to the Church, either by profession or letter; while 22 have removed their relations from us to other Churches. Four have been removed by death; and four have either already gone or are about to leave us, to engage in the service of their country. Others, whose names appear on the list of Church members, have for a long time past absented themselves from Church gatherings, and from the Communion.

YEAR ENDING NOVEMBER, 1862.

CHARLES F. HOTCHKISS, G. H. BUTRICKS AND ROBERT LATTA, COMMITTEE.

It speaks volumes for our good, kind-hearted officers, on whom we have placed the charge of all our organizations, and who at all times, and amid the various sectional interests that have crossed the path of the Church, have ever been at their posts, true to us and the Church of Christ. How difficult the duty of satisfactorily supplying the pulpit for so long a time, and yet how well it has been done.

On the 1st Sunday in June last, our present dear Pastor was by our united hearts and the best affections of his people, regularly installed in our pulpit, though not by an Ecclesiastical Council. A perceptible change in the various branches connected with the Church was at once seen. From the 10th of January last, when your Committee's labors commenced, (they having been appointed at a special meeting in place of a Committee who had resigned,) until the 1st of June, the attendance at the main Church had been gradually on the decrease, and it was seldom visited by strangers. The largest number present in the forenoon during that time, was 91, and in the afternoon, 179. The average attendance was 80 in the morning and 130 in the afternoon. The smallest number in the forenoon was 45, and in the afternoon 92.

The Sunday evening services in the Chapel were mostly supported by the constant presence of a few devoted brothers and sisters, who deemed it their duty to be in their seats. The smallest number present during the above mentioned period, from January to June, was 15; largest, 37; average, 23.

Compared with these statistics, we have the satisfaction to state that since our new minister entered upon his labors, a great improvement has been visible in every particular. The attendance on Sabbath morning, June 1st, (his first Sabbath,) was 146 in the forenoon, and 189 in the afternoon. These are the smallest numbers present on any Sabbath since he commenced his labors. On both parts of the day, the average increase is about 300 per cent. In many instances the Church has been filled, far beyond our highest expectations. The Sunday evening services from June 1st to the time when the meetings were transferred to the Church, show an increase of more than 200 per cent. The young people's prayer meeting has largely increased. The Sunday School, under the care of brother George S. Minor, still continues to be attractive, and is well attended. A Bible Class of about 25 persons gather regularly in the Pastor's study between the regular Sabbath services, under the direction of brother M'Neill.

Our Church and congregation have contributed largely to the rank and file of our army, and perhaps none have been more saved from the ravages of war; for, thus far, not one to our knowledge has fallen by death, although disease has laid several aside for a time.

One great cause for congratulation to the Church is, that in our meetings for business, or for any other purpose, of late, nothing foreign to a mild and Christian spirit has been displayed, and nothing has occurred to mar that true Christian feeling which alone can give it prosperity.

Thus as a Church and congregation we have abundant cause for heart-felt thanksgiving to God; *Financially*,—in that we are entirely free from debt. *Numerically*—that in the five months of Mr. Carroll's ministry among us, our congregations have steadily increased up to 300 per cent. *Socially*—as seen in our last Ladies' Sewing Society in this room; the largest ever assembled here on a similar occasion, and as harmonious and as joyous as possible. And *Spiritually*—the best of all. We have reason,—O so much!—to bless our dear God for His presence in the services in the Church and in the prayer meeting; in the edification and warming of our hearts who are Christians, and in our up-building; for we are fed by the preached word, and have had the strong meat and marrow of the Gospel of Christ, which keeps our souls active and full, while the babes have the sincere milk of the word dispensed by our Pastor to them too, that they may grow thereby. And they are growing; for, thank God, His Spirit is now striving with many of the youth in this Church; quite a number have been hopefully converted and are rejoicing, while many of their companions are inquiring anxiously after salvation. O then, like the disciples of old, let us continue, with one accord, and of one mind, in one place, and pray without ceasing, that upon us as upon them, God will pour down a Pentecostal blessing, thereby adding to our dear Church, multitudes of such as shall be saved.

YEAR ENDING NOVEMBER, 1863.

CHARLES H. WARNER, JOHN H. LEEDS AND AMOS SMITH, COMMITTEE.

This report having been communicated verbally by the chairman, we are unable to give extracts from it. We remember, however, that it was full of encouragement, and represented the affairs of the Church to be in a very prosperous condition, as to its general features and prospects.

YEAR ENDING NOVEMBER, 1864.

C. F. Hotchkiss, Wm. M. Hubbard and Pascal Withey, Committee.

Your Committee beg leave to report that the number of additions to the Church since our last annual meeting is 25; of whom two came to us from other Churches, and 23 by confession of faith, including one who returned a certificate previously given her by this Church. Included in this number are also several who, having been denied letters by their own Churches, were admitted on profession of their faith, after examination and recommendation by the Standing Committee.

Since the last annual meeting our congregations on the Sabbath have steadily increased in numbers, and on several recent occasions have been very large. The Tuesday evening prayer meetings have been well sustained throughout the year, with an average attendance much larger than last year.

During the period the Sunday evening meetings have been held in the Chapel, we all know how admirably they have been attended; and the subjects selected by Mr. Carroll, with his full and interesting remarks on them, have been instructive to us, as well as the many strangers who have been attracted thither. We are now permitted to commence a new series of discourses on Scripture characters, to which, we trust, we shall see increased attention.

The Sabbath School, under the direction of brother C. H. Warner, is in a flourishing condition, and has safely surmounted all the evil influences that many of the seceding members brought to bear upon it. The Bible Class, under the direction of our good brother Kirkuff, has an increasing attendance, numbering nineteen the last Sabbath.

The Ladies' Sewing Society favored us a few evenings since with the report of their doings, and shared with us the bounties of their beautifully arranged tables. That institution also has surmounted all its share of trials the past year, and opens for the future with a better prospect than it did one year ago. At its annual meeting there were present 104 persons, including many who had recently cast in their lot with us. This department continues to be useful for its social as well as charitable connections, and we should by every means in our power, forward and encourage its managers in their good work.

The pulpit, by the blessing of God, has been filled, we believe, to the cheerful acceptance of all. Under the direction of our dear Pastor, and the assistance during a short vacation, of our valued friend and his former associate, Rev. Myron Barrett, we have the past year been favored with the preached word without having our minds disturbed by the absorbing worldly topics of the day; and if by the exclusion of such matters, our dear Church has been an asylum to which many of our fellow citizens could resort, we may take courage to believe that for the future we may be able to welcome many more, to worship with us at our altars. This class of persons are numerous, we are happy to say, and the revenue from slips will much exceed that of any former year in the history of our Church. The peace within these walls should not cause us to forget that in a large section of our beloved land, Churches are made desolate by the ruthless hand of war, the men of God without support, and the people scattered and driven from their homes, to seek a shelter for themselves and their little ones wherever charity may be found. Within these enclosures no disturbing element is now felt, and none molest us or make us afraid. Here we enjoy the sweet communion of kindred fellowship, and unite in our Christian cheer. Hither we bring all our sorrows and rejoicings,—our songs of praise and prayers. It is here that we can shut out the world, and in faith try to catch a word from our dear Saviour, whose blessed Spirit seems at times to fill our hearts too full for utterance, and sweetly whispers, "My peace I give unto you." O blessed sanctuary, our happy earthly home! Who among us to-night, when he scans our privileges as a band of Christians, can refuse to lift up his voice and thank God for his protecting care over us, through the many dark and fearful days in the past, and for the bright openings of the future. Blessed with peace and good will in the Church; blessed with occasional **conversions** from the ranks of sin;

blessed with the use of **these comfortable and commodious buildings;** blessed **with the shepherd whose voice we all can hear and love, because we know he careth for the sheep, in that he breaks to us the bread of life;** blessed, **though last yet not least, because all these God-sent blessings are ours without pecuniary burthens,—we may almost say without money and without price.** This is our home; our "Memorial Stone" is erected here; and to-night we can truthfully re-inscribe on its front, "Hitherto hath the Lord helped us."

It is probable that no one connected with us is ignorant of the fact that fellowship is denied us and our dear Pastor by nearly all the Churches of our denomination in New England. Parties acknowledged by sister Churches to be of their membership in good and regular standing, and desiring to cast their lot with us, are denied the usual certificates. Also members from us with the same qualifications, and presenting certificates from us in the usual form, can only make those certificates available by having them endorsed by the Scribe of a certain Council, which assumed to sit in judgment on our Church and its beloved Pastor. While it is not to be denied that these are real inconveniences, and that such proscription is as undesirable as it is undeserved, we may well doubt whether the effect upon our numbers and general prosperity has not thus far been favorable. And with the help of God, it may be still more so in time to come.

And now, as to the progress of our Church. The aim and object of our associating ourselves together in the capacity of a Church, we all agree, is, that the cause of our Redeemer may be advanced, and that we may receive spiritual instruction as a support in our pilgrimage here, our stay in the hour of death, and preparation for an endless eternity. These considerations should bind Pastor and people more closely to each other; and if we do our duty faithfully, giving him our support, and co-operating with him in his exertions for the salvation of souls, God will prosper us, and the Redeemer's kingdom will be extended by our progress. We must be a united and happy Church; united in our endeavors to comfort and sustain each other in hours of trial and despondency; united in protecting the interests and good name of our little flock, avoiding every thing that tends to strife and ill feeling, ready to put aside our own selfish ends to comfort and cheer our brethren,—in other words, act according to the Golden Rule,—and then no root of bitterness will spring up among us, but we shall be a happy people whose God is the Lord. Our usefulness will be felt, our zeal for the Church quickened, and we shall see conversions to Christ more frequently than we now do. This is what we want. We want all our households converted. We want our souls to go out in earnest, united prayer that God will save not only us, (for this is selfish,) but our kindred, friends and neigbors,—nay, a perishing world. These appliances are for that end. Our dear Pastor is here with us for that object; and it is for us, from this time forth, to shake off our indifference about men's souls, and WORK.

All our distracting anxieties as a Church,—all the elements of strife,—like the dark clouds of the storm, have passed over us, and we can have no claim to an excuse for future inactivity. May God in his infinite goodness, who has so kindly directed us in the year that is past, be our director and support for the year to come; and may we all, from this good hour, be willing to be guided in the ways of truth and righteousness, ready to meet the summons whenever God shall call us hence, to death and to judgment.

SOUTH CHURCH FINANCES.

The Ecclesiastical Society connected with the South Church, was organized on the 5th of December 1857. Dr. Stiles had resigned his position as Stated Supply on the 15th of the previous month. Until the organization of the Society, the principal proprietor of the buildings paid the ministers' salaries and most other expenses, in his own way, receiving from the Treasurer of the *Church* such part of the revenue from slips as was not required for incidental expenses. Said proprietor kept no exact account of his payments; but from such data as are at his command, he estimates them at $5,000 a year on an average, for the first five years, ending about the date of Dr. Stiles' resignation. By way of offset, he received out of the slip rents (and there was no other revenue) an average of $300 or $400 per annum. The first annual report of the Treasurer of the Society covered the year ending Nov. 1, 1858. The receipts and expenditures of the Society during that and each subsequent year, ending Nov. 1st, were, according to the Treasurer's reports, as follows:

				RECEIPTS.	EXPENDITURES.
Year ending Nov. 1,			1859	$2,127 71	$2,127 71
"	"	"	1860	2,309 13	2,229 30
"	"	"	1861	2,325 80	2,320 94
"	"	"	1862	1,706 09	1,704 79
"	"	"	1863	2,788 40	2,799 31
"	"	"	1864	2,708 90	2,768 87
				16,219 77	16,279 74
Due Treasurer,				59 97	
				$16,279 74	

From the first, a large part of the receipts have been derived from voluntary contributions made by members of the Church and congregation; the rent of slips being low,—highest $25, lowest $2,—to bring them within the means of persons in moderate circumstances. No assistance towards the support of public worship, has ever been asked or received from persons not belonging to the Church or congregation. It should be remarked, however, that under the ministry of Dr. Stiles, (and the same is true at present,) several families rented slips, and occupied them a part of the time, who belonged to other Churches. This explains the fact, that the revenue from slips was larger during the first two years after the formation of the Church, when Dr. Stiles was preaching his great sermons, than it has been at any period since. For the current year it will probably be larger than under Dr. Stiles' ministry. During the whole period of twelve years, ending 1st of November last, the average rent from slips has been about $500 per annum.

It has always been customary to pay the ministers' salaries either weekly or monthly, and in the latter case as early as the middle of the month.

The Treasurer of the *Church* has kept an account distinct from that of the *Society*, embracing collections for benevolent objects and the disbursement of the same; collections at Communions, relief of poor members, Communion expenses, and sundry other matters pertaining to the Church proper, in distinction from the Society. The largest aggregate collected for benevolent Societies in any one year, was $1,717 85 in 1856. In 1855 the aggregate was $1,670 32. In each of those years an individual gave $1,000 for the Southern Aid Society.

Neither the Church, nor the Society, was ever in debt except for current expenses, and these for so small an amount, and for so short a time, as not to be worth mentioning.

RESOLUTIONS CONCERNING THE BELL.

At a special meeting of the Committee of the Ecclesiastical Society connected with the South Congregational Church of New Haven, on Tuesday evening, June 28th, 1864, it was unanimously

Resolved, That the ringing of the South Church bell, on the occasion of the recent meeting of a political party to ratify the nomination of their candidates for the Presidency and Vice-Presidency of the United States, was without the consent or previous knowledge of this Committee, or any of its members, and was contrary to the well known wishes of the South Church and Society, and their Minister, as to the mingling of ecclesiastical affairs with politics, and that said act is disapproved and deeply regretted by this Committee.

Resolved, That the Sexton of this Church has no more rightful control over the bell, than over any other portion of the property entrusted to his care; and that over none of said property has he any jurisdiction or control, except as delegated to him by its owners or lessees, or by this Committee, who are their legal representatives. Much less has he a right to exercise any control over that property in opposition to their instructions or known wishes.

Resolved, That no person ought to be employed as Sexton of this Church, who is unwilling to conform strictly, and at all times, to the spirit of the foregoing resolutions.

Resolved, That henceforth the Sexton of this Church be prohibited from ringing or tolling its bell, or permitting it to be rung or tolled, for any political or secular purpose whatever, except in celebration of the Fourth of July, or in cases of fire, insurrection or invasion, without the written consent of this Committee or its chairman; and that any intentional departure from this rule by the Sexton, shall be regarded as affording ample cause for his removal.

Resolved, That as the act so justly complained of, was not only public in its nature, but has been made more so by newspaper comments, these resolutions be also published, as signed by the members of this Committee.

THOS. HORSFALL, Chairman,
C. F. HOTCHKISS,
T. H. FULTON,
GERARD HALLOCK,
} Committee.

Speaking of bells, we are reminded of a little communication which was written just after the Vicksburg rejoicing, in July, 1863, but was not published. On the principle of "better late than never," we append it here:

For the Journal and Courier.

Messrs. EDITORS:

You say in your paper of this morning, "We are requested to ask who stopped, or tried to stop, the ringing of the South Church bell at the rejoicing over the capture of Vicksburg?" Would it not be more pertinent to ask,— "*Who rung that bell,* and *by whose authority?*" Was it done by order of the Society's Committee? or even with their knowledge? Had any application been made to that Committee by the Mayor, or Common Council, or by any one else, to permit it to be rung? Or was it rung by some unauthorized person or persons, who saw fit to take possession of other people's property without their consent? I am not raising the question of the propriety of ringing Church bells on the occasion mentioned, or on any or all other occasions of public rejoicing or mourning; but only ask whether such bells are the property of every individual who can gain access to them and is capable of ringing them, or whether they belong to their legal owners or lessees. Perhaps you will be so kind as to answer this question before you determine the other; and if you decide in favor of "the largest liberty" against the rights of property, don't complain if one of these days you should hear the Center Church bell rung as a token of rejoicing over some Federal *disaster;* for, in a city of 40,000 inhabitants, there may be some individual who will think this a proper use of the Center Church bell, and that *he* has a better right to determine that question than the Society or its Standing Committee.

ONE OF YOUR SUBSCRIBERS.

HEATING APPARATUS.

Near the close of 1864, a large new furnace was placed under the South Church, main edifice, instead of two small ones, which were worn out. But it was found, as before, that in certain conditions of the wind, smoke and coal gas would blow down, and escape into the body of the Church. The same cause kept the fires from burning freely. To remedy these evils, a chimney more than 100 feet high was erected in an angle of the tower, and with it the furnaces were connected by flues. The result was all that could be desired. Cost of the new furnace and chimney, a little more than $600.

CHAPTER VII.

REV. MR. CARROLL'S "MEMORIAL" SERMON.

BELIEVING that the Memorial Sermon preached by Rev. Mr. Carroll in the South Church on the second anniversary of his ministry there, should have a place in a work like this,—not because it is intrinsically better than many other sermons he has preached in that Church, but as embodying numerous facts in our history, and also as setting forth the principles which govern his pulpit ministrations in some important particulars,—principles which are cordially approved by his present Church and congregation,— we have asked and obtained permission to republish it, as here presented. The reader will perceive that some parts of it are a good deal expanded as compared with the edition already published by request of his people. In other words, portions of it which were then omitted or abridged, are here restored to their original form, as delivered from the pulpit, or as nearly so as can be done at this time. Much of the sermon, when spoken, was not written out in full. It was first preached on Sabbath afternoon, June 5th, 1864, being two years from the commencement of Mr. Carroll's labors as minister of the South

Church. On the next Sabbath evening it was repeated, by request, before a very large audience, including many members of other churches and congregations. The reader will please bear in mind, that the statistics of this sermon come down only to the 1st of June, 1864, and, so far as the South Church is concerned, relate chiefly to the two years immediately preceding, viz.: from 1st June, 1862 to 1st June 1864; whereas, the Catalogue at the close of the volume deals with *calendar* years, extending from January 1st to January 1st, and covers the whole period from the organization of the Church in 1852 to the beginning of 1865.

SERMON.

I. SAMUEL VII. 12.

"Then Samuel took a Stone, and set it between Mizpeh and Shen, and called the name of it Ebenezer, saying, Hitherto hath the Lord helped us."

There are occasions in associated life, signaled by remarkable deliverances, or distinguished by marked tokens of Divine favor, which call not only for passing remembrance, but for formal and permanent recognition. Many such belong to the Church of God, and one is referred to in the historic context.

Behold that scene at Mizpeh! The sacrificial altar is reared,—upon it smokes the lamb, slain for a burnt offering; around it, already gathered, is idolatrous and obdurate Israel, now repentant and returned to God; while before it, a holy prophet prays a prayer in which heart, voice, vision, all are lifted—a prayer of consecration and intercession for his people, which, mounting on the breath of the evening sacrifice, ascends with it, a sweet-smelling savor unto God. But lo! in the midst of solemn sacrifices and prayers, Philistia's embattled hosts surround them, and threaten a sore and immediate overthrow. Already their defiant shout rings through the tents of Israel, and now the dread gleam of their weaponry flashes on their eyes. Ere the challenge is answered, or the ranks are formed, the lords of the Philistines are seen advancing to the attack. A panic seizes the Hebrew host. Escape is impossible. Nought is left but inglorious flight, with instant and irresistible pursuit ; or ignominous surrender with its merciless horrors. In despair the Israelites crowd around Samuel, and in tones of terror beseech him, as their theocratic viceroy, to seek and secure divine interposition and deliverance ; " cease not to cry unto the Lord our God for us, that he will save us out of the hand of the Philistines." And see! responding to their cry ; undisturbed by the imminent danger ; undismayed by the impending onset ; how the patriarch prophet, calm and resolute, remains behind the smoke of his sacrifice ; his face uplifted ; his hands outstretched imploringly ; until heaven becomes his ally ; until he hears the artillery of the skies, the clouds mustering to the battle ; until he sees lightning arrows shot from the quiver of God, making havoc remediless in the ranks of the exultant foe : For " the Lord thundered with a great thunder on that day upon the Philistines and discomfited them."

Here was a manifest miraculous interposal, and for it, as a memorial of Divine deliverance, as a monument unto God, for His glory, and the inspiration of their children adown the ages, Israel set up a stone, and called it Ebenezer, saying, "Hitherto hath the Lord helped us."

As the occasion, so the place is memorable. It was conspicuous in location, as its very name indicates. Mizpeh, i. e. Watch-tower, occupied an elevated site, the highest eminence in the landscape near Jerusalem; and if rightly identified with "Nebi-Samuel," was, according to an apocryphal writer, within sight of the holy city. A city of Benjamin, it was likewise famed in sacred history as Israel's central gathering place; where Samuel sacrificed and judged; where Saul was designated King; and is noted in profane history as the spot on which "King Richard buried his face in his armor, and exclaimed, 'Oh! Lord God, I pray I may never enter thy holy city, if so be that I may not rescue it from the hands of thine enemies.'"*

It was here, then, in this most remarkable and prominent place, Samuel lifted the memorial pillar, alike a *history* and a *phophecy*; a record of past, a prediction of future, deliverances.

And surely, brethren, in our history we have every reason for lifting the monumental stone, and in this public place, as a memorial of God's gracious favors which have crowned the years just past, and as a prophecy of similar interposition during the new year we enter upon to-day, fraught as it is with so many

---

* See Stanley's Sinai and Palestine. p. 213.

blessings, and brightened with so many sanguine hopes.

That the inscription of our hearts upon the stone we set up should be Ebenezer, i. e. "stone of help," will appear if we, as a Church, recall our *manifold deliverances*. And

1st.—Our deliverance from FINANCIAL EMBARRASSMENTS.

A most gracious deliverance. Read the initial chapter of our history. The Church sprang almost from nothing, in a destitute and neglected portion of the city, where there were few worshippers, and still fewer who were able and willing to assist in the enterprize; without a congregation; with scarcely a word of encouragement and Christian cheer; and encountering the opposition of those who regard it a pious duty to annul all proceedings, and annoy all persons who do not humbly seek and secure their imprimatur, and who, over the freshly laid foundation stones, and even over the finished walls, sneeringly asked, "What do these feeble folk? Will they fortify? Will they sacrifice? Verily, if a fox go up, he will break down their stone wall." But these stone walls still stand, spite of all the foxes; and though their erection, and the sustaining of the means of grace within them since, have cost *one hundred thousand dollars*, both Church and Society are out of debt, and always have been.

Although the aggregate expenditure has been large, it has been borne cheerfully by our own members, without being burdensome to any. Except from two individuals in the *erection* of the buildings, not a dollar was ever asked or received towards the establishment or support of public worship here, from any source outside of our own Church and congregation. Meanwhile, a standing invitation has been and still is held out to ALL who desire to listen to the Word of Life, or are willing to do so, to come in and enjoy our religious privileges, with or without money and without price.

With such an experience, humbly yet thankfully must we set up a stone to-day, memorial of God's special blessing in our *temporalities*, saying, "Hitherto hath the Lord helped us."

2nd.—Deliverance from INTERNAL STRIFE.

God says, "Where envying and strife is, there is confusion and every evil work." At present and at length we are mercifully delivered from such signs of Divine displeasure ;—this withering blight and blasting mildew has been removed at last from this portion of the Lord's vineyard. We begin our new pastoral year amid the rejoicings of a *peaceful* people, and, we fain hope, beneath the smiles of an approving God. We are now a *united* people, since those who relished and indulged in unchristian asperities, and who sought schism, together with those who conscientiously differed from the principle of this Church in excluding politics, have been re-absorbed in more congenial folds. No longer need our labors and strength be expended on a factious opposition minority, to neutralize their disastrous efforts to dismember and destroy, but can be devoted wholly to the direct advancement of the legitimate and spiritual objects of the Redeemer's Kingdom.

Oh, this merciful deliverance!—This longed-for, welcome blessing, who can over-estimate! Actually permitted to *possess our souls in peace*,—to "maintain the *unity of the faith*," yet in "the *bonds of peace!*" Alas for that people who are given up to envying and strife and cruel criticism; for they are thereby declared deserted of God, and may expect, as they will have, barren ordinances,—and their pastors, of course, a barren ministry. Ah, here then is a great deliverance; deliverance from strife, and as a sequence, from "confusion and every evil work," which must be entailed upon any people where even a part would rather, as Matthew Henry says, "hear themselves speak, though it be to misrepresent and malign, than to enjoy the peace of God, and the teachings of His Spirit."

For redemption from dissension we raise the pillar, and on it the significant inscription—"Ebenezer!"

3d.—Deliverance from DECLENSION and SPIRITUAL LETHARGY.

This Sabbath, two years ago, in great physical weakness, I preached my first sermon to a small congregation, occupying a few places, here and there, in this large edifice, while the average attendance upon the week-day service approached the minimum gospel number. But note the change which God hath wrought. While our weekly meetings are uniformly well attended, our congregations on the Sabbath have so rapidly and steadily increased, that they compare most favorably with some of the oldest central churches,—and this, notwithstanding our remote position from the centre of the city; notwithstanding the persistent and prolonged efforts of members within to diminish our numbers; notwithstanding organized and official efforts of ministers of God without.

And from *lethargy*, likewise, have we been delivered. God's children have been earnest and active for their Heavenly Father,—not merely exhorting, edifying one another, but winning sinners to the Saviour. We have had additions by profession, as well as by certificate, at every Sacramental season save two,* of such, as I believe, will take the wine anew in the kingdom above. In the two years last past, fifty-nine have been added to the membership of this Church —eighteen on certificate, forty-one on profession. Think of this, dear brethren! So many deathless souls redeemed, through your instrumentality, to glorify Christ on earth, and shine in His crown in Heaven. Is not this a glorious reward for your

---

* By profession, *or* certificate, at every Communion, save one.

labors in season and out of season,—for providing and sustaining these means of grace, which, to even one immortal, have eventuated in hopes of glory?

And ye, who have been thus redeemed, and have a new life in your hearts, and a new song in your mouths, do you not bless God for this dear Zion, your spiritual birth-place, and will you not, even in heaven? Most precious to me, as your minister, are ye! Though not rewarded for success, but for labor, —(not he that is successful, but he that is *faithful* unto death, winning and wearing the crown,)—still no inconsiderable portion of my support and comfort during the hours of trial through which I have passed, were these soul seals. For surely, however imperfect the presentation of the truth, however much in my ministrations may have been thought omitted and wrong, *God blessed what was uttered;* and it seems enough was uttered to build up and comfort saints, and convert sinners unto God; for, we are only sanctified by the truth, 'Thy word is truth!' While I have such encouraging acknowledgments that the word of God, and not man's teaching, has been presented, I ask that your prayers may ascend with mine, that while I stand here, I may preach nothing but "the excellency of the knowledge of Christ," and be sustained in the resolution and determination "not to know any thing among you save Jesus Christ, and Him crucified."

I abjure all isms and ignore all secular and political themes in the house of God, on the day of God, either preached or prayed; (and they can be as easily prayed as preached;) I do not *pray* them; I recognize *Government* as an institution of God, and "the powers that be," as "ordained of God." I pray for our *Rulers,*—obeying the Apostle's exhortation,—" I exhort, therefore, that, first of all, supplications, prayers, intercessions, and giving of thanks, be made for all men; for kings and for all in authority: that we may lead a quiet and peaceable life in all godliness and honesty." I pray that God would endue them with His Spirit; grant them wisdom from above, which is profitable to direct; make them fearless of men, because so fearful of God; cause them to be executors of the Divine Will; crown with His blesssing and with success every plan which shall be for the real good of our land, and the glory of God.

I pray for our *Country,*—that God would mercifully interpose in her behalf; converting her from one vast Golgotha into the land of Emanuel.

I pray for the *Soldiers,*—that the Angel of the Lord would encamp round about them; that God would preserve them in health and morals; that He would bless them in all their interests for time and eternity, and graciously care for their families and friends as well.

I pray for *Peace,*—for peace in God's own time and way, (and "His ways are not as our ways")—for peace in accordance with God's mind and will, (and "His thoughts are not as our thoughts,")—for peace, which, if God sends, must be righteous and right.

But to go further than this,—when leading the devotions of an entire people, to intone the shiboleth of a party; when failing to represent the desires and wants common to all, and spiritual, to become the high priest of a party before God's throne, expressing what is partial and political; to dictate to the All-Wise and Most High God, the time and way in which His plans shall be executed,—this I never can do.*

Nor do I *preach* politics. In all places and at all times I have opposed, to the full extent of my ability, the introduction of civil, secular, and political questions into the house of God. I do not mean necessarily *party* politics, or those that play directly into party hands, but also that mingling of public and political affairs with the ministrations of the pulpit, which brings up and discusses in this sacred place and time, those topics of secular interest which occupy the minds of worldly men during the week. My reasons for this course I can here only indicate; a course

---

* The Boston "Congregationalist," under the heading, *Haranguing in Prayer*, says, "He who uses the form and attitude of prayer to ventilate his individual opinions upon public policy, to animadvert upon public measures and public men, to lecture the assembly upon its duty, or to forestall its action, to harangue his fellow worshippers as auditors, or to offer a disquisition upon the state of affairs—in a word, he who makes prayer any other than a reverential expression to Almighty God of feelings and desires that may be fairly assumed to be common to the Christian consciousness whose mouth-piece he is, not only violates the conventional proprieties of public prayer, but gives offense to devout minds, and occasion for cavil to the undevout, and is guilty of irreverence toward Almighty God."

which is regarded as such a startling innovation, and so subversive and destructive of the primary, essential, *spiritual* object and end of the Gospel ministry, as to draw upon its humble representative the formal and official promulgation of "anathema."

(1) I regard it *Unscriptural*,—as degrading my high calling in Christ Jesus; as an unwarrantable substitute for a Gospel message. What is the minister's calling,—what should be his message? Paul answers in 2 Cor. v, 18–21, "And all things are of God, who hath reconciled us to himself by Jesus Christ, and hath given to us the ministry of reconciliation; to wit, that God was in Christ, reconciling the world to himself, not imputing their trespasses unto them; and hath committed unto us the word of reconciliation; now then we are ambassadors for Christ, as though God did beseech you by us: we pray you in Christ's stead, be ye reconciled to God. For He hath made Him to be sin for us, who knew no sin; that we might be made the righteousness of God in Him."

Is not the minister's calling indeed "a high calling of God in Christ Jesus." Is not the message given unto him spiritual? Does it not pertain to men's souls; their sins; their Saviour; and the method of salvation by Him? Certainly; and this is the very essence of that Gospel the Master commands His ministers to preach to every creature.

We then who are called to deliver God's message, should keep to God's record, which forbids, either as a supplement or as a substitute, the presentation of "another gospel," be it of side issues, or popular reforms, or "Sharpe's rifles." We therefore believe the Divine message is not delivered, nor is the Master's word adhered to, when His servants substitute matters of state for those of the soul; the secular for the sacred; the political for Christ; "the power of God and wisdom of God" unto salvation to every one that believeth.

But has not the gospel to do with man in his relations to man, as well as to God; in his relations to human government, as well as to the divine; with the duties of a citizen, as well as of a sinner? Of course it has. Then must not the minister preach the rendering "unto Cæsar the things which be Cæsar's," as "unto God the things which be God's?" Must he not preach that "the powers which be, are ordained of God: Whosoever therefore resisteth the power, resisteth the ordinance of God"? To be sure he must; and presenting them *as the gospel does*, neither degrades his high calling, nor vitiates the spirituality of his divine message, nor converts it into a political harangue. For, "while these passages put government on its right basis, they do not inquire into the origin, rightfulness, or excellence of any government; nor do they give the preacher in expounding them the smallest authority for so doing. They take every government on earth as it is. It may be good, or bad; founded in right, or wrong. Nor do these passages bind the citizen to approve every act of his government, even in time of war. Did no good citizens in England disapprove of their war upon the Colonies? or their opium war with China? or the Crimean war? Did no good citizen disapprove of *our* war with England in 1812?" or our war with Mexico? "Did Paul approve of all the acts of his government when he wrote the passages to the Romans, already quoted? If he did, he approved the acts of a government at which it has been thought virtuous ever since to shudder. These passages say not a word of these things, and if the minister sticks to his text, *he* will not. Again: the true interpretation of them is true ALWAYS. Therefore, either they do not teach the doctrine of passive obedience, or they condemn the revolutions of 1648 and 1688, in England, and the revolution of 1776, in America. Again: the true interpretation is true EVERYWHERE. Eternal truth is universal. The Bible is for all the earth. Ministers then, rightly interpreting these texts, will, in every land, and under every government of earth, say the same thing if they speak according to the oracles of God." Yet how many ministers, discoursing on these words, remind us of the saying of Daniel Webster: "too many ministers get their text from the Bible and their sermon from the newspapers;" verify the statement of Toplady,— "few men are more prone to dabble in politics than some divines; and it must be added, few men in general have acquitted themselves more lamely than these reverend daubers with untempered mortar;"—

endorse the truthfulness of the statement of Washington Irving when he says,—"a cunning politician is often found skulking under the clerical robe, with an outside all religion and an inside all political rancor. Things spiritual and things temporal are strangely jumbled together, like poisons and antidotes on an apothecary's shelf; and instead of a devout sermon, the church-going people have often a political pamphlet thrust down their throat, labeled with a pious text from Scripture."

But I need not tell you, my hearers, adopting the language of a distinguished divine to his people, "that it has come to pass in these latter days, that these standing places of God's messengers to a ruined world, become oft-times the mere platforms for political harangues, where all questions of practical morals are discussed as side issues with some aim of the demagogues. That the cross of Christ is taken down from its high place as the crowning glory of the sanctuary, and in its stead, as an engine of reform, is lifted the ballot box; and the popular passions are lashed into storm, that with their suffrages as freemen they may carry a Maine Law or defeat a Nebraska bill. That these altars of our God, where the broken heart is demanded as a sacrifice to Jehovah, become oft-times only "seats of custom" where the worldly tribute is rendered to Cæsar. That the precepts of the Divine law, thundered from Sinai; the promises of the Gospel issued in the death-cry from Calvary; alas! they are all set aside and forgotten, that these ambassadors of God may discourse political declamation upon moot points that divide our great political parties. Either because these men find the duties of their sacred profession so light and their consequent leisure so abundant; or because they regard the care of souls so trivial a concern in comparison with the general enlightenment of society on these political questions; or, it may be, because they regard themselves as men of such prodigious powers and special inspiration, as to make it their extraordinary call to leave to their humbler and less gifted brethren the care of the ark in the fields of Bethshemish, while they strive about the golden mice with the lords of the Philistines."

We believe such a course to be unscriptural, and ask for the Bible warrant.

We cannot appeal on this point to Old Testament examples. For, it has been observed justly, there is no parallel between their government and our own. Theirs was Theocratic. With them, Church and State were one and the same. "What was political was ecclesiastical," and therefore pertained legitimately and necessarily to the ministers of religion. But does it follow that what was lawful and a necessity for the Jewish prophet, is either with the New Testament minister who does not live under a Theocracy; where Church and State are *not* identified, or so much as united; where things political are *not* ecclesiastical?

Again: there is no parallel in this respect between a Jewish prophet and a Christian minister; for the prophet was inspired, the minister is not. When he is, then may the preacher under the New Testament speak as did the prophet under the Old. But while he does not live under a Theocracy; while he is without special *revelation* of some particular political doctrine, and without special *inspiration* to declare it, the gospel minister must continue to preach the things spiritual which God *has* already revealed.*

Turning from the Old to the New Testament, where, in the life and precepts of Christ and His Apostles, do we find an example of political preaching, or the duty enjoined?

Do you find the indispensable warrant in any of the

---

* "The Jewish commonwealth constituted in all the stages of its history a *pure Theocracy*. David was anointed of God, as the type of Christ, and his kingdom was the dim foreshadow of that kingdom which is not of this world. He was not only king, but prophet. When he uttered imprecations upon the enemies of the Jewish State, *God spake through him against His enemies and the enemies of the Church*. When he poured out his passionate love for Jerusalem, his prophetic soul was enraptured with the glories of the new Jerusalem coming down from God out of heaven. And now, it is sheer ignorance, if it be not blasphemy, for a New Testament minister, whose head Samuel has not anointed, and whom God has not moved by inspiration of the Holy Ghost, to seize the sceptre and harp of David, and put on the mantle of Elijah, and dwarfing the prophecies into mere temporal predictions, to apply them to a nation whom God has never chosen as he did the Jews, or to a human government which he has not set up as he did the old Theocracy."—*Vandyke on the Spirituality and Independence of the Church*, p. 13.

sermons or epistles of the *Apostles?* No! Among them it cannot be found.

Do you find it in the Sermon on the Mount, or in any of the precepts of Christ? Surely not in them. On a certain occasion "one of the company said unto Him, Master, speak to my brother that he divide the inheritance with me?" Is the warrant found in His reply: "who made me a judge or divider over you?" No; on the contrary, is not that reply a rebuke, or at least a significant hint to ministers, not to "intermeddle in civil affairs that concern the commonwealth,"—a plain intimation, that this is not any more the minister's, than the Master's business.

On another occasion, the Pharisees "took counsel how they might entangle Him in His talk." They therefore "sent out to Him their disciples with the Herodians"—a committee from Church and State—fanatical members of the one, and political partizans of the other—to learn whether He was loyal to Cæsar's government. True, He obeyed the laws, and paid His tax, poor as he was, though it required a miracle to do it. But this, it seems, was not sufficient. Neither Pharisaic nor Herodian loyalty can be satisfied until He declares His political sentiments. Does He declare them? Does He seize this most auspicious moment to set Himself right with fanatic or partizan? Does He improve this occasion, so inviting, by preaching a sermon upon the agitating subject of that day, "is it lawful to give tribute unto Cæsar, or not?" Did He discourse on governmental policy, or decide the question, however important, of disputed political allegiance? What an opportunity for preaching politics! for settling this vexed question by a Divine example which His ministers might imitate and perpetuate! Did He do it; and thereby endorse a similar course in His servants as lawful and Scriptural? What is the record? "But Jesus perceived their wickedness, and said, why tempt ye me, ye hypocrites?" "Render unto Cæsar the things that are Cæsar's, and *to God the things that are God's.*" Does this answer furnish us with the necessary warrant? Have we here a sample of a modern political sermon, or a command to preach one? So far from it, should this very answer of the Master be returned to our modern catechising committees, they would pronounce it at best but suspicious and evasive, cowardly and conservative; if not denounce it as disloyal and traitorous. So doubtless felt and spake the original Committee;—the furious Pharisee and the baffled Herodian;—for we read, "they marveled, and left Him, and went their way."

Or do we find such a warrant in the records of the first Ecclesiastical Council of the Christian Church holden at Jerusalem? No. And though it be to the shame and disgrace of the Church in these latter days; yet, for the honor and purity of the early Church, must we not conclude, in this respect there is no analogy between them. So far at least as we may judge from personal knowledge and experience of modern ecclesiastical Councils, and so far as their records and result furnish a basis of comparison, we must say, to us any resemblance in spirit or spirituality, is inconceivable between primitive Councils of the apostolic day, and Puritan Councils of the present day.

On another occasion, when a Council, not of the Christian, but of the Jewish Church, arraigned Jesus for alleged heresy and offenses against the Mosaic law, coupled with charges of disloyalty and treason against the State, so that if they failed to prove Him guilty of the one, they might, by the power of political prejudice, insure His condemnation by the other,— when thus before Pilate's bar, do we find the sought for warrant in His answer to the heathen Governor, explaining to him the spiritual nature of His kingdom: "My kingdom is not of this world: if my kingdom were of this world, then would my servants fight;" but now is my kingdom not from hence."

Again: Peter and John were similarly arraigned for insisting upon preaching Christ, and Christ only. "The priests and the Captain of the Temple and the Sadducees came upon them, being grieved that they taught the people and preached through Jesus the resurrection from the dead." "And they took knowledge of them that they had been with Jesus." "But when they commanded them to go aside out of the Council, they conferred among themselves, saying, what shall we do to these men?" "That it spread no farther among the people, let us straightly threaten them, that they speak henceforth to no man in this name. And they called them, and commanded them not to speak at all nor teach, in the name of Jesus." Do we find the desired warrant in their answer? "Peter and John answered and said unto them, whether it be right in the sight of God to hearken unto you more than unto God, judge ye. For we cannot but speak the things which we have seen and heard."

Yet again, they brought them and "set them before the Council: and the high priest asked them, did not we straightly command you that ye should not teach in this name? and, behold, ye have filled Jerusalem with your doctrine." "Then stood there up one in the Council, a Pharisee, named Gamaliel," and he said, "refrain from these men and let them alone; for if this counsel or this work be of men, it will come to nought; but if it be of God, ye cannot overthrow it; lest haply ye be found even to fight against God. And to him they agreed; and when they had called the Apostles and beaten them, they commanded them that they should not speak in the name of Jesus, and let them go." Do we find a warrant for preaching anything but Jesus—do we find any warrant the remotest, for preaching politics, from the Apostles' words or deeds after that memorable and inquisitorial Council adjourned? Read: "And they departed from the presence of the Council, rejoicing that they were counted worthy to suffer shame for His name. And daily in the temple and in every house, they ceased not to teach and preach—Jesus Christ."

In the absence of all Scriptural warrants, either

from example or precept; from Christ or His Apostles; from sermon or epistle; or from the records of the assembled Church; therefore we also exclude all secular, or political, or semi-political themes and discussions from our ministry; therefore it is we deem it our duty to preach only the Gospel—" not to know any thing among" the people " save Christ, and Him crucified;" therefore it is we judge and say with Paul, "Now then, we are ambassadors for God"—" We, then, of all persons in the world," says Toplady, " should religiously abstain from whatever may conduce to cherish the seeds and fan the fires of civil discord. Shocking it is when they who profess to experience and to preach the love of Christ, can so far prostitute the dignity and design of their sacred calling as to offer fulsome incense at the shrine of aggrandized authority, or seek to exasperate differing parties against each other, instead of laboring to preserve unity of spirit, to strengthen the bonds of peace, and promote righteousness of life. Our direct business is with the policy of an invisible and better country. On the one hand, we are to sound the trumpet, not of secular, but of spiritual alarm; and on the other, to proclaim to them that mourn, and to them that believe, in Zion,

'The joyful news of sins forgiven,
Of hell subdued and peace with heaven.'"

(2) It is *unnecessary*. There are other places provided for political instruction, and open to all. Why make the House of God a caucus room? There are

other means, and ample for all. Why take those intended for spiritual ends, and so pervert them that they shall effect only what is selfish and secular? It is the peculiar mission of the press to give such information. Why then should the pulpit voluntarily give up its mission that it may assume that of the press, which needs no extraneous help, throwing off on the wings of every hour innumerable and much wiser treatises on these subjects, and which neither asks nor gives thanks for foreign advocacy? Besides, we ask, in the words of Dr. Dwight, " Will party politics carry you to Heaven ? Has Christ said, ' He that is a Federalist, he that is a Democrat, shall be saved ?' Has he not said, ' He that believeth shall be saved; and he that believeth not, shall be damned ?' Has He not said, ' Except ye repent, ye shall all likewise perish ?' Has He not said, ' Without holiness no man shall see the Lord ?' Has He not required you to '*Follow peace with all men?*' Has He not told you 'that the fruit of righteousness is sown in peace, of those that make peace ; and, therefore, that it cannot be sown in contentions—nor by them that work contentions ?' "

Not essential, sowing the seeds of discord, and already absorbing the minds of men six days out of seven *elsewhere*, is it *necessary* that another place, God's house, and another day, the Lord's Day, be appropriated for the discussion of such themes, and the dissemination of worldly knowledge, thus leaving the great God without a temple or a day for

His special worship, and the soul without a home where it may find a momentary truce, in its warrings with the world, even a temporary refuge from the din of party strife; where it may hear concerning a Kingdom which is not of this world, and of a rest that remaineth to the people of God?

(3) It is *inexpedient*. Already invading the sanctuaries of our land, it has eaten out the very heart of spirituality, so that a revival of God's work in *such* Zions is an anomaly; already does it threaten to usurp a permanently paramount place in the house of God and the hearts of His worshipers, demanding, even now, conformity to its political creed, as essential to Christian fellowship. Thereby Christians are driven away from their spiritual homes in bitter disappointment. They come to hear the things of eternal life; to be edified, upbuilt. And especially in such days of suffering and sorrow, to enjoy the consolations of the Gospel, and the sweet comfortings of the Spirit. But alas! they find no oasis now in the house of God; for wells of salvation and shading palms, only the monotonous waste of burning sand; for the sincere milk of the Word, only the bitter waters of Marah; while for the spirit of heaviness there is no garment of praise; for the wounded spirit, no balm of Gilead.

And what is the effect *upon worldlings?* They depart in disgust from the house of God, doubting the reality and value of Religion because of this counterfeit and caricature; and how can the effect upon them be otherwise, " when the parishioner sits in his pew, silent and still by custom, decorum, and the manners of New England, and the preacher turns upon him every eye in the congregation for the politics he practices, and for the party to which he has attached himself? How can it be otherwise when the very first word he hears in prayer, the very first word he hears in a hymn selected to be sung, however well it may be sung, and by whatever choir, the very first illustration in the sermon to which he may listen, sends him away gloomy and irritable, turns the whole service into a political mockery, and awakens a train of reflection that renders him, from first to last, inaccessible to the truth, closes his ear to the voice of the charmer, charm he never so wisely on that day?"

Is this expedient? No. And we wonder not that multitudes endorse and repeat the saying of Henry Clay, and give it, as he did, as the reason for ceasing to attend a certain Church:

"I have so much politics all the week, that I do not care to go to Church except to hear the Gospel."

O how different the result, if ministers, especially throughout New England, held the views and imitated the example of Rev. Dr. Dwight, President of Yale College. In the sermon already quoted, and preached in the Chapel on the National Fast, August 20th, 1812, he says:

"I wish it to be distinctly understood that, in the progress of my observations, no party will be arraigned; the character of no person attacked; no public measure censured; and the feeling of no individual wounded. All who are here, or all who are elsewhere, will be considered merely as creatures of the same God; as bound to the same eternity; as alike interested in renouncing sin and returning to holiness; and as bound alike to regard the work of the Lord as the operation of His hand."

O how different the result, if the tribute the great Rufus Choate paid his Pastor, could be truthfully given to every minister in New England; if every parishioner could assign it, as he did, as one reason, not for leaving, but attending Church. He says:

"Every one of us assuredly felt, as we came here from Sunday to Sunday, and took our seats in our pews, that we should hear nothing in the world but Religion preached from the pulpit, and no manner of politics, State or National, directly or indirectly; nothing connected in the remotest degree with the party considerations or organizations of the day. We came here, if we came as we professed we did, to hear of those things which pertain to Religion, to the salvation of the soul, and to the rest everlasting. And I have uniformly found it to be true, that I heard nothing, was assailed by nothing, was secularized by nothing, was defended or attacked by nothing which I had done, nothing for which I had voted or acted in the political world without. Never in an introductory prayer, never in a hymn, occasionally or in the ordinary course of public worship selected, never by any illustration in any sermon, by any train of association, right or wrong, was I carried back into the world that I had left, and which I should have been willing, for that day at least, to have forgotten forever." *

(4) *My Ordination Vows forbid it.* What says the Constitution of my Church, which every Presbyterian minister in his ordination vows declares " he sincerely receives and adopts as containing the system of doctrines taught in the Holy Scriptures ?" " Synods or councils are to handle or conclude nothing but what is ecclesiastical ; and are not to intermeddle with civil affairs which concern the commonwealth." Can this be a reason why ordination by the Presbyterian Church is here practically repudiated ? And was the literal fulfillment of this vow by me, regarded as equivalent to a forfeiture of my credentials as an ordained minister of Jesus ?

However this may be, " It is a very small thing that I should be judged of man's judgment !" Man's judgment cannot affect my views of duty while I believe them to be right in the judgment and sight of God ; and therefore I still say with a brother minister, " that the point from which I regard and deal with men has never been as citizens of the commonwealth having civil duties to perform, but as ' fallen sinners, having need of salvation ; ' and the great thing at which I have aimed, and to which I have subordinated every thing else, is, to bring them to the Cross, to reconcile them to God through the blood of the Lamb, and to imbue them with the Spirit of the

---

* See Memorial Volume, pp. 32, 38.'

Divine Master. In saying this, I neither forget nor ignore the fact that I am the authorized expounder of Revelation, which touches the entire circle of human duty. But I hold this to be true, that when men have an intellectual acquaintance with their civil or social duties, the speediest, most effectual way to bring them to their performance, is, to press upon their hearts and consciences the great doctrines of the Cross. The all-comprehending source of sin is alienation from God. Bring men back to God, and you bring them back to the performance of all known duties." This has been my theory and practice during the nine years of my ministry, and *ever will be.* Amen.

(5) *It is mocking the Wants of the Immortal Soul.* In the house of God the gospel feast is spread. Ministers of God, servants at the table, extend the invitation,—" Come, for all things are now ready ;" " come, buy wine and milk without money and without price. Wherefore do ye spend your money for that which is not bread? and your labor for that which satisfieth not? hearken diligently unto me, and eat ye that which is good, and let your soul delight itself in fatness!" See! yon hungry soul hears, believes, comes, " to *taste* and see that the Lord is good." It approaches, and from the rich provisions, asks for bread—the minister gives him this " stone ;" he asks for meat—the minister gives him this "serpent ;" and with immortal hungerings unsatisfied, the soul departs, mocked, betrayed, poisoned, stung.

Behold that blind man; it is Bartimeus. "They have let him know that the healer of the blind is near; and I am sure that nothing they could say about anything else, could make up for not telling him that. The most eloquent harangue on the politics of the times, though Pilate, and Herod, and Cæsar, and Roman eagles, and Jewish banners, and liberty, and nationality, and destiny, had rolled with splendid imagery through sounding periods, would have been a sad exchange for those simple words,— 'Jesus of Nazareth passeth by.' Nor would Aristotle's keenest logic, nor Plato's finest speculations, have served a whit better. The man was blind, and wanted his eyes opened; and these things, however set forth, were but trash and mockery."—"*Blind Bartimeus,*" pp. 83–84.

(6) *It degrades and divides the Church of God.*

It *degrades* the Church. Edward Everett in a sermon "On the dedication of the First Congregational Church in New York," administers a pertinent rebuke to those ministers and disciples of Christ who insist upon generating secular associations and kindling worldly excitements in the house of God, by the introduction of political themes. He says: "We dedicate our house to God; to no earthly power, to no human name, but to God, who reigns on high. It is henceforth not ours, but His; we resign, devote and consecrate it to Him." "We dedicate it to the glorious cause of the gospel. It is sacred henceforth to that alone. Let no other message be ever heard within its walls ; **no human science,** no learning or art of this world ; **no case** or interest which begins or ends with man ; **but the holy faith of the Son of God and the truth as it is in Jesus."** Any other course than this we believe degrades the Church by making her the partner of the State, and at length its tool and servant. This accomplished, and her dishonor and degradation are complete. Polluted by the hand of secular power ; her fair robes rent and soiled ; her head bowed and crownless ; her hands chained to Cæsar's chariot wheels ; behold the once fair bride of Christ !

Such a course of necessity *divides* the Church. It is the procuring and prolific cause of ecclesiastical schism. Breaking down the partition wall, the world comes in upon her like a flood. The excitements and storms shaking the State, sweep over and convulse the Church. How fully does the history of the Church, especially in our own country, manifest this fact : once introduce questions agitating the commonwealth into the sanctuary—once sow this wind, and you reap the whirlwind. You light the flame which burns out spirituality and Christian charity ; start the wedge that drives through and disrupts whole denominations of Christians ; seize the sword that rends in twain the seamless robe, and hews the perfect body of Christ. Hence the jealous care with which the Apostles guarded the infant Church from the political conflicts of their day. Hence their refusal to identify the Christian Church with the government of

Jew or Gentile. The great secret of their success in organizing and establishing Churches in the various countries through which they passed, and amid civil revolutions and convulsions, was this: Apostolic *ex*clusion of the secular, and *in*clusion *only of the spiritual*. It was the ignoring of this principle—the obliteration of this demarcation and distinction—the departure of ministers and Churches from Apostolic and primitive Church examples, that caused her subsequent and signal defeats; her comparatively few and feeble triumphs; and in this land at least, has written "Ichabod" on the Church of God.

True, as memorable, are the words of Edmund Burke: "Politics and the pulpit are terms that have little agreement. No sound ought to be heard in the Church but the voice of healing charity. The cause of civil liberty and civil government gains as little as that of Religion by this confusion of duties. Those who quit their proper character to assume what does not belong to them, are, for the greater part, ignorant both of the character they leave and the character they assume. Wholly unacquainted with the world in which they are so fond of meddling, and inexperienced in all its affairs, on which they pronounce with so much confidence, they have nothing of politics but the passions they excite. Surely the Church is a place where one day's truce ought to be allowed to the dissensions and animosities of mankind."

I am aware that these views concerning the sphere and duties of the gospel ministry in this respect, are in direct antagonism to those of the Congregational ministry here, and that this difference is regarded by them as radical and essential ; so much so, that from a candidate who is not prepared to conform to their views and practice in this particular, license is sometimes withheld. My convictions of duty are strong and conscientious ; and being so, cannot be abandoned to please men, or to escape their frown. And if for excluding politics from my ministrations in a Congregational Church, I am utterly isolated, and stand alone in this city, or even in all New England, I can well afford to be singular. If for the maintenance of this principle I am persecuted, I glory in persecution. *For one, I had rather be proscribed for unswerving fidelity, and adherence to my convictions of duty, than, for a craven abandonment or a criminal compromise of them, to be enthroned.* I would fain say with Paul, "None of these things move me; neither count I my life dear unto myself, so that I might finish my course with joy, and the ministry which I have received of the Lord Jesus, to testify the gospel of the grace of God." Archbishop Leighton was once asked why he did not preach more to the times. His answer was : "O, while so many are preaching to the times, give *me*, at least, leave to preach to the eternities." Be his reply ever mine !

4TH.—DELIVERANCE FROM DEATH.

Only four adults have died within the past two years, (although *twenty-seven* of our members have been exposed to sudden death in the army and navy,) and *"all these died in faith."*

Mid the thunder of artillery, in the thickest of the furious contest, just where Death was holding such high carnival; from the bloody hill-side of Fredericksburg; there went up the gentle spirit of a young man,*—son, husband, father, church member, Sabbath School teacher,—to the holy hill of Mount Zion above, where grim visaged war, with its rude alarms, and fierce baptisms, and crimsoned graves, is known no more; where peace, sacred and serene, forever dwells; where is the rest that "remaineth;" where, with the God of peace, he shall spend the Eternity of heaven, in the rest of serving of God.

> "Do you mourn when another star
>   Shines out in the glittering sky?
> Do you weep when the noise of war
>   And the rage of conflict die?
> Then let not your tears roll down
>   And your hearts be sorely riven,
> For another gem in the Savior's crown,
>   And another soul in Heaven!"

Within sight of this church, from the bosom of his family,—listening to the voice of prayer and praise, heavenly melodies filling the soul, like the notes that come floating down to us from the harps of the angels,—passed away the aged disciple and church officer.† As we bent over him a dying, "my father! my father! the chariot of Israel and the horsemen thereof," fell from our lips, as he made his glorious exodus to the

---

* Thomas F. Barrett.   † Deacon Benedict Burwell.

Eternal. As we stood around his grave, we transcribed the lines from Machpelah to his headstone,—the epitaph of Abraham, written by no human hand,—"*An old man and full.*" "An old man!"—Yes, we see the patriarch in the wasted face; in the dimmed eye; in the furrowed brow; in the trembling hand; in the hoary head, whitened by the frosts of four-score winters, yet unto him a crown of glory, because "found in the way of righteousness,"—covered with snow, yet, like the mountain-top, because nearest unto heaven.

And "full,"—full, like Abraham, not merely "of years," but of *experience*, not earthly only, but heavenly,—the favor and friendship of God; like him, full of *graces*, not human, but divine,—obedience, prayer, faith; like him, full of *anticipations*, not bounded by the horizon of earth, but sweeping beyond the shadows of time and the gloom of death,—looking for *Christ*; and he too "saw His day and was glad," clasping Him in his dying arms, "the antidote of death;" looking for "*a city*" too,—and lo! breaking on the dying vision, bathed in supernal splendor, are the jasper foundations, the sapphire walls, the golden street of that "city whose builder and maker is God." What anticipations these! full-orbed hopes of seeing Jesus, and of entering where, with no shadow on the heart, no tear-drop in the eye, with golden crown on the brow, and palm branch of victory in the hand, he should be "presented before the presence of God's glory with exceeding joy." And of these hopes he was "full." And see, as he rises to the realization of them—as the celestial convoy, upbearing him on immortal wings, nears the radiant hills, exultingly chanting, "lift up your heads, O ye gates"—lo! these gates of flashing pearl wide open swing, while angel and archangel wake their harps to louder, loftier strains, sweeping them to the hallelujah anthem of Heaven's Harvest Home, because another matured soul has been ingathered to the garner of glory, "as a shock of corn cometh in in his season," ripe and "full." Mid heavenly music, re-echoing his epitaph—"full"—bending before the throne to receive into his soul "fullness of joy," yea, "the fullness of the God-head,"—we leave him.

Not on the battle-plain, none by to quench the death-thirst or wipe the death-dew from the brow, but at home, mid its gentle, loving ministries,—a home fragrant with the incense of prayer, and perfumed with the name of Jesus,—we saw the other soldier[*] member die.

Standing by the bedside, where pain had made stone the downy pillow, we saw that scene of suffering transfigured into a Bethel, with its vision, and typical ladder leaned against the sky; saw the chamber, darkened by the death-wing, made lustrous with the flashing of angel pinions, hovering there to carry the fluttering soul, all radiant and ready, to the pearly gates of its home! As the pulse grew weaker, and the breath shorter, the heart was fuller and the

---

[*] John Crosby.

lips more eloquent with prayer and gratitude. He consoles the little group gathered round to catch his last, hallowed accents, with thoughts of a brighter world, where sorrow never enters; where farewell tears are never shed; where are no griefs nor graves; where no harp ever wails the sorrows of a bleeding or a broken heart. Kindling visions of that world are his; heaven reveals its light and song, its triumphs and eternal transports, to allure; God unveils His throne; Christ, "the brightness of the Father's glory," flooding the death-couch with heavenly splendor, appears, fulfilling His promise, "I will come again, and receive you unto myself;" while celestial voices, breaking on the dying ear, say, "come up hither." Leaning forward, as if responsive to the celestial call, the wan face reflecting the smile of God, from his faltering lips falls the mystic monosyllable,—"*up.*" Hark! again, with beaming eye still riveted upon "the excellent glory," and with arms uplifted, anticipating ascension, is heard the key-note of the heavenly harper's song, "*up*,"—'come up *hither;*' and *he went.*

In faith, also, the female member[*] and mother died. Disease had long marked her for its victim. Consumption laid its skeleton hand upon her, and flattered even unto death, imparting a hectic glow for the warm bloom of health,—autumn's leaf for the rose. Plying its stealthy, deceptive sapping at the

---

[*] Mrs. Anna F. Gillette.

very root of life, the tree at length fell, with thick foliage and clustering fruitage still upon it. Wasting daily during a lingering illness, yet no murmuring, no repining. To the last "her spirit, like frankincense, gave forth increasing sweeetness the more the corporeal part was consumed." And when the summons came, calmly she looked upon Death, not as the terror-crowned one, but as a kind messenger from her Father's house, and clasped his hand, that he might lead her, a weary and long absent child, home.

Besides these, and these prepared, no adults have died, and only four of our little ones,—lambs transferred to the arms and fold of the Good Shepherd. And I always thank God, when, descending to the brink of Jordan, little hands press mine, and when it is the loving spirit of a confiding child I there anoint. For "verily to the eye of faith, nothing is fairer than the death of young children. Sight and sense indeed recoil from it. The flower, that like a breathing rose filled the heart and home with an exquisite delight,—alas, we are stricken with sore anguish to find its stem broken and the blossom gone! But unto Faith, eagle-eyed beyond mental vision, and winged, to mount, like the singing lark, over the fading rainbow unto the blue heaven—even this is touchingly lovely. The child's earthly ministry was well done—for the rose does it work as grandly in blossom as the vine with its fruit. And having helped to sanctify and lift heavenward the very hearts that broke at its farewell, it has gone from this troublous sphere, ere the winds chilled or the rains stained it, leaving the world it blessed, and the skies through which it passed, still sweet with its lingering fragrance, to its glory, as an ever-unfolding flower in the blessed Garden of God! Surely prolonged life on earth hath no boon like this! For such mortal loveliness to put on immortality—to rise from the carnal with so little memory of earth that the mother's cradle seemed to have been rocked in the house of many mansions—to have no experience of a wearied mind and chilled affections, but from a child's joyous heart, growing up into the power of an archangelic intellect—to be raptured as a blessed babe through the gates of Paradise. Ah! this is better than to watch as an old Prophet for the car of fire in the valley of Jordan."

Come, my people, come, and sadly, yet smiling through our tears, let us set up the stone, and on it an "Ebenezer" too, when it is a memorial unto us of "*garnered immortality.*"

Great deliverances, or exemptions from evil, imply great positive blessings. To some of these I have alluded in passing. Others must be omitted for want of time. But I cannot forbear to dwell for a moment,—

Lastly,—Upon the POSITIVE FEATURES OF OUR DELIVERANCE FROM SPIRITUAL DECLENSION, so far at least as they are shown by *outward results*,—and for them to raise the monumental pillar.

To place these results in a stronger light, I will compare the number of admissions into this Church during the two years of my ministry here, with those of the years immediately preceding, and also with those of other Congregational Churches in this city and State. This I do, not in a spirit of vain-glory,— God forbid such a thought,—but to correct an impression industriously and perseveringly circulated in the community, to the effect that this Church was in a highly prosperous condition when I took charge of it, but that it has since dwindled in numbers, and almost fallen to pieces. Let us never forget, that whatever of good there is within us or about us,— whatever blessing is bestowed upon us,—is the free gift of our dear God in Christ, to whom be all the glory.

There have been received into this Church during the two years of my ministry here, fifty-nine members, viz : forty-one by profession, and eighteen by certificate from other Churches. The number separated from us during the same period, commencing 1st June, 1862, is sixty-three, viz : fifty-seven by certificate, two by discipline, and four by death. The number admitted is exactly equal to the number dismissed by certificate and by discipline : Death is the only enemy that has made any encroachments upon us, beyond what, by the grace of God, we have been able to meet and overcome. But death has been foiled in his efforts, for each victim was crowned a conqueror, exclaiming, "O, death, where is thy sting." These results, viewed in connection with the extraordinary efforts which have been made, both within and without the Church, to crush it out, unless we would yield to the dictation of others as to the topics which should be introduced into the pulpit, and the manner in which they should be discussed, are indeed most encouraging. Of those who have voluntarily withdrawn during the period mentioned, *forty-three* are supposed to be in sympathy with the movement which culminated in the calling of an ex-parte Council; leaving a gain of fourteen, so far as that movement was concerned. It is due to verity, however, to state, that quite a number of the families represented in this movement, and even of these Church members, have seldom attended the services of this sanctuary, during my ministry; so that what would seem to be a loss to us, is in many, if not most cases, a gain. It is surely a gain to be freed from a disturbing element, which never could be pacified except by yielding to its dictation. It is a gain to feel that we are speaking to friends, and that as a Church and people we are *united*. As an illustration of our essential unity since the withdrawal of disaffected members, it may be remarked that only in a single instance within the last ten months, has there been a dissenting voice on any question before the Church.

If we now proceed to compare the above results with those of the *two years next previous to my coming among you*, we shall find still further cause for gratulation and encouragement. During those two years, commencing 1st June, 1860, and ending 1st June, 1862, forty-five members were dismissed by certificate, discipline and death, and only nineteen received, viz : six by profession (three in each year,) and thirteen by certificate : showing a net loss of twenty-six members during those two years, over and above the admissions.

If we go back yet another year, viz : from 1st June, 1859, to 1st June, 1860, we find again that only three persons were admitted by profession, and eleven by certificate. Thus it appears, that during these three years, commencing June, 1859, only nine persons were added by profession (three in each year), and twenty-four by certificate, (averaging eight in each year.)

Undoubtedly, taking the whole period of eleven and a half years since its organization, this Church has been blessed in a remarkable degree ; especially during the incumbency of Rev. Dr. Stiles. God blessed it ; numbers came to listen to the powerful preaching of the minister ; and very soon a revival commenced, which resulted in the conversion of many, and their admission to the Church. On the first day this sanctuary was opened, (last Sabbath in June, 1852,) the services resulted in the conversion of a confirmed sceptic, who, a few months afterwards, united with this Church, and has ever since adorned his profession. The Church was organized November 8th, 1852, with twenty-nine members, gathered from ten different Churches, in three States, and representing three denominations of Christians. In the following month eight more were admitted, five of them by profession, making a total in 1852 of *thirty-seven*. In 1853 *forty-seven* were received—including twenty-six by profession. In 1854, *thirty-two*, including seventeen by profession. In 1855, *fifty-four*, including thirty-five by profession. Thus far, and indeed for some time longer, there was no collision of opinion among the members,—for all were satisfied with the faithful preaching of the word. Secular and political or semi-political affairs were considered, as a matter of course, excluded from the pulpit. Nobody expressed a desire for their introduction. But in process of time the enemy came and sowed tares. He could not permit a work of so much promise to go on unimpeded. He whispered to some, as he did to the mother of our race, that they ought to know both good and evil; they ought to be enlightened on *all* subjects in any way connected, or supposed to be connected, with religion and morals; and who but the minister should teach them! The rest is too recently and too well known, to require repetition here. Suffice it to say, that a kind Providence, in a way that we knew not, and should not have chosen, has freed us from these destructive influences, and opened before us new visions of prosperity and peace.

Our present number is 170; of whom 50 are males, and 120 females. The whole number who are, or have been members, is 338. Of these, 184 were admitted by profession, and 154 by certificate. Of the 168 who *have been* members, but are not so at present, 73 were admitted by profession, and 95 by certificate. Of the whole number dismissed, 23 were removed by death, 5 by discipline, and 140 by certificate.

The addition of 59 members, in the two years just closed, (41 by profession, 18 by letter,) is more manifestly a cause of special gratitude to God, because it has occurred during a period of great depression in the Churches generally, throughout the State and nation.

Now compare this *general resume* with that of the Congregational Churches *in the State*. From the minutes of the General Association, covering the last year of which we have returns, (the calendar year 1862,) we find that the aggregate number of persons admitted to all the Congregational Churches in Connecticut by profession, was 83 less than the number *removed by death*. In the same document, page 104, we find this further general review : " For the last four years, 187 Churches, two thirds of the whole number, have lost more by death than they have gained by profession. In these years, ten large Churches— only one of them a city Church—with 2,633 members, have added only nine by profession, while they have lost 233 by death ; twenty-six times as many as they have added. In the last five years—1858 to 1862—4 Churches, with 170 members, have added none by profession. In the last four years—1859 to

1862—28 Churches, with 2,672 members, have added none by profession. In the last three years—1860 to 1862—45 Churches, with 4,747 members, have added none by profession. In the last two years—1861 and 1862—83 Churches, with 9,447 members, have added none by profession. In the last year, 127 Churches, with 15,851 members, have added none by profession. For the last four years—1859 to 1862—from one-third to one-half of our Churches, yearly, have not added one by profession." Dr. Cleaveland, in his report to the Association, (page 51,) says: "In 1859, 110 Churches, with 14,184 members, gained not one from the world. In 1860, 136 Churches, with 19,323 members, were alike fruitless. In 1861, 146 Churches, more than one-half our whole number, with 19,685 members, received not one by profession."

Compare, now, the statistics of this Church during the *past two years* of my ministry here, with those of other Congregational Churches in Connecticut during *the two* calendar years 1861 and 1862. (No later returns have yet been published.) We find that *only one* of the 285 Churches in this State received so large a number of members by *profession* in these years as have been admitted into this Church during the past two years. That one Church received 42 members by profession; this Church, 41. I also find that *only two* of the 285 Churches received a larger *aggregate* of members, including those admitted on *certificate*, than have been received into this Church during the past two years. One of these Churches received an aggregate of 74 in two years; the other, 65. This Church, 59.

And how does our record compare with that of the Congregational Churches *in New Haven?*

According to the Association statistics, the number of members admitted into the North Church by profession *during the two calendar years* 1861 and 1862, was 25; Centre Church, 16; College Street Church, 8: Howe Street Church, 7; Yale College Church, 9; Chapel Street Church, 7; Temple Street Church, 2; Davenport Chapel, (no Church in 1861,) 5; Third Congregational Church, 3; Fair Haven First, 1; Fair Haven Second, 1; Fair Haven Centre, 4; Westville, 2; Total in two years, 90. To the South Church, in two years, have been admitted by profession, 41; or nearly half as many as the total admitted to the other 13 Churches in two years.

Yet Churches, whose barrenness and unfruitfulness appall us, sit in judgment on this Zion, whose record is so favorable when compared with years immediately preceding in our own history, or when compared with the Churches of this city and State. Is it for this we are adjudged guilty of having signally failed to accomplish the legitimate objects of the institution of the Church of God, and declared to have forfeited all claims to be considered as a Christian Church?

Dr. Cleveland, in his report, mourning over the lamentable condition of the Churches, and hinting at one of the causes, says:

"It becomes us to be on our guard, lest any of the great doctrines of grace, which in all ages have been the wisdom and power of God unto salvation, should be eclipsed by nearer, but infinitely less important objects."

And it is a fair question to ask, how much of this failure of the great object of pulpit ministrations is chargeable to the admixture of foreign ingredients, which have blunted the edge of truth, and kindled worldly excitements and associations by the very means which should have led men to repentance, and on the day set apart by God Himself for His especial service and worship? I presume not to decide; but I am sure that there is nothing in these results which should lead this Church or its minister to depart from the course they have pursued, of preaching and desiring to hear in this sacred place, and on this holy day, *only* the truth as it is in Jesus,—the truth which converts, sanctifies and saves.

O, then, brethren, as we set up this stone,—memorial of so many fruits of the spirit—of *positive spiritual blessings* in Christ Jesus—for this Ebenezer of the *past*, let us call upon our hearts, and all that is within us, to bless God's holy name.

> "Come, thou fount of every blessing,
> Tune my heart to sing thy grace;
> Streams of mercy never ceasing
> Call for songs of ceaseless praise.
>
> Here I raise my Ebenezer,
> Hither by thy help I'm come;

> And I hope by thy good pleasure,
> Safely to arrive at home.
>
> O, to grace how great a debtor
> Daily I'm constrained to be!
> Let that grace, Lord, like a fetter,
> Bind my wandering heart to thee.
>
> Prone to wander, Lord, I feel it;
> Prone to leave the God I love;
> Here's my heart, O take and seal it,
> Seal it for thy courts above."

To conclude :—

Let God's watch and ward through these ordeal years, His precious deliverances and positive blessings, *quicken our faith*, and impel to *greater effort during the new year* which dawns so brightly on us to-day. Think not the stone we set up here, and now, is merely an Eben-ezer of the past ; it is likewise an *Eben-ezer unto the future..* Then, let memory and hope be busy ; while one recalls divine goodness, let the other anticipate divine aid ; and while recollection of past guardianship inspires re-dedication and re-consecration, let expectation of a helping Omnipotence urge to a more zealous and strenuous performance of our work ; a work, the results of which, grasp Eternity for their duration. Brethren, remember,—"the time is short ;" the time for the accomplishment of this mighty work. "The night cometh." Be admonished, then, by these fast fleeting years, "to work while it is called to-day." O, how rapidly the years go by! Nine years ago this month, I knelt at the altar, and was ordained a minister of Jesus; eleven years and a half since, you were organized as a Church of Christ. All these years of my ministry, and your history, gone—beyond recall. Let us " redeem the time ;"

> "Do something, do it soon, with all our might:
> An angel's wing would droop if long at rest;"

remembering we are co-workers with God—and

> "God himself inactive were no longer blest"—

remembering too the days of toil are nearly over, and days of remaining rest and reward nearly ours.

Then, brethren, let us work—work for our own soul's sake, for this dear Church's sake, for Christ's sake, with all the energy which the hastening glories of our on-coming Eternity can inspire. Very close to this Eternity do we lift our memorial pillar to-day; like Samuel's, even within sight of the holy city. "Why see, see—the very glory that plays upon its summit, is light flashed from the pinnacles so near, of the heavenly Jerusalem!" while the golden radiance streaming through the now open portal, reveals in letters of living light traced by the hand of God, that epitome of our history and our hope,—" EBEN-EZER," "EBEN-EZER." Amen, Amen.

CONFESSION OF FAITH.

WE believe in one only living and true God, the Father, the Son, and the Holy Ghost; unchangeably perfect in goodness, wisdom, and power; the universal Creator, Preserver, Benefactor, and King, who works all things after the counsel of his own will, without impairing the liberty of the creature.

We believe that God has an infinite right to the services of his rational creatures, and that he requires of them, under penalty of his eternal displeasure, to love him supremely, and each other as themselves.

We believe that God made man upright; that our first parents freely sinned and fell; that in consequence of this act, their descendants, until regenerated, are utterly devoid of holiness, dead in trespasses and sins, and helplessly exposed to the righteous wrath of God.

We believe that God, who is rich in mercy, of his own good pleasure has provided a glorious salvation for ruined man.

We believe that the Son of God, who is equal with the Father, having taken upon himself our nature, and thus becoming man as well as God, did, by his sufferings and death in our stead, make atonement for our sins; that he rose from the dead and ascended into heaven; where he ever liveth to make intercession for his people.

We believe that through him God offers forgiveness to all men; and that every sinner who turns to God by repentance, and relies upon the Lord Jesus Christ by faith, is justified by His righteousness.

We believe that the Holy Ghost, who is very God, by special agency works in all those who are chosen to salvation, that change of heart from sin to holiness, without which no man can enter into the kingdom of God; and though God will save no man who does not work out his own salvation to the end, yet, whenever he commences a good work, we believe, through sovereign grace, the Holy Ghost will surely work in that man to will and to do until the day of Jesus Christ.

We believe that God has revealed all things necessary to salvation in the Scriptures of the Old and New Testament; which, being given by the inspiration of the Holy Spirit, are the only infallible rule of faith and practice.

We believe that it is the Scriptural duty of the disciples of Christ to associate themselves for worship and communion; for mutual watchfulness and improvement; for the administration of Baptism and the Lord's Supper; and for the perpetuation and extension of the Redeemer's kingdom; and that every association of believers for these purposes is a Christian Church.

We believe that there will be a general resurrection of the righeous and of the wicked; and a general judgment, by the award of which the righteous will be admitted to everlasting happiness, and the wicked sentenced to misery without end.

Do you cordially assent to these Articles of Belief?

COVENANT.

THROUGH Christ strengthening us, without whom we can do nothing, here in the presence of God, angels, and men, we humbly covenant, from this time henceforth and for ever, that we do renounce the world, the flesh, and the devil ; that we do give up ourselves, soul and body, all that we have and are, unto God, our Father, to love and to serve him, and to be his, and at his disposal in all things ; unto the Lord Jesus Christ, our Saviour, Prophet, Priest and King, for our salvation and his glory, to be taught, strengthened, governed and employed in all the relations and circumstances of life ; and unto the Holy Ghost, our Sanctifier, to be influenced, edified, and comforted by his gracious power, unto all Christian perfection and usefulness.

And we do further promise, that we will walk with this Church in all the commandments and ordinances of the Lord, and in love and charity with all its members ; resolving, for their encouragement and our own spiritual progress, that we will endeavor, by personal effort and influence, to promote its purity, efficiency, and enlargement.

Do you thus solemnly covenant and promise ?

Then doth this Church affectionately receive you to its membership, and welcome you to all the privileges, labors, and blessings of the Household of Faith.

Thus you are admitted to this Church, and have a right to all its privileges. May you have grace to improve them to the glory of God and your own edification.

STANDING RULES.

1. OFFICERS.—The officers of this Church, in addition to the Pastor and Deacons, shall consist of a *Clerk*, *Treasurer*, *Standing Committee* of three, and a *Committee on the State and Progress of the Church*, who shall be elected annually. The pastor and deacons shall be ex-officio members of the Standing Committee.

2. DUTIES OF THE OFFICERS.—In the absence of the pastor, the oldest deacon present shall *preside*.

The *Clerk* shall keep a record of the proceedings of the Church, a list of members, and of baptized children, and note the changes by death, removal, or marriage, and make a report thereof at the annual meeting. It shall be his duty to enter the names in full of all persons admitted to the Church, or dismissed from it, not only in the alphabetical list of members, but in the general record of proceedings.

The *Treasurer* shall receive all contributions of the Church and congregation, and disburse them under the direction of the Standing Committee, and make a specific annual report.

The *Standing Committee* shall receive all applications for admission to the Church, and after satisfactory examination, recommend them for acceptance; examine, and report on all cases of discipline; direct for what objects and at what dates, benevolent contributions shall be taken up; appoint collectors; ascertain the wants of poor members, and make appropriations, when necessary, for their relief; and attend to such other matters as may be referred to them by the Church.

The *Committee on the State and Progress of the Church* shall take note of interesting facts and occurrences, and embody them, with suitable suggestions, in an annual report.

3. MEMBERSHIP.—Persons desirous of *professing* their faith in Christ, in connection with this Church, who shall have been recommended by the Standing Committee, shall be publicly propounded at least two Sabbaths before Communion. If no objections are offered within this period, to their reception, they shall be admitted by the Pastor in the usual manner.

Persons recommended for admission, by *certificate* from other churches, shall be received, by vote of the Church, at a regular meeting.

4. DISMISSION OF MEMBERS.—It is expected that members, on removing, will ask for letters of dismission and recommendation. Requests for such letters may be announced at the weekly prayer-meeting or lecture, and if, at the end of one week, no objection has been made, the Pastor or Clerk shall issue the customary certificate.

5. DISCIPLINE.—The directions given, Matt. XVIII. 15–17, shall be observed in regard to private offenses. Public offenses shall be referred to the Standing Committee, who shall investigate and report on the same to the Church. Censure, of every degree, shall be passed only by vote of the Church.

Members who statedly absent themselves from the appointed services of this Church, without presenting satisfactory reasons therefor, shall be amenable to discipline.

6. COMMITTEE ON THE SABBATH SCHOOL.—There shall be a Committee of *three* persons, appointed quarterly, by the Church, whose duty it shall be to visit the families connected with this Church and Congregation, and endeavor to awaken an interest in the Sabbath School, on the part of parents; to secure the regular attendance of their children; to visit the Sabbath School, and in coöperation with the Superintendent, to use every means in their power to promote the welfare of the School, and they shall make a report of their proceedings at the quarterly meeting ending their term of service.

There shall be a quarterly meeting held in the months of January, April, July, and October, of which public notice shall be given, when the Sabbath School interest shall be specially considered, and reports received from the aforesaid Committee and from one of the officers of the School.

7. COMMUNION SERVICES shall be held on the first Sabbath of each alternate month, beginning with January next.

8. There shall be an *Annual Meeting* in the month of November, for the choice of officers, the presentation of annual reports, and the transaction of other business.

9. No additions or alterations shall be made to these Rules, except at an annual meeting, or a meeting called specifically for the purpose, and by a vote of *two-thirds* of the members present.

NEW HAVEN, Nov. 22, 1864.

SOUTH CHURCH PULPIT.

INCUMBENTS.

Rev. JOSEPH C. STILES, D.D.,
Stated Supply, from 1852 to Nov. 15, 1857.

Rev. GURDON W. NOYES,
Associate Supply, from June 25, 1854 to Dec. 1, 1857.
Then Stated Supply, till May 24, 1858.
Then installed Pastor till June 3, 1861.

Rev. JOSEPH HALSTED CARROLL,
Stated Supply, from June 1, 1862.

Rev. MYRON BARRETT,
Associate do. from Feb. 18, 1863 till May 1, 1864.

DEACONS.

BENEDICT BURWELL, from Nov. 19, 1852, till his death, April 14, 1863.
EASTMAN S. MINOR, from Nov. 19, 1852 till July 31, 1863.
THOMAS HORSFALL, from June 3, 1852.
CHARLES H. WARNER, from Nov. 1, 1863.
NICHOLAS COUNTRYMAN, from Nov. 1, 1863.

OFFICERS ELECTED FOR ONE YEAR AT THE ANNUAL MEETING OF THE CHURCH, NOVEMBER 22, 1864.

STANDING COMMITTEE.

Rev. J. HALSTED CARROLL,
THOMAS HORSFALL,
CHARLES H. WARNER,
NICHOLAS COUNTRYMAN.

Ex-Officio: CHARLES F. HOTCHKISS, JOHN H. LEEDS, SAMUEL BRACE.

CLERK.
GERARD HALLOCK.

TREASURER.
THOMAS HORSFALL.

COMMITTEE ON THE STATE AND PROGRESS OF THE CHURCH.
JOHN H. LEEDS,   EDWIN W. TREAT,
JOHN D. TYLER.

OFFICERS OF THE ECCLESIASTICAL SOCIETY CONNECTED WITH THE SOUTH CHURCH.
Elected Nov. 22, 1864, for one year.

SOCIETY'S COMMITTEE.
THOMAS HORSFALL,   GERARD HALLOCK,
THOMAS H. FULTON,   CHARLES F. HOTCHKISS,
NICHOLAS COUNTRYMAN.

CLERK.
CHARLES H. WARNER.

TREASURER AND COLLECTOR.
THOMAS HORSFALL.

MUSIC COMMITTEE.
THOMAS HORSFALL,   GERARD HALLOCK,
CHARLES H. WARNER.

USHERS.
CHARLES F. HOTCHKISS,   EDWIN W. TREAT.

COLLECTORS IN CHURCH.
PASCAL WITHEY,   CHARLES F. HOTCHKISS,
EDWIN W. TREAT.

ORGANIST.
FRANK L. MARTYN.

SLIP AGENT.
CHARLES F. HOTCHKISS.

SEXTON.
HENRY W. BLAKESLEE.

GENERAL LIST OF MEMBERS,

Comprising all who are or have been Members, at any period from the organization of the Church, to Jan. 1, 1865.

EXPLANATION.—The letter c prefixed to a name, denotes that the person was received by *certificate* from some other church. All others were admitted on profession of their faith.

The letter [r] at the end of a name, signifies that the person had before been a member of this Church, but having asked and received a certificate of dismission, now returned it, or brought a new one, and was re-admitted.

The letter [w] inserted in the name of a female, signifies *widow*.

In the names of married women, who were so at the time of admission, the name of the husband is inserted in a parenthesis.

To ascertain whether any person is still a member or not, and if not, when and how he was dismissed, and whither he has removed, see the two Alphabetical Lists, which follow this. In those Lists the names of women who have been married since their admission, as well as those who had been married before, take the names of their husbands.

1852.

The South Church was constituted November 8th, 1852, consisting of twenty-nine members, who presented letters from other churches, as follows:

c Benedict Burwell, Third Congregational Church, New Haven.
c Polly (Benedict) Burwell, Third Congregational Church, New Haven.
c Charles B. Burwell,   "   "   "   "
c Harriet A. (Chas. B) Burwell, "   "   "   "
c William S. Porter, Fourth Church, Hartford.
c Jane B. (William S.) Porter, Fourth Church, Hartford.
c Caroline W. Burwell, Third Congregational Church, New Haven.
c Jane S. Burwell, (afterwards Mrs. Thos. E. Barrett,) Third Congregational Church, New Haven.
c Thomas Horsfall, Chapel Street Church, New Haven.
c Sarah G. (Thomas) Horsfall, Chapel Street Church, New Haven.

c Nancy L. [w] Barrett, Union Church, Worcester.
c Thomas E. Barrett, " " " "
c Amos Smith, Chapel Street Church, New Haven.
c Maria (Amos) Smith, Chapel Street Church, New Haven.
c Eliza (Gerard) Hallock, College Street Church, New Haven.
c Lucy Coffin, " " " "
c Catharine *McCann*, (now the widow of Robert Steele,) College Street Church, New Haven.
c E. Porter Belden, Presbyterian Church, Sing Sing, N. Y.
c Eliza (E. Porter) Belden, " " " "
c William M. Hubbard, United Society, (North Church,) New Haven.
c Harriet Jane (Wm. M.) Hubbard, " "
c Sarah M. Hubbard, (now Mrs. Wm. A. Wright,) North Ch., "
c Martha Jane Hubbard, " "
c Eastman S. Minor, " "
c Judith M. (Eastman S.) Minor, " "
c Ann M. (Stephen, Jr.) Hotchkiss, Trinity Church, "
c Augusta W. [w] Currier, College Street Church, "
c Grace G. [w] (Andrew L.) Mason, Howe Street Church, "
c Mrs. Mary E. Merrow, East Granby Church, Mass.

At the first Communion, first Sabbath in December, 1852, the following persons were received as members:

Dec. c Mary (Stephen, Sen.) Hotchkiss.
     c Lucy Hotchkiss.
     c Harriet Hotchkiss.
     James V. R. Chapman.
     Frank Edwin Hotchkiss.
     George S. Minor.
     Alfred Minor.
     Mary (John) Ward.

1853.

Feb. c James L. Burnett.
     c Juliet (James L.) Burnett.
     c Thomas Owen.
     c Josephine (Thomas) Owen.
     Caroline E. Alley, (now Mrs. George S. Foote.)

GENERAL LIST OF MEMBERS.

        George Bradley.
        Lovisa (George) Bradley.
        Margaret Collinson.
        Amelia Hotchkiss.
        Charles F. Hotchkiss.
        Olivia E. (Charles F.) Hotchkiss.
        Porter G. Hull.
        Abby (John) White.
April. c Henry Judson.
      c George W. Nettleton.
      c Charlotte (George W.) Nettleton.
      c Evan Thomas.
      c Jane (Evan) Thomas.
        Emily Bliss Augur.
        Charlotte A. *Cadwell*, (now Mrs. Henry Loomis.)
        Lydia G. Chidsey.
        Clarissa Chapman Porter.
        Laura *Eliza Russell*, (now Mrs. L. P. Deming.)
June.   Mary E. (Robert) Blair.
      c Nicholas Countryman.
        Henry L. Stewart.
      c Sarah E. (Henry L.) Stewart.
      c Harriet S. [w] Thompson.
        Josephine Benedict Clark.
        Martha C. (Caleb S.) Duell.
        Jane S. *Price*, (now Mrs. Terrill.)
        Mary [w] Severance.
Aug.   c George R. Bill.
        Caleb S. Duell.
        John C. Nelson.
        Elizabeth W. (John C.) Nelson.
        Henry Martyn Barrett.
        David H. Hine.
        John Thomas Mix.
Oct.   c Christiana Young, (now Mrs. Theophilus H. Benham.)
      c Isaac Martin.
      c Eliza Jane (Isaac) Martin
      c Chester E. Pond.

	c Nancy M. (Erastus R.) Phelps.
	c Polly [w] Armstrong.
	c Susan Carrington, (now Mrs. David H. Hine.)
Dec.	c James H. Beers.

1854.

Feb.	c Deborah (John L.) Cadwell.
	c Elizabeth (Charles B.) Pomeroy.
	Lewis Chapman.
	David Douglass.
	Mary Elizabeth [w] (Wm. G.) Hunter.
	Mary A. Smith.
	Mary Scott, (now Mrs. Chester E. Pond.)
April.	L. Amelia (Geo. R.) Bill.
	Celia Hall, (afterwards Mrs. James H. Beers.)
	Julia Virginia Phelps, (now Mrs. James W. Wilson.)
	c Mary M. (Charles) Ward.
August.	Origen A. Barrett.
	Lindsley Monroe Burnett.
	Margaret (John) Crosby.
	Charles Edwin Daily.
	Gerard Hallock.
	Charles Augustus Hotchkiss.
	c Agnes (Gurdon W.) Noyes.
	c Charles Phillips.
	c Patty (Charles) Phillips.
	Sarah Maria (Ransom H.) Thomas.
	John Wilkinson.
	c Elizabeth (John) Wilkinson.
Oct.	c Jane (Adam) Baird.
	c Marilla [w] Hall.
	c Louisa Hall.
	c Marietta Hall.
	c Elizabeth [w] Knox.
Dec.	John Crosby.
	c Lewis M. Mills.
	c Charlotte I. (Lewis M.) Mills.
	c Lucy B. Minor.

1855.

Feb.   Augusta Alling.
James Buchanan.
Ann (James) Buchanan.
Susan B. (Thomas C.) Hollis.
William C. Scobie.
c Amelia (Wm. C.) Scobie.
c Jane L. [w] Scobie.
c Pascal Withey.
c Lucy Wells (Pascal) Withey.

April.   Horace A. Augur.
c Fannie E. (Horace A.) Augur.
Thomas Bence.
Sarah (Thomas) Bence.
Charlotte A. Churchill, (now Mrs. Minot A. Butricks.)
Henry Clarence Daily.
Ann (Wm.) Edwards.
c Julia [w] Fowler.
Sarah Fowler.
c Mary Hill.
Harriet Frances [w] (Wm.) Hull.
c William Merwin.
c Lucy (Wm.) Merwin.
c Emily O. Merwin.
c Mary E. Merwin.
c Rufus S. Pickett.
c Catharine (Rufus S.) Pickett.
Cornelia Eliza Taylor, (now Mrs. T. Hanson.)
Charles Henry Warner.
Sarah M. (Charles H.) Warner.

June.   Lucie Jane Benedict.
c John Evans.
Eliza (John) Evans.
Mary Emeline Hurd, (now Mrs. Frank Hayes.)
Maria Louisa Mills.

August.   Cornelia Bevins.
Maria Helen Bevins.
Robert Dyas.

GENERAL LIST OF MEMBERS.

          Ellen Jeffreys.
          John H. Leeds.
          Sarah Jane Magie, (now Mrs. Orville F. Parsons.)
          Harvey Merchant.
          Catharine Cornelia (Harvey) Merchant.
          George Youngerman.
          Emma B. (George) Youngerman.
October. Minot Augustus Butricks.
          Charles Burwell Foote.
       c Mrs. Ann Fenn.
Dec.   Alexander Adams.
          Hester Bishop.
       c Eliza H. Bristoll.
       c William A. Hallock.
          Frances Amelia Hine, (now Mrs. John H. Leeds.)
       c Mrs. Mary Stuart.
       c Lucina S. [w] Tisdale.

1856.

Feb.   Susan Jane Street, (now Mrs. John Butler.)
          James Steele.
       c Jessie (James) Steele.
          Arabella [w] Tyrrell.
April. c Mary (Ira) Bryan.
          Sarah (Teunis) Bowns.
          Charlotte E. (Thomas H.) Fulton.
          John W. Scofield.
          Lavinia C. (Edgar) Scofield.
June. c Andrew Baird.
       c Jane A. (Andrew) Baird.
          Margaret Baird, (wife of David.)
          Jennette Baird, (wife of Hugh.)
August. Frederick Grant.
          Elizabeth W. McArthur.
October. James Coggeshall.
       c Betsey A. Mansfield.
          Edgar Scofield.
Dec.   c Jane (Wm. B.) Catlin.

GENERAL LIST OF MEMBERS.

c John Nicoll.
c Cornelia C. (John) Nicoll.
c John Stetson.
c Harriet (John) Stetson.

1857.

Feb.   Reugene L. Young.
       Mrs. Margaret Wright.
June. c Maria K. Munson.
       c William E. Scranton.
       c Sarah E. (Wm. E.) Scranton.
August. Lucy J. Bryan.
       Mary A. Bryan.
       Paulina L. Thompson, (now Mrs. C. B. Foote.)
       Frances M. Clark.
       Sarah D. Gaskill.
October. Laura E. Gaskill.
       c Charles M. Shumway.
       c Mary (Charles M.) Shumway.
Dec.   c Maria (Henry S.) Catlin.
       c Lydia M. Lord.
       c A. L. Frisbie.

1858.

Feb.   Jane McPhee.
June. Julietta Currier, (now Mrs. G. W. Hazel.)
       Isabella Baird.
       Sarah Baird.
       Jessie Ann Torbett, (now Mrs. Alaric McNeill.)
       Eliza Hare, (now Mrs. Henry Corbett.)
       Sarah L. Horsfall.
       Laura Burnett.
       James H. Burnett.
       Preston B. Burnett.
       Fidelia Taylor, (now Mrs. Theo. Morris.)
       Elizabeth S. Duell, (now Mrs. Ed. A. Hart.)
       Charlotte Macomber.
       Mary E. Bunnell.
       Jennette Eddy.

George H. Butricks.
Sophia (George H.) Butricks.
Edward Gillette.
Anna (Edward) Gillette.
William H. Hazel.
George W. Hazel.
Waldemir B. Alling
Seth Gillette.
Catharine (Seth) Gillette.
Susan Martin.
Louisa B. Tuttle, (now Mrs. D. Umberfield.)
Phebe M. Dean.
c Ezra Staples.
c Vesta (Ezra) Staples.
c Elias Gaylord.
c Mary A. (Elias) Gaylord.
c Martha Coggeshall.
c James Torbett.
c Ann (James) Torbett.
c Lucy P. [w] Young.

August. James A. Bryan.
c Catharine C. Jones.
c Catharine Moffat.

Oct. c Mary M. Abbott.
c Polly Woodruff.
c Martha Woodruff.
c Mary S. Woodruff.
c Martha Stewart.

1859.

Feb. Lydia L. (John) Pierson.
Ellen F. Corey, (now Mrs. James H. Burnett.)
c Amos Smith, [r.] *See Note* 1.

June. Agnes [w] Baird.
c Ira Alling.

---

1. Admitted by letter, November 8, 1852. Dismissed in 1856, to Congregational Church in Orange. August, 1859, returned certificate, and was re-admitted. Left again in 1864, without a certificate from South Church, and joined College Street Church.

c Hannah Alling.
August. Martha O. Francis.
  c Robert Latta.
  c Elizabeth (Robert) Latta.
  c Arabella [w] Tyrrell, [r.]   *See Note 2.*

[At this point of time the date of the Communion was changed. The next Communion after December, was held in March, and has been continued on each alternate month ever since.]

1860.

March. c John H. Leeds, [r.]   } *See Note 3.*
       c Frances (John H.) Leeds, [r.] }
       c Thomas E. Barrett, [r.]   } *See Note 4.*
       c Jane S. (Thomas E.) Barrett, [r.] }
       c Polly W. Williams.
       c Abbie S. Williams.
         John Wallace.
July. c Henrietta E. Walker.
       c John R. Garlock.
       c Catharine (John R.) Garlock.
       c Albert R. Harrison.
       c Eli H. Scofield.
       c Jane (E. H.) Scofield.
Nov.   c C. F. Hotchkiss, [r.]   } *See Note 5.*
       c Olivia E.(C.F.) Hotchkiss, [r.] }
       c Marion O. Hotchkiss, (now Mrs. A. J. Nichols.)
       c Margaret Moffat.
       c Nancy Crone.
         Hannah (Joseph H.) Smith.

---

2. Admitted by profession, in 1856. Dismissed, September, 1859. Returned the letter in August, 1859, and was re-admitted to South Church. Dismissed again in 1864, to a Church in Canada.

3. Admitted by profession, in 1855. Dismissed in 1859, to a Church in Northampton. Returned certificates in March, 1860, and were re-admitted to South Church.

4. Admitted by letter, November 8, 1852. Dismissed, August 3, 1858, to a Church in New Britain. Re-admitted to South Church, March, 1860. Mr. Barrett was killed in the battle of Fredericksburg, December 13, 1862. Mrs. B. was dismissed again, April 19, 1864, and joined College Street **Church.**

5. Admitted by profession, February, 1853. Dismissed to Congregational Church in Waubonsee, **Kansas, in May,** 1859. Re-admitted to South Church, November, 1860.

Mary M. Stowe.
Ann (Capt. Wm.) Bates.

1861.

Sept. Thomas T. Minor.
Nov. c George W. Hazel, [r.]
      c Julietta (George W.) Hazel, [r.] } *See Note* 6.

1862.

Jan. c Lucy A. Sweetland, (now Mrs. Ed. Gillette.)
      c Henry Upson.
      Edna M. Walker, (now Mrs. Dibble.)
March. Agnes McDonald.
July. Mary E. (Capt. Frederick S.) Ward.
      c Edward Coe.
      c Louisa A. (Edward) Coe.
      Julia A. (Edwin W.) Treat.
Sept. Mary Cordelia (M. Porter) Snell.
      Edna S. (Joseph) Gray.
Nov. Ann E. (George) Deming.

1863.

January. Sarah Moffat.
      Elizabeth M. Bishop.
      Ella M. Hotchkiss.
      Anna D. Hotchkiss.
      Bettie Lee.
      Agnes Baird.
      Emma Jane Minor.
      Jennie E. Minor.
      Theresa E. Burnett.
      Mary J. Blair.
      Martha Duell.
      Mary C. Deming.
      Carrie E. Burwell.

---

6. Admitted by profession, June 6, 1858. Dismissed to Howe Street Church, June 11, 1861. Re-admitted to South Church, in November, same year. Dismissed again, by general letter, July 1, 1863.

    c Wilbur Johnson.
    c Leicester A. Carrington.
    c Laura A. (Leicester A.) Carrington.
March. c Juliette Bonney.
    Edwin W. Treat.
    Mary L. Lockwood.
    Joseph H. Smith.
    George Petrie.
    Louisa E. Bryan.
    c Lafayette S. Comstock.
    c Hannah M. (Lafayette S.) Comstock.
    Josephine Hollister.
May. Ellen M. Minor.
    c Huldah Jennings.
    William H. Deming.
    Pulaski Leeds.
    c Andrew Moffat.
    c Mary Moffat.
    c Huldah Scott, (now Mrs. Benjamin.)
    Gilbert Moore.
July. c Julia (Elias) Hotchkiss.
    c Joseph G. Isham.
    c Christina (Joseph G.) Isham.
    John B. Isham.
Sept. c Josephine B. Clark, [r.] *See Note* 7.

1864.

January. Louisa (Nicholas) Countryman.
    Franklin Countryman.
    Sarah (Frederick) Grant.
March. Samuel Brace.
    c Sarah R. (Samuel) Brace.
    c M. Porter Snell.
    Martha C. (Ralph V.) Kent.
    Sarah A. Webster, (now Mrs. Geo. Petrie.)

---

7. Admitted by profession, **June 5, 1853. Dismissed to a Church in Scotland, Dec. 13, 1860.** Re-admitted to South Church, **in September, 1863.**

	Jane (John) Magie.
	Joseph Gray.
	Thomas Horsfall, Jr.
May.	Samuel L. Hawkins.
	Laura (Samuel L.) Hawkins.
	Caroline S. (Alvin L.) Willoughby.
July.	R. W. Wright.
	Sarah Louisa (R. W.) Wright.
	Marie Antoinette Kingsbury.
	Adelaide [w] Louisa Lyon.
Sept.	Margaret (Frederick) Veitch.
Nov.	John D. Tyler.
	Mrs. Ann E. Mersham.
	Sarah I. (H. D.) Smith.
	Eleanor [widow of Bennett] Caldwell.
	Jane A. Supple.
	c Martha Jane Hubbard. [r.] *See Note* 8.

---

8. **Admitted by certificate, November 8, 1852. August** 3, 1861, took a letter to the **Second Congregational Church in Fair Haven.** Returned it in November, same year, and was re-admitted to South Church.

GENERAL LIST OF MEMBERS.

RECAPITULATION BY FIGURES.

Year.	Profession.	Certificate.	Total.
1852,	5	32	37
1853,	26	21	47
1854,	17	15	32
1855,	35	19	54
1856,	13	10	23
1857,	8	8	16
1858,	28	15	43
1859,	4	6	10
1860,	4	17	21
1861,	1	2	3
1862,	7	4	11
1863,	24	14	38
1864,	22	3	25
	194	166	360
Deduct for re-admissions,		12	12
Certificate,		154	348
Profession,		194	

Total, 348

It is proper to remark, that quite a number of persons, especially since the action of the late ex-parte Council, have been admitted by profession, who had before been members of other churches.

Of the twelve re-admissions, two occurred in 1859, six in 1860, two in 1861, one in 1863, and one in 1864.

PRESENT MEMBERS.

ALPHABETICAL LIST OF MEMBERS, JANUARY 1, 1865.

Note.—The figures before the name, denote the *year* when the person was admitted to this Church.

A.

1859.—Abbott, Mary M.

B.

1854.—Baird, Jane, wife of Adam.
1856.—Baird, Margaret, wife of David.
1856.—Baird, Jennette, wife of Hugh.
1856.—Baird, Andrew.
1856.—   Jane A., wife of Andrew.
1858.—Baird, Sarah, wife of James.
1858.—Baird, Isabella.
1859.—Baird, Agnes, widow of Archibald.
1863.—Baird, Agnes.
1860.—Bates, Ann, wife of William.
1863.—Benjamin, Huldah *Scott*.
1855.—Bevins, Cornelia.
1855.—Bevins, Mary Helen.
1855.—Bishop, Hester.
1863.—Bishop, Elizabeth M.
1863.—Blair, Mary Jane.
1856.—Bowns, Sarah T.

1863.—Bonney, Juliette.
1864.—Brace, Samuel.
1864.—   Sarah R., wife of Samuel.
1856.—Bryan, Mary, wife of Ira.
1857.—Bryan, Mary A.
1857.—Bryan, Lucy Jane.
1858.—Bryan, James A.
1863.—Bryan, Lousa E.
1855.—Buchanan, James.
1855.—   Ann, wife of James.
1854.—Burnett, Lindley Monroe.
1852.—Burwell, Dolly, widow of Deacon Benedict.

C.

1864.—Caldwell, Eleanor, widow of Bennett.
1856.—Catlin, Jane, wife of William B.
1857.—Catlin, Maria, wife of Henry S.
1857.—Clark, Frances M.
1853.—Clark, Josephine B.
1852.—Coffin, Lucy.
1858.—Corbett, Eliza *Hare*, wife of Robert.
1853.—Countryman, Nicholas.
1863.—   Louisa, wife of Nicholas.
1863.—Countryman, Franklin.
1858.—Coggeshall, Martha.
1860.—Crone, Nancy.
1854.—Crosby, Margaret, widow of John.

D.

1858.—Dean, Phebe M.
1858.—Deming, Ann E., wife of George.
1863.—Deming, Mary C.
1863.—Deming, William H.

1853.—Duell, Caleb S.
1853.—   Martha C., wife of Caleb S.
1863.—Duell, Martha.

E.

1855.—Evans, John.
1855.—   Eliza, wife of John.

F.

1855.—Fenn, Ann.
1855.—Foote, Charles B.
1857.—   Paulina L. *Thompson*, wife of Charles B.
1853.—Foote, Caroline E. *Alley*, wife of George S.
1859.—Francis, Martha O.
1856.—Fulton, Charlotte E., wife of Thomas H.

G.

1856.—Grant, Frederick.
1864.—   Sarah, wife of Frederick.
1858.—Goodrich, Martha *Stewart*, wife of John.
1864.—Gray, Joseph.
1862.—   Edna S., wife of Joseph.

H.

1854.—Hallock, Gerard.
1852.—   Eliza, wife of Gerard.
1855.—Hallock, Rev. William A.
1855.—Hanson, Cornelia E. *Taylor*, wife of Thomas.
1858.—Hart, Elizabeth S. *Duell*.
1864.—Hawkins, Samuel L.
1864.—   Laura L., wife of Samuel L.
1855.—Hayes, Mary E. *Hurd*, wife of Frank.
1855.—Hill, Mary.
1863.—Hollister, Josephine.

1855.—Hollis, Susan B., wife of Thomas C.
1852.—Horsfall, Thomas.
1852.—   Sarah G., wife of Thomas.
1858.—Horsfall, Sarah L.
1864.—Horsfall, Thomas, Jr.
1852.—Hotchkiss, Ann M., wife of Stephen, Jr.
1852.—Hotchkiss, Lucy.
1852.—Hotchkiss, Harriet.
1853.—Hotchkiss, Charles F.
1853.—   Olivia E., wife of Charles F.
1863.—Hotchkiss, Julia, wife of Elias.
1863.—Hotchkiss, Ella M.
1863.—Hotchkiss, Annie D., wife of Frederick T.
1852.—Hubbard, William M.
1852.—Hubbard, Martha Jane.
1853.—Hull, Porter G.
1854.—Hunter, Mary E., widow of William G.
1855.—Hull, Harriet F., wife of William.

I.

1863.—Isham, Joseph G.
1863.—   Christina B., wife of Joseph G.
1863.—Isham, John B.

J.

1863.—Jennings, Huldah.

K.

1863.—Keeler, Carrie E. Burwell, wife of Morris.
1864.—Kent, Martha C., wife of Ralph V.
1864.—Kingsbury, Marie Antoinette.

L.

1859.—Latta, Robert.
1859.—   Elizabeth, wife of Robert.

1863.—Lee, Bettie.
1855.—Leeds, John H.
1855.— Frances A. *Hine*, wife of John H.
1863.—Leeds, Pulaski.
1863.—Lockwood, Mary L., wife of Edgar.
1864.—Lyon, [w] Adelaide Louisa.

M.

1862.—McDonald, Agnes, (under discipline.)
1864.—Magie, Jane, wife of John D.
1858.—McNeill, Jessie Ann *Torbett*, wife of Alaric.
1858.—McPhee, Jane.
1853.—Martin, Eliza J., widow of Isaac.
1858.—Martin, Susan.
1856.—Mansfield, Mrs. Betsey A.
1852.—Minor, Alfred.
1863.—Minor, Ellen M.
1853.—Mix, John T.
1864.—Mersham, Mrs. Ann E.

N.

1853.—Nelson, John C.
1853.— Elizabeth, wife of John C.
1860.—Nichols, Marion O. *Hotchkiss*, wife of A. J.

O.

1853.—Owen, Thomas.
1853.— Josephine, wife of Thomas.

P.

1855.—Parsons, Sarah Jane *Magie*, wife of O. F.
1863.—Petrie, George.
1864.— Sarah A. *Webster*, wife of George.
1853.—Phelps, Nancy M., wife of Erastus

R.

1854.—Rawling, Mary A. *Smith*, wife of Benjamin.

S.

1856.—Scofield, Edgar.
1856.— Lavinia A., wife of Edgar.
1864.—Smith, Sarah Jane, wife of Horatio D.
1864.—Snell, M. Porter.
1862.— Mary Cordelia, wife of M. Porter.
1852.—Steele, Catharine *McCann*, [w] of Robert.
1864.—Supple, Jane A.

T.

1855.—Tisdale, Lucina S., [w.]
1858.—Torbett, James.
1858.— Ann, wife of James.
1863.—Treat, Edwin W.
1862.— Julia A., wife of Edwin.
1864.—Tyler, John D.

V.

1864.—Veitch, Margaret, wife of Frederick.

W.

1860.—Wallace, John.
1855.—Warner, Charles H.
1855.— Sarah M., wife of Charles H.
1853.—White, Abby, wife of John.
1864.—Willoughby, Caroline S., wife of Alvin L.
1855.—Withey, Pascal.
1855.— Lucy, wife of Pascal.
1857.—Wright, Margaret.
1864.—Wright, Robert W.
1861.— Sarah Louisa, wife of Robert W.

Y.

1855.—Youngerman, George.
1855.—   Emma B., wife of George.

Total in the above list of present members, 153,—viz. 41 males, and 112 females. Of the whole number, 107 were received on profession of their faith, and 46 by certificate from other churches. To ascertain whether any particular person was admitted by certificate or by profession, see General List of Members, under the year mentioned at the beginning of the name concerning which the information is sought.

PAST MEMBERS.

ALPHABETICAL LIST

Of Persons who HAVE BEEN *Members of the South Church, but are not not so January* 1, 1865.

NOTE.—The figures which immediately precede the name, denote the *year* of admission. If the *month* is wanted, see General List, under the year mentioned. The *day* of the month can be ascertained by referring to an A'manac, as no persons are admitted except at Communions, and these are always held on the first Sabbath of the month.

The figures opposite the name, *on the right*, show the date of dismission; the middle column, the mode of dismission, or place of removal, or both.

The letter (g) immediately before the date of dismission, denotes that the person so designated was dismissed by *general* certificate; the letter (l), that he *left* this Church without asking or receiving a certificate from us.

Those removed by death, are marked with a * immediately preceding the date when they ceased to be members; those by discipline, with a (d); those without any letter or mark immediately preceding such date, were dismissed by certificate to some particular church or churches.

A.

1855, Adams, Alexander,		Mar. 29, 1857
1855, Alling, Augusta,	Ch. in W. Haven,	Apr. 30, 1861
1859, Alling, Ira,	Died,	*Nov. 11, 1861
1859, Alling, Hannah,	Howe st. Ch.,	Mar. 11, 1862
1858, Alling, Waldemir B.	Died,	*Dec. 31, 1858
1853, Armstrong, Polly,	Died,	*Jan. 1, 1859
1853, Augur, Emily B.	Joined Bapt.ch. (l)	Mar. 26, 1854
1855, Augur, Horace A.	College st. ch.	Dec. 16, 1863
1855, Fannie E., wife of do.	do.	Dec. 16, 1863

B.

1852, Barrett, Thomas E.,	Killed in battle,	*Dec. 13, 1862
1852, Jane S. *Burwell*, [w] of do.	College st. ch.	Apr. 19, 1864
1852, Barrett, [w] Nancy L.,	Ch.in W.Killingly,	Nov.25, 1863
1853, Barrett, Henry M.	Died,	*July 26, 1861

PAST MEMBERS.

1854,	Barrett, Origen A.	Died,	*July 29, 1854
1853,	Beers, James H.,	Pres. ch. Brooklyn, July 2, 1856	
1854,	Celia Hall, [w] of do.	do.	July 2, 1856
1852,	Belden, E. Porter,	Pres.ch.SingSing, Dec. 17, 1854	
1852,	Eliza A., wife of do.	do. do.	Dec. 17, 1854
1855,	Bence, Thomas,	Discipline,	(d) Jan. 10, 1862
1855,	Sarah, wife of do.	do	(d) Jan. 10, 1862
1855,	Benedict, Lucy Jane,	College st. ch.	June 2, 1861
1855,	Benham, Christiana Young,(Th.H.)Died,		*Nov. 5, 1859
1853,	Bill, George R.,	Exeter ch. Leb'n, June 22, 1858	
1854,	Amelia L., wife of do.	Died,	*Feb., 1856
1853,	Blair, Mary E. wife of Robert,	College st. ch.	April 19, 1864
1853,	Bradley, George,	do. do.	March 24, 1863
1853,	Lovisa, wife of do.	do. do.	March 24, 1863
1855,	Bristol, Eliza H.,	Third ch.,	About Feb. 2, 1858
1858,	Bunnell, Mary E.,	St. Paul's ch.	Dec. 1, 1861
1853,	Burnett, James L.,	College st. ch.	March 24, 1863
1853,	Juliette, wife of do.	do.	March 24, 1863
1858,	Burnett, James H.,	do.	March 3, 1863
1859,	Ellen F. Corey, wife of do.	do.	March 3, 1863
1858,	Burnett, Preston B.,	do.	March 24, 1863
1858,	Burnett, Laura,	do.	March 24, 1863
1863,	Burnett, Theresa E.	do.	March 24, 1863
1852,	Burwell, Caroline W.	Third ch.,	(l) Nov. 22, 1864
1852,	Burwell, Deacon Benedict,	Died,	*April 14, 1863
1852,	Burwell, Charles B.,	Third ch.	Dec. 16, 1863
1852,	Harriet A., wife of do.	do.	Dec. 16, 1863
1858,	Butricks, Geo. H.,	College st. ch.	Feb. 5, 1864
1858,	Sophia, wife of do.	do.	Feb. 5, 1864
1855,	Butricks, Minot A.,	do.	(l) Nov. 22, 1864
1855,	Charlotte A. Churchill,wife of do. do.		(l) Nov. 22, 1864

C.

1854,	Cadwell, Deborah, (John L.,)	Ch.in Woodbury, Apr. 26, 1859	
1863,	Carrington, Leicester,	College st. ch.	(l) Nov. 22, 1864
1863,	Emily, wife of do.	do.	(l) Nov. 22, 1864
1852,	Chapman, James V. R.,	Pr. ch. Rochester, Jan. 17, 1860	
1854,	Chapman, Lewis,	do	Jan. 17, 1860

PAST MEMBERS.

1853, Chidsey, **Lydia G.**,   Discipline,   (d) Dec. 20, 1861
1862, Coe, Edward,   College st. ch. (l) Nov. 22, 1864
1862,   Louisa A., wife of do.   do.   (l) Nov. 22, 1864
1856, Coggeshall, James,   Died,   *April 24, 1857
1853, Collinson, Margaret,   A ch. in Canada,   1853
1863, Comstock, Lafayette S.,   Chapel st. ch. (g) Aug. 4, 1863
1863,   Hannah M., wife of do.   do,   (g) Aug. 4, 1863
1854, Crosby, John,   Died,   *Aug. 6, 1863
1852, Currier, Augusta W.,   College st. ch. (g) July 31, 1863

D.

1854, Dailey, Charles E.,   Ch. in Was. City, Aug. 26, 1862
1855, Dailey, Henry C.,   Ch. in Unionville, Aug. 26, 1862
1853, Deming, Laura E. *Russell*, wife of L. P. Deming, (g) Aug. 11, 1863
1862, Dibble, Edna M. *Walker*,   College st. ch.   March 8, 1864
1854, Douglass, David,   Presb. ch. Rock I.   June, 1855
1855, Dyas, Robert,   Chapel st. ch. (l) Nov. 22, 1864

E.

1858, Eddy, Jennette,   Dav. Chapel,   (l) Nov. 22, 1864
1855, Edwards, Ann, wife of Wm.,   March 29, 1857

F.

1855, Fowler, [w] Julia,   Ch. in Guilford,   Oct. 26, 1858
1855, Fowler, Sarah,   do.   Oct. 26, 1858
1857, Frisbie, Rev. A. L.,   Ch. in Ansonia,   May. 1860

G.

1867, Gaskill, Sarah D.,   Ch. in Norwich,   Jan. 3, 1861
1857, Gaskill, Laura E.,   St. Paul's   April 9, 1861
1860, Garlock, John R.,   Geo. st. Me. ch. Aug. 12, 1862
1860,   Catharine G. B., wife of do.   do.   Aug. 12, 1862
1858, Gaylord, Elias,   Ch. in Cheshire, May 13, 1862
1858,   Mary Ann, wife of do.   do.   May 13, 1862
1858, Gillette, Edward,   Davenp. Chapel, Oct. 22, 1862
1858,   Ann F., wife of do.   Died,   *July 23, 1862
1862,   L. A. *Sweetland*, 2d wife do. Davenp. Chapel. Oct. 28, 1862
1858, Gillette, Seth,   do.   (l) Nov. 22, 1864
1858,   Catharine, wife of do.   Died,   *Nov. 24, 1861

H.

1854, Hall, Merilla, [w]   Ch. in Wallingford, May 6, 1856
1854, Hall, Louisa,   do.   May 6, 1856
1854, Hall, Marietta,   do.   May 6, 1856
1860, Harrison, Albert R.,   (g) June 16, 1863
1858, Hazel, Geo. W.,   Coll. st. ch. (g) July 31, 1863
1861,   Juliette *Currier*, wife of do.   do. (g) July 31, 1863
1858, Hazel, Wm. Henry,   Howe st. ch.   Jan. 7, 1862
1853, Hine, David H.,   3d Meth. ch.   Feb. 19, 1856
1853,   Susan *Currington*, wife of do.   do.   Feb. 19, 1856
1852, Hotchkiss, Mary, [w] Stephen, Sr., Died,   *April 16, 1856
1852, Hotchkiss, Frank E.,   Third ch.   Oct. 26, 1858
1853, Hotchkiss, Amelia,   Died,   *Oct. 5, 1853
1853, Hotchkiss, Charles A.,   Ch. in Waubonsee, May, 1859
1852, Hubbard, Harriet J., (Wm. M.,) Died,   *Jan., 1861

J.

1855, Jeffries, Ellen,   Pr. ch. Rochester, Dec. 6, 1859
1863, Johnson, Wilbur,   Pr. ch. Harford, Pa. Feb. 5, 1864
1858, Jones, Catharine C.,   Third ch.   (l) 1864
1853, Judson, Henry,   Ch. in Bridgeport. Nov. 15, 1854

K.

1854, Knox, Elizabeth, [w]   (g) Feb. 24, 1857

L.

1853, Loomis, C. A. *Cadwell*, (Henry,) Ch. in Woodbury, Sept. 22, 1859
1857, Lord, Lydia M.,   (g) June 24, 1862

M.

1856, McArthur, Elizabeth W.,   Ch. in Wallingf'd, May 14, 1861
1858, Macomber, Charlotte,   College st. ch.,   1864
1852, Mason, Grace G. [w]   Died,   *March 10, 1855
1853, Martin, Isaac,   Died,   *May 28, 1857
1855, Merchant, Harvey,   Ch. in Westville, Oct. 2, 1860
1855,   Catharine C., wife of do.   do.   Oct. 2, 1860
1852, Merrow, Mrs. Mary E.,   First ch. F. Haven, Oct. 28, 1856
1855, Merwin, William,   •   Ch in Milford.   April 9, 1861

PAST MEMBERS. 37

1855, Merwin, Lucy, wife of Wm.   Ch. in Milford,   April 9, 1861
1855, Merwin, Emily O.,   do.   April 9, 1861
1855, Merwin, Mary E.,   do.   April 9, 1861
1854, Mills, Lewis M.,   Ch. in Clinton,   April 26, 1859
1854,   Charlotte I., wife of do.   do.   Jan. 18, 1859
1855, Mills, Maria Louisa,   do.   Jan. 18, 1859
1852, Minor, Dea. Eastman S.,   Coll. st. ch.   (g) July 31, 1863
1852,   Judith M., wife of do.   do.   (g) July 31, 1863
1852, Minor, George S.   do.   (g) July 31, 1863
1854, Minor, Lucy B.,   Died,   *Sept. 28, 1857
1861, Minor, Thomas T.,   Coll. st. ch.   (g) July 31, 1863
1863, Minor, Jennie E.,   do.   (g) July 31, 1863
1863, Minor, Emma Jane,   (g) Aug. 4, 1863
1857, Munson, Maria K.,   Ch. in W. Haven,   May 7, 1861
1858, Morris, Fidelia *Taylor* (Theodore) Ch. in S. Canaan,   Oct. 28, 1862
1858, Moffat, Catharine,   Coll. st. ch.   (l) Nov. 22, 1864
1860, Moffat, Margaret,   do.   (l) Nov. 22, 1864
1863, Moffat, Sarah,   do.   (l) Nov. 22, 1864
1863, Moffat, Andrew B.,   do.   (l) Nov. 22, 1864
1863, Moffat, Mary.   do.   (l) Nov. 22, 1864
1863, Moore, Gilbert F.,   do.   (l) Nov. 22, 1864

N.

1853, Nettleton, Geo. W.,   Howe st. ch.   March 11, 1862
1853   Charlotte, wife of do.   do.   March 11, 1862
1856, Nicoll, John,   College st. ch. (g) Aug. 4, 1863
1856,   Cornelia C., wife of do.   do.   (g) Aug. 4, 1863
1854, Noyes, Agnes, (Rev. G. W.,)   F. Haven, 2d, (g) June 11, 1861

P.

1854, Phillips, Charles,   Died,   *Oct. 18, 1861
1854,   Patty, wife of do.   Howe st. ch.   March 11, 1862
1855, Picket, Rufus S.,   College st. ch.   March 17, 1863
1855,   Catharine, wife of do.   do.   March 17, 1863
1859, Pierson, Lydia, (John,)   (g) Sept. 1861
1854, Pomeroy, Elizabeth, (Chas. B.)   Ch. in Webster, Mass. Nov., 1854
1854, Pond, Chester E.,   Kansas,   (g) March 18, 1856
1854,   Mary *Scott*, wife of do.   do.   (g) March 18, 1856

1852, Porter, Wm. S., College st. ch. April 1, 1856
1852, Jane B., wife of do. do. April 1, 1856
1853, Porter, Clarissa C., do. Nov. 1854

S.

1855, Scobie, [w] Jane L., Died, *Nov. 1, 1856
1855, Scobie, Wm. C., College st. ch. (1) Nov. 22, 1864
1855, Amelia, wife of do. do. (1) Nov. 22, 1864
1856, Scofield, John W., College st. ch. Jan. 19, 1864
1860, Scofield, Eli H., Davenport Chapel, July 2, 1862
1860, Jane, wife of do. do. July 2, 1862
1857, Scranton, Wm. E., Me. ch. Geo. st. Jan. 26, 1858
1857, Sarah E., wife of do. do. Jan. 26, 1858
1853, Severance, [w] Mary, Ch. in Mass., 1856
1857, Shumway, Charles M., (g) Jan. 3, 1861
1857, Mary J., wife of do. (g) Jan. 3, 1861
1852, Smith, Amos, College st. ch. (1) Nov. 22, 1864
1852, Maria, wife of do. do. (1) Nov. 22, 1864
1863, Smith, Jos. H., do. (1) Nov. 22, 1864
1860, Hannah, wife of do. do. (1) Nov. 22, 1864
1858, Staples, Ezra, Ch. Farmi'gt'n.Me.,Dec.24, 1861
1858, Vesta, wife of do. do. Dec. 24, 1861
1856, Steele, James, Discipline, (d) Jan. 21, 1863
1856, Jessie, wife of do. do. (d) Jan. 21, 1863
1856, Stetson, John, Pr. ch. Brooklyn, } March 12, 1861.
1856, Harriet, wife of do. do. }
1853, Stewart, Henry L., Ep. ch. M. Had.,(g) Aug. 1, 1860
1853, Sarah E., wife of do. Died, *June 20, 1855
1860, Stowe, Mary M., Ch in Milford, May 14, 1861
1855, Stuart, Mary, (g) Aug. 26,1856
1856, Street, Susan J., Third ch., Feb. 2, 1858

T.

1854, Thomas, Sarah M. (Ransom H.) Ch. in Westville, 1864
1853, Thomas, Evan, North Church, Dec. 1853
1853, Jane, wife of do. do. Dec. 1853
1853, Thompson [w] Harriet S., Howe st. ch., Nov. 19, 1857

1853, Terrill, Jane S. *Price*,   Ch. in Hamden,   May 3, 1864
1856, Tyrrell, [w] Arabella,   Church in Canada, Aug., 1864

U.

1858, Umberfield, Louisa B. *Tuttle*, (Dennis,) Chapel st. ch. Oct. 28, 1862
1862, Upson, Rev. Henry,   Ch. N. Preston,   Feb. 12, 1864

W.

1860, Walker, Henrietta E.,   College st. ch.   April 26, 1864
1852, Ward, Mrs. Mary, (John,)   1861
1854, Ward, Mary M., wife of Charles, Chapel st. church,   1860
1862, Ward, Mary E., (Capt. F. S.,) College st. ch. (g) July 31, 1863
1860, Williams, Abby S.,   Con. ch. Newark, May 28, 1861
1860, Williams, Polly,   do.   May 28, 1861
1854, Wilkinson, John,   Coll. st. ch.   (l) Nov. 22, 1864
1854,   Elizabeth, wife of do.   do.   (l) Nov. 22, 1864
1854, Wilson, Julia V. *Phelps*, (Jo. W.) Ch. in Norwalk, April 23, 1861
1858, Woodruff, Polly,   College st. ch.   May 2, 1863
1858, Woodruff, Martha E.   do   May 2, 1863
1858, Woodruff, Mary T.,   do.   May 2, 1863
1852, Wright, Sar. M. *Hubbard*, (W. A.) Fair Haven 2d ch. Apr. 30, 1856

Y.

1857, Young, Reugene L.,   Chapel st. ch.   Dec. 16, 1862
1858, Young, Lucy P.,   (g) Dec. 16, 1862

RECAPITULATION.

Number of names in the foregoing list of ex-members, ... 195
Males, ... 72
Females, ...123

Of the whole number, (195,) eighty-seven were admitted by profession, and one hundred and seven by certificate. Of the same whole number, there were dismissed by certificate from this to other churches, ... 116
By general letter, (g) 26
By discipline, (d) 5
By death, (*) 22
Joined other churches, without asking or receiving certificates of dismission from us, (l) 26

                Total, as above, 195

Of the 26 thus (l) separated from us, it is understood that 25 received a certificate from the Scribe of the late Ex-parte Council, Rev. Mr. Eustis, and that on the strength of that certificate, they have been admitted to other churches, as specified in the above list. Most of them were admitted to the College Street Church, August 7, 1864. In regard to these 25 persons, the following preamble and resolution were unanimously adopted at the annual meeting of the South Church, November 22, 1864 :—

"WHEREAS, we are credibly informed that Amos Smith, and Maria, his wife, Edward Coe, and Louisa A., his wife, Leicester Carrington, and Emily, his wife, Minot A. Butricks, and Charlotte A., his wife, Joseph H. Smith, and Hannah, his wife, William C. Scobie, and Amelia, his wife, John Wilkinson, and Elizabeth, his wife, Andrew B. Moffat; Margaret, Catharine, Mary and Sarah Moffat; Gilbert F. Moore, Jennette Eddy, Catharine C. Jones, Caroline W. Burwell, Robert Dyas, and Seth Gillette, whose names stand on our books as members of this Church, have united with other churches, without asking letters of dismission from us, as was required by one of our Standing Rules, to which they were parties.

"*Resolved*, That notwithstanding the irregularity of their course in this particular, we accept it as at least an expression of their desire to be released from their connection with this Church, and that accordingly our Clerk be directed to enter their names on our Records as dismissed members *from this date*, (November 22, 1864,) in the same sense as if they had asked and received from us letters of dismission and recommendation, in the usual form."

DISMISSIONS IN EACH YEAR,

AND NAMES OF THE DISMISSED.

NOTE.—Deceased Members marked with a *. Those who have died since their dismission, are *not* marked with a *.

1852.
None.

1853.
Margaret Collinson,
Amelia Hotchkiss,*
Evan Thomas,
Jane (Evan) Thomas.

1854.
E. Porter Belden,
Eliza (E. P.) Belden,
Origen A. Barrett,*
Emily B. Augur,
Henry Judson,
Clarissa C. Porter,
Elizabeth (Chas. B.) Pomeroy.

1855.
David Douglass,
John H. Leeds,
Frances A. *Hine* (J. H.) Leeds.
Grace G. Mason,*
Sarah E. Stewart.*

1856.
James H. Beers,
Celia *Hall* (J. H.) Beers,
L. Amelia (Geo. R.) Bill,*
Marilla [w] Hall,
Louisa Hall,
Marietta Hall,
David H. Hine,
Susan *Carrington* (D. H.) Hine,
Mary (Stephen, Sr.) Hotchkiss,*
Wm. S. Porter,
Jane B. (Wm. S.) Porter,
Chester E. Pond,
Mary *Scott* (Chester E.) Pond,
Mary [w] Severance,
Mrs. Mary E. Merrow,
Amos Smith,
Mary L. Stewart,
Jane L. [w] Scobie,*
Sarah M. *Hubbard* Wright.

1857.
Alexander Adams,
James Coggeshall,'
Ann Edwards,
Isaac Martin,*
Lucy B. Minor,*
Harriet S. [w] Thompson,
Elizabeth Knox.

1858.
Waldemir B. Alling,*
Thomas E. Barrett,
Jane S. (Thos. E.) Barrett,
George R. Bill,
Julia Fowler,
Sarah Fowler,
Frank E. Hotchkiss,
Wm. E. Scranton,
Sarah E. (Wm. E.) Scranton,
Eliza H. Bristol,
Arabella [w] Tyrrell,
Susan J. Street.

1859.
Polly Armstrong,*
Christiana Young (T. H.) Benham,*
Charlotte A. Cadwell,
Deborah Cadwell,
Charles A. Hotchkiss,
Ellen Jeffries,
Lewis M. Mills,
Charlotte I. (Lewis M.) Mills,
Maria L. Mills,
Charles F. Hotchkiss,
Olivia E. (Chas. F.) Hotchkiss.

1860.
James V. R. Chapman,
Lewis Chapman,
Rev. A. L. Frisbie,
Harvey Merchant,
Catharine C. (Harvey) Merchant,
Mary M. (Charles) Ward,
Henry L. Stewart,
Josephine B. Clark.

1861.
Augusta Alling,
Ira Alling,*
Henry M. Barrett,*
Lucy Jane Benedict,
Mary E. Bunnell,
Lydia G. Chidsey,
Sarah D. Gaskill,
Laura E. Gaskill,
Catharine (Seth) Gillette,*
George W. Hazel,
Juliette Currier (George W.) Hazel,
Harriet J. (Wm. M.) Hubbard,*
Eliz. W. McArthur,
Wm. Merwin,
Lucy (Wm.) Merwin,
Emily O. Merwin,
Mary E. Merwin,
Maria K. Munson,
Agnes W. Noyes,
Charles Phillips,*
Lydia (John) Pierson,
Charles M. Shumway,
Mary J. (Chas. M.) Shumway,
Ezra Staples,
Vesta (Ezra) Staples,
John Stetson,
Harriet (John) Stetson,

DISMISSIONS IN EACH YEAR. 45

Mary M. Stowe,
Mary (John) Ward,
Abby S. Williams,
Polly Williams,
Julia V. *Phelps* Wilson.

Louisa B. *Tuttle* Umberfield, Oct. 28.
Reugene L. Young, Dec. 16.
Lucy P. Young, Dec. 16.

1862.

Hannah Alling, March 11.
John R. Garlock, Aug. 12.
Catharine G. B. (John R.) Garlock, Aug. 12.
Elias Gaylord, May 13.
Mary Ann (Elias) Gaylord, May 13.
Thomas E. Barrett,* Dec. 13.
Thomas Bence, Jan. 10.
Sarah (Thos.) Bence, Jan. 10.
Charles E. Dailey, Aug. 26.
Henry C. Dailey, Aug. 26.
Wm. Henry Hazel, January.
Edward Gillette, Oct. 22.
Ann F. (Edward) Gillette,* July 23.
Lucy A. *Sweetland* (Edward) Gillette, Oct. 28.
Lydia M. Lord, June 24.
Fidelia Taylor Morris, Oct. 28.
Geo. W. Nettleton, March 11.
Charlotte (Geo. W.) Nettleton, March 11.
Patty (Chas.) Phillips, Mar. 11.
Eli H. Scofield, July 2.
Jane (Eli H.) Scofield, July 2.

1863.

Horace A. Augur,
Fannie E. (Horace A.) Augur,
Nancy L. Barrett,
Geo. Bradley,
Lovisa (Geo.) Bradley,
James L. Burnett,
Juliette (James L.) Burnett,
James H. Burnett,
Ellen F. Corey (James H.) Burnett,
Preston B. Burnett,
Laura Burnett,
Theresa E. Burnett,
Dea. Benedict Burwell,*
Charles B. Burwell,
Harriet A. (Chas. B.) Burwell,
Lafayette S. Comstock,
Hannah (Lafayette) Comstock,
John Crosby,*
Augusta W. Currier,
Laura E. *Russell* (L. P.) Deming.
Albert R. Harrison,
Geo. W. Hazel,
Juliette *Currier* (Geo. W.) Hazel,
Dea. E. S. Minor,

Judith M. (E. S.) Minor,
George S. Minor,
Thomas T. Minor,
Jennie E. Minor,
Emma Jane Minor,
John Nicoll,
Cornelia C. (John) Nicoll,
Rufus S. Pickett,
Catharine (Rufus S.) Pickett,
James Steele,
Jessie (James) Steele,
Mary E. (Capt. F. S.) Ward,
Polly Woodruff,
Martha E. Woodruff,
Mary T. Woodruff.

1864.

Jane S. *Burwell* Barrett,
Mary E. (Robert) Blair,
Caroline W. Burwell,
Geo. H. Butricks,
Sophia (G. H.) Butricks,
Minot A. Butricks,
Charlotte A. (Minot) Butricks,
Leicester Carrington,
Emily (Leicester) Carrington,
Edward Coe,
Louisa A. (Edward) Coe,
Edna M. *Walker* Dibble,

Robert Dyas,
Jenette Eddy,
Martha J. Hubbard, Aug. 23.
Seth Gillette,
Wilbur Johnson,
Catharine C. Jones,
Charlotte Macomber,
Catharine Moffat,
Margaret Moffat,
Sarah Moffat,
Andrew B. Moffat,
Mary Moffat,
Gilbert Moore,
Amos Smith,
Maria (Amos) Smith,
Joseph H. Smith,
Hannah (Joseph H.) Smith,
Sarah Maria (Ransom H.) Thomas,
Jane S. *Price* Terrill,
Rev. Henry Upson,
Henrietta E. Walker,
Wm. C. Scobie,
Amelia (Wm. C.) Scobie,
John Wilkinson,
Elizabeth (John) Wilkinson,
John W. Scofield,
Arabella (w) Tyrrell.

NUMERICAL EXHIBIT

OF

ADMISSIONS AND DISMISSIONS IN DIFFERENT YEARS.

The following table shows the total number of admissions and dismissions, (including deaths,) in each calendar year, since the organization of the church to Jan. 1, 1865.

Year.	Admissions.	Dismissions.	Gain.	Loss.	Whole No. at close of year.
1852.	37	0	37	0	37
1853.	47	4	43	0	80
1854.	32	7	25	0	105
1855.	54	5	49	0	154
1856.	23	19	4	0	158
1857.	16	7	9	0	167
1858.	43	12	31	0	198
1859.	10	11	0	1	197
1860.	21	8	13	0	210
1861.	3	32	0	20	181
1862.	11	24	0	13	168
1863.	38	39	0	1	167
1864.	25	39	0	14	153

Total admissions, 360   207   211   58
" dismissions, 207   Loss, 58

Present Members, 153   153 net gain.

The number of *admissions* (360) is twelve greater than the number of *persons* admitted (348). The reason is, that twelve persons have been admitted twice; having, at some period after their first admission, taken certificates to other churches, and subsequently re-united with this. For the same reason the number of *dismissions* is twelve greater than the number of *persons* dismissed. But in this table, as well as in the General List, it is necessary to follow these changes, in order to show the gain or loss of members in each year, and the number remaining at the close of each year. In the Alphabetical Lists no name is inserted more than once.

Mr. Carroll commenced his labors as Stated Supply on the 1st of June, 1862. During the 31 months which have since elapsed, to 1st of January, 1865, there have been admitted into this church by profession 51 members, by certificate 19,—total 70; which is only 23 less than the number of dismissions within the same period, including two by discipline and four by death. Considering the extraordinary efforts which have been made by disaffected persons within our own church, and by terrorism, Ex-parte Councils, and other appliances without, to draw or drive away our members,—indeed to destroy us altogether,—the result is a signal triumph. As these elements of mischief are now in a great measure exhausted, it is reasonable to anticipate, from this time forward, with the blessing of God, a rapid increase of members, proportionate to the large increase of our congregations. It is also worthy of remark that our net loss of members (23) in the 31 months of Mr. Carroll's ministry among us, is *eleven less* than our net loss (34) during the *seventeen* months immediately preceding. On the whole, we have much to be thankful for in the past, and more to hope for in the future. The faithful preaching of the Word, which the South Church enjoys in an eminent degree, is sure to yield its legitimate fruits.

www.ingramcontent.com/pod-product-compliance
Lightning Source LLC
Chambersburg PA
CBHW022052230426
43672CB00008B/1147